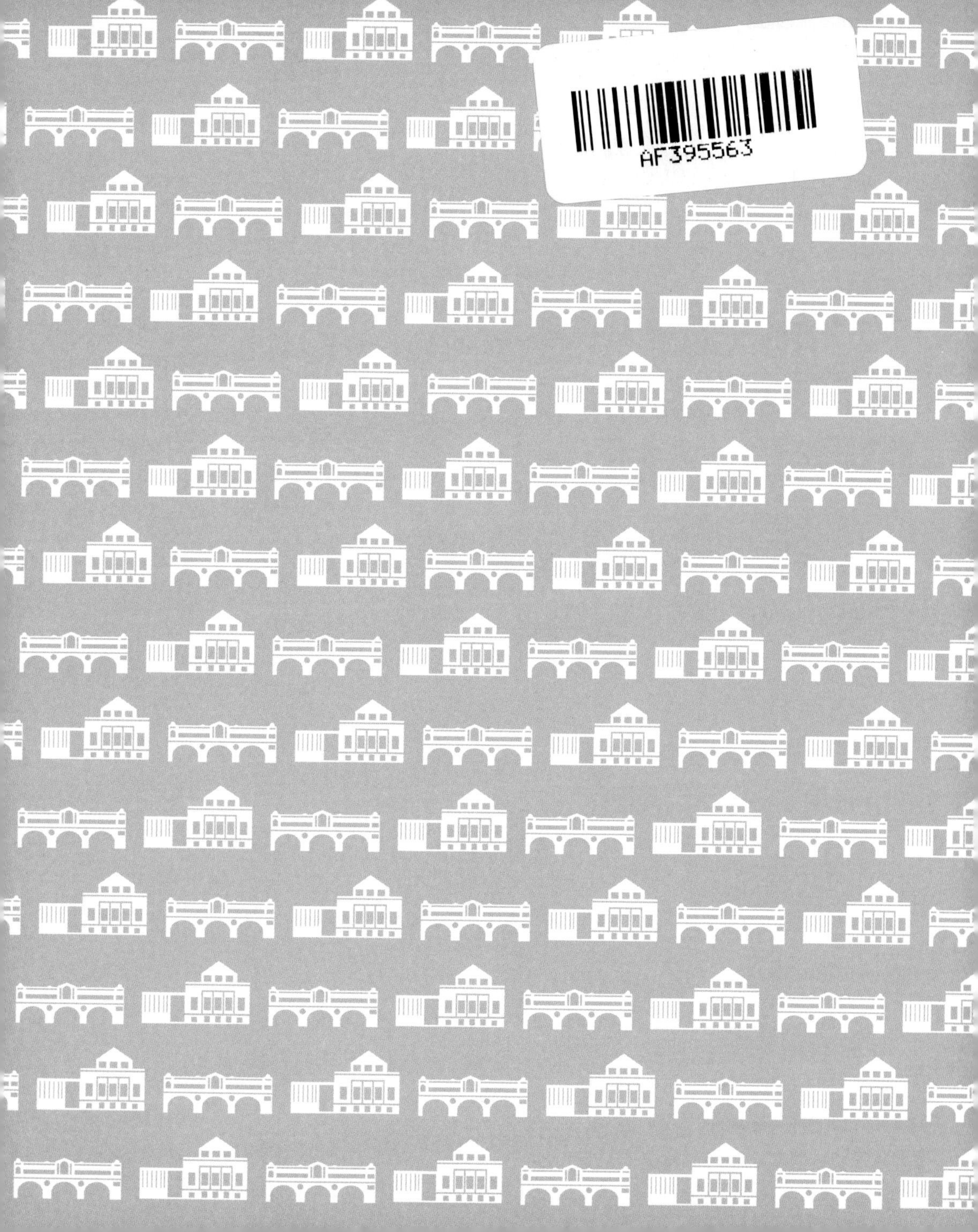

AF395563

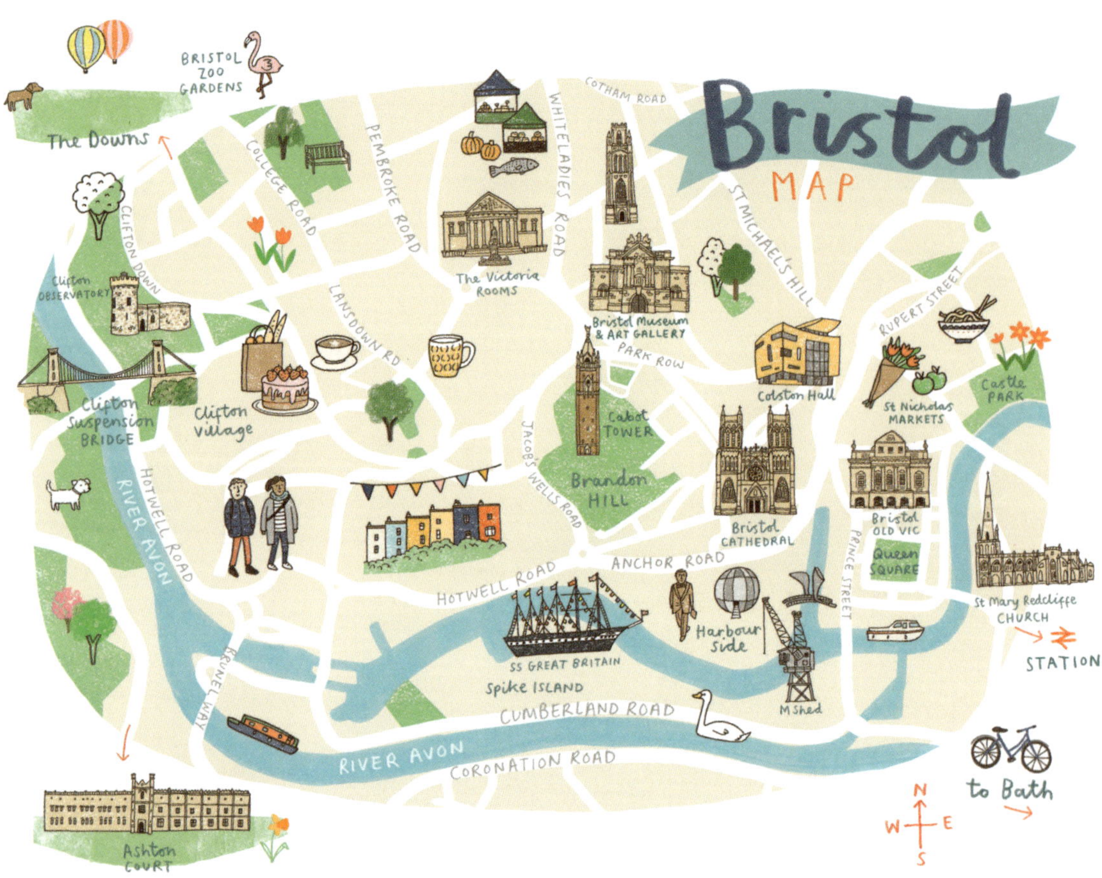

BRISTOL ZOO GARDENS
The Downs
CLIFTON DOWN
COLLEGE ROAD
PEMBROKE ROAD
COTHAM ROAD
WHITELADIES ROAD
ST MICHAEL'S HILL
Bristol
MAP
RUPERT STREET
Clifton OBSERVATORY
LANSDOWN RD
The Victoria ROOMS
Bristol Museum & ART GALLERY
PARK ROW
Colston Hall
St Nicholas MARKETS
Castle PARK
Clifton SUSPENSION BRIDGE
Clifton Village
Cabot TOWER
JACOB'S WELLS ROAD
Brandon HILL
Bristol CATHEDRAL
Bristol OLD VIC
HOTWELL ROAD
RIVER AVON
ANCHOR ROAD
Queen SQUARE
PRINCE STREET
St Mary Redcliffe CHURCH
HOTWELL ROAD
Harbour Side
STATION
SS GREAT BRITAIN
Spike ISLAND
M Shed
BRUNEL WAY
CUMBERLAND ROAD
RIVER AVON
CORONATION ROAD
to Bath
N
W E
S
Ashton COURT

*Fantastic images of two splendid cities*
DAME JACQUELINE WILSON, AWARD-WINNING AUTHOR,
*TRACY BEAKER, HETTY FEATHER*

*The creativity and skill of the artists in this book are both astonishing and inspirational*
DAISY MAY COOPER & CHARLIE COOPER, WRITERS AND ACTORS
OF AWARD-WINNING COMEDY *THIS COUNTRY*

*It's like being given a brilliant new set of eyes. Seeing the familiar afresh*
ADRIAN SCARBOROUGH, TV AND FILM ACTOR –
'PETE' IN *GAVIN AND STACEY*

*Bristol and Bath in a beautiful book*
*Picturesque studies of both vista and nook.*
*I played in their theatres on many a night.*
*These page turning fancies of artistic high flight*
*And stunning renditions of colour and light*
*Believe me when I tell you, as tell you I do*
*This book that you're holding, it's well worth a look.*
JEREMY IRONS, OSCAR-WINNING FILM & TV ACTOR

*Wonderfully unique and vivid studies of my vibrant*
*hometown and its elegant neighbour.*
STEPHEN MERCHANT, COMEDIAN, ACTOR, TV PRESENTER,
DIRECTOR, WRITER OF *THE OUTLAWS*

*Truly stunning pictures of two of our most beautiful cities*
MARK STRONG, TV & FILM ACTOR –
1917, *SHERLOCK HOLMES, OUR FRIENDS IN THE NORTH*

*Fresh, invigorating and inspiring*
SIR TONY ROBINSON, AUTHOR, ACTOR –
'BALDRICK' IN *BLACKADDER*, PRESENTER *TIME TEAM*

HERBERT PRESS
Bloomsbury Publishing Plc
50 Bedford Square, London, WC1B 3DP, UK
29 Earlsfort Terrace, Dublin 2, Ireland

BLOOMSBURY, HERBERT PRESS and the Herbert Press logo are trademarks of Bloomsbury Publishing Plc

First published in England in 2022 by UIT Cambridge Ltd.
This edition published 2024



A CIP catalogue record for this book is available from the British Library
Library of Congress Cataloguing-in-Publication data has been applied for

ISBN: 978-1-91293-421-8 (hardback) ISBN: 978-1-91293-422-5 (ePub)

3 5 7 9 10 8 6 4 2

Printed and bound in India

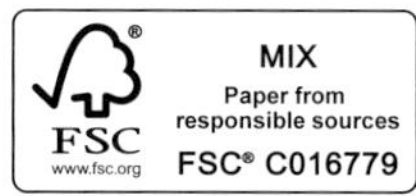


To find out more about our authors and books visit www.bloomsbury.com and sign up for our newsletters

# THE
# BRISTOL & BATH
# ART BOOK

## The Cities Through the Eyes of their Artists®

EDITED BY

## EMMA BENNETT

HERBERT PRESS

LONDON · OXFORD · NEW YORK · NEW DELHI · SYDNEY

# Acknowledgements

*The Bristol and Bath Art Book* has been made possible by the enthusiasm and talent of the contributing artists and to them I am eternally grateful.

In the city of Bristol, an illustrious panel of local art and city professionals helped select images for publication. I am indebted to them for their creative input. They are:

- Colin Moody, Artist and Photographer

- Amanda Nicholls, Editor, *The Bristol Magazine*

- Joanna Plimmer, Arts Officer, Bristol City Council

- Sarah Thorp, Owner, Room 212 Gallery and Alchemy 198

- Naomi Triggol, Artist and Director of Memory Maze Ltd

- Jo Tunmer, Lead Panellist, *The City Through The Eyes of Its Artists*® series

I grew up spending my summer holidays visiting my grandparents who lived in the shadows of the Mendip Hills in Somerset. These summers which included daily craft activities form some of my happiest childhood memories and encouraged a love of all things creative. It should never be underestimated how influential grandparents can be. For these summers of fun I thank Madge (Vi) and George Birch, who along with my maternal grandparents Betty and Norman Adams encouraged all genres of arty creativity. Thank you Nanny and Grandad Birch for introducing me to the beautiful Somerset countryside.

To Jo Tunmer: thank you for fun-filled days in Bristol, you are the best of travel companions. Naomi and Andrew Triggol, thank you for some fabulous times on Triggols Farm in Clevedon when I lived in Cheltenham. Julia Sadler and Alison Schuldt thank you for the endless devotion to proofreading.

# CONTENTS


Foreword 6

Preface 7

The Vic Rooms (Bristol) to the Bristol Old Vic 8

Arnolfini and the Harbourside Area 35

Clifton and the Clifton Suspension Bridge 57

Clevedon 76

A visit to the Stokes Croft area en route to Bath 78

From Bristol to Bath 82

The City of Bath 84

Pulteney Bridge 86

Around Bath Abbey and the Roman Baths 91

The Circus and The Royal Crescent 106

Around Landsdown Road 117

Sydney Gardens 123

Artist Credits 126

# FOREWORD

Some cities open their arms to art and creativity more than others. It may happen as a result of historical and contemporary 'incidence' or an ineffable alchemy of economics, happenstance and will. Whatever the mix is — that both allows it to happen and to celebrate it — it often creeps forward as a defining characteristic of the place itself, and this certainly applies to Bristol and Bath.

Creativity is strongly embedded in the historical institutions, museums, architecture and public spaces of both cities. They have also escaped the Georgian and Victorian 'city making' and found a new life in the creativity of communities and contemporary life. If you add into this mix a commitment to independent shops, the slow food and maker movements, an urban culture based on mobility and contemporary economics then you start to scratch the surface of why Bristol and Bath are 'art cities'. Global policy makers and leaders have tried to replicate this recipe to set their own cities on a course of social and economic change fuelled by creativity. The results have been exciting and patchy.

Over many decades, institutions such as the Royal West of England Academy (founded in 1844) and Arnolfini (1961) in Bristol, and the Holborne Museum in Bath (1882), have been part of a rich cultural sector committed to celebrating and encouraging creativity in many arts forms. But all institutions recognise that it is the artists themselves that give them purpose and content. And more importantly that art mostly happens outside of institutions in an unstoppable way with an energy of its own. This is the wonderful thing about *The City Through The Eyes of Its Artists*[®] series — it gives a voice to the artists to share their relationship to the cities they call home. In the best way it gives the city 'story' back to the artists to do what they do best — both reflect upon it and constantly recreate it.

**Gary Topp**
Director, Arnolfini, Bristol's International Centre for Contemporary Arts

# PREFACE

Less than 20 kilometres separate the cities of Bristol and Bath but in many ways these two cities are as different as chalk and cheese. Look a little closer and you will see two places that share a breathtaking natural landscape of rivers and hills, and which stand out in the history of the world.

2,000 years ago, the Romans settled in Bath constructing a stunning complex of baths and temples. Add to this the Bath Stone of the Georgian era and it's difficult to know where to look first.

Bath had the Romans, Bristol had Isambard Kingdom Brunel who led the way in the Industrial Revolution, with his groundbreaking construction of the Great Western Railway and the Clifton Suspension Bridge.

It's not just about the history. Bristol is one of the most modern, vibrant, quirky and independent cities you will visit, bustling at the seams with bold creativity. Banksy's signature street art can be seen everywhere whilst Wallace and Gromit creators Aardman Animations are based in the city. Bath is modern in a less vocal, more understated way — a city that ticks all the boxes and has it all.

This is the sixth in *The City Through The Eyes of Its Artists*® series (after Cambridge, Oxford, Edinburgh, Liverpool and Dublin). These books show iconic cities through the eyes of the local artists they inspire and represent just some of the talented artists working in and around Bristol and Bath. With the help of the maps, potter through these cities with *The Bristol and Bath Art Book* in your hand and stand for a while in the footsteps of an artist.

**Emma Bennett**

Creator and Editor of the *The City Through The Eyes of Its Artists*® series

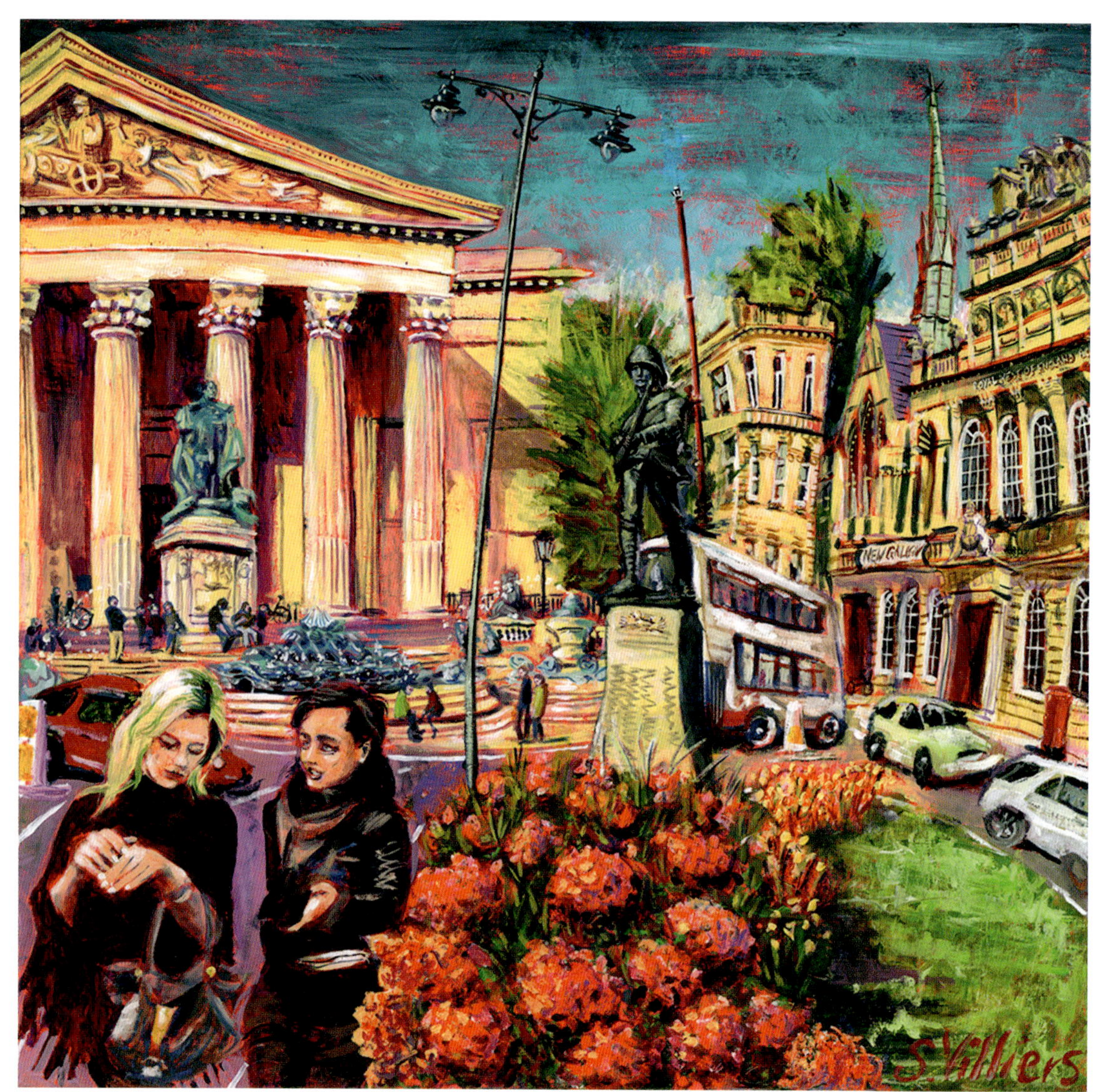

QUEENS ROAD, SONIA VILLIERS

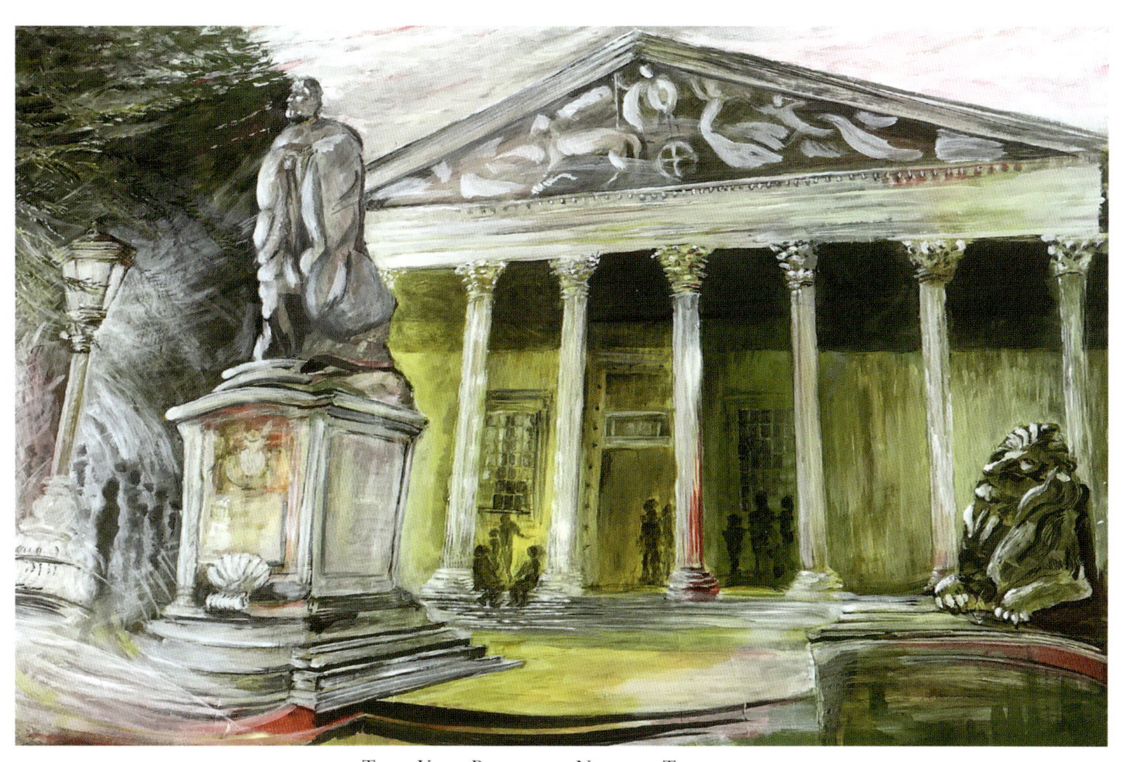

THE VIC ROOMS, NAOMI TRIGGOL

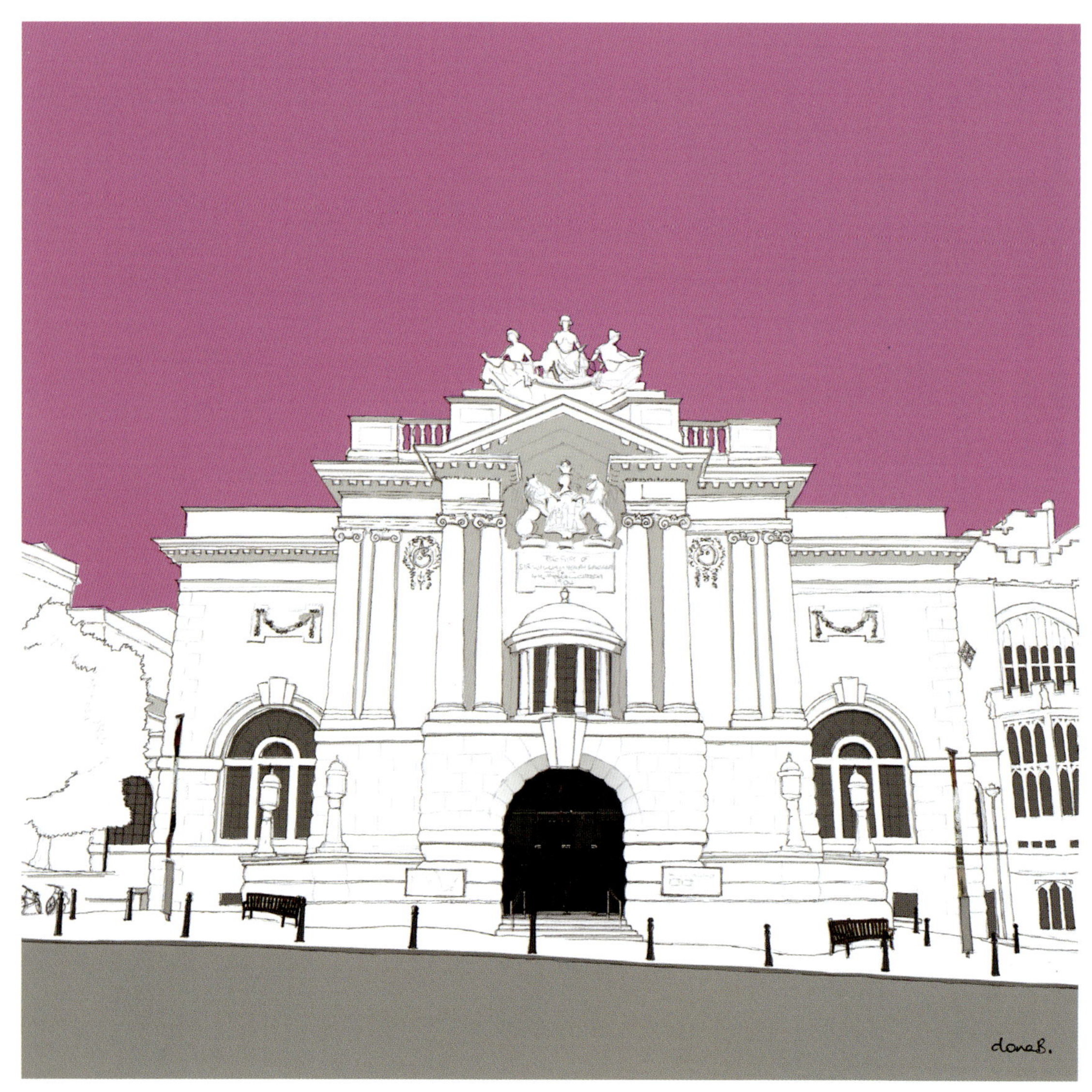

BRISTOL MUSEUM & ART GALLERY, DONA BRADLEY

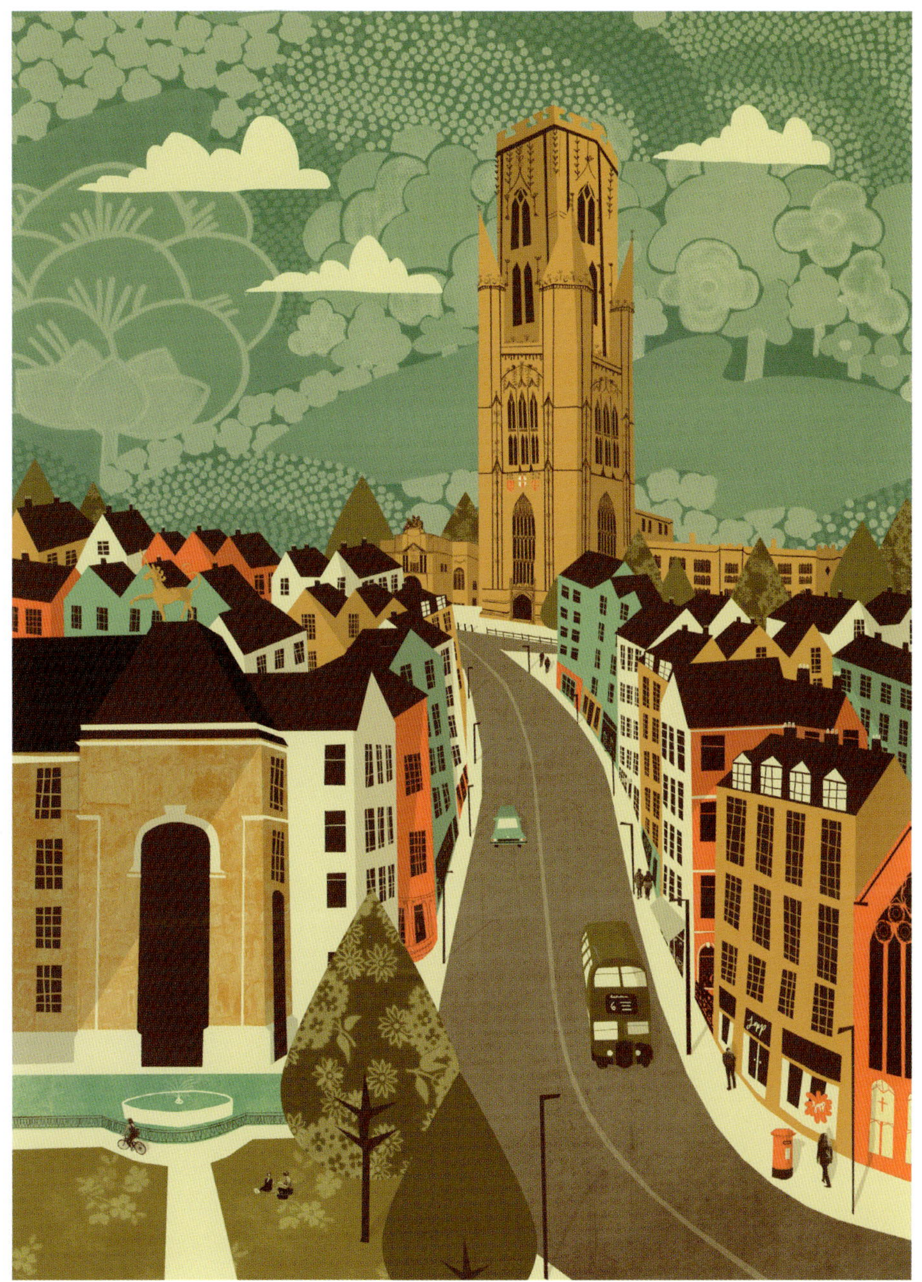



PARK STREET, EMY LOU HOLMES

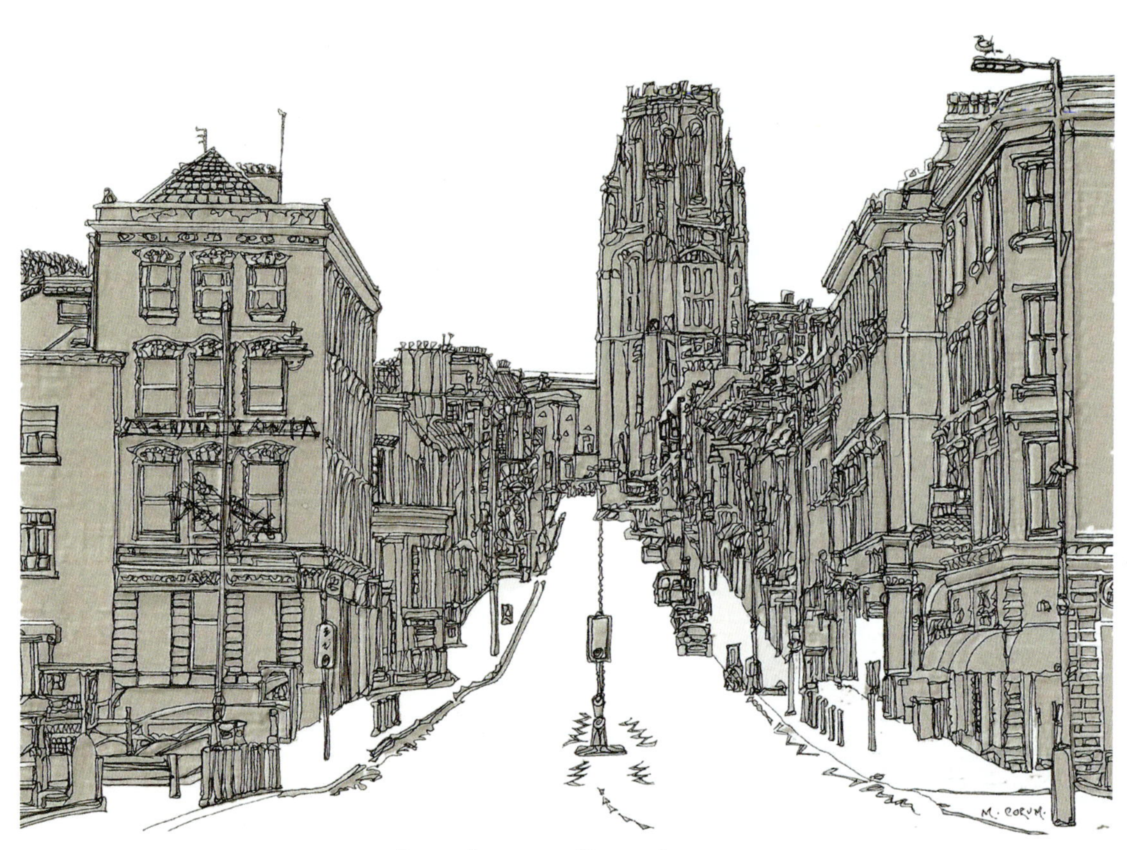

PARK STREET, MARY CORUM

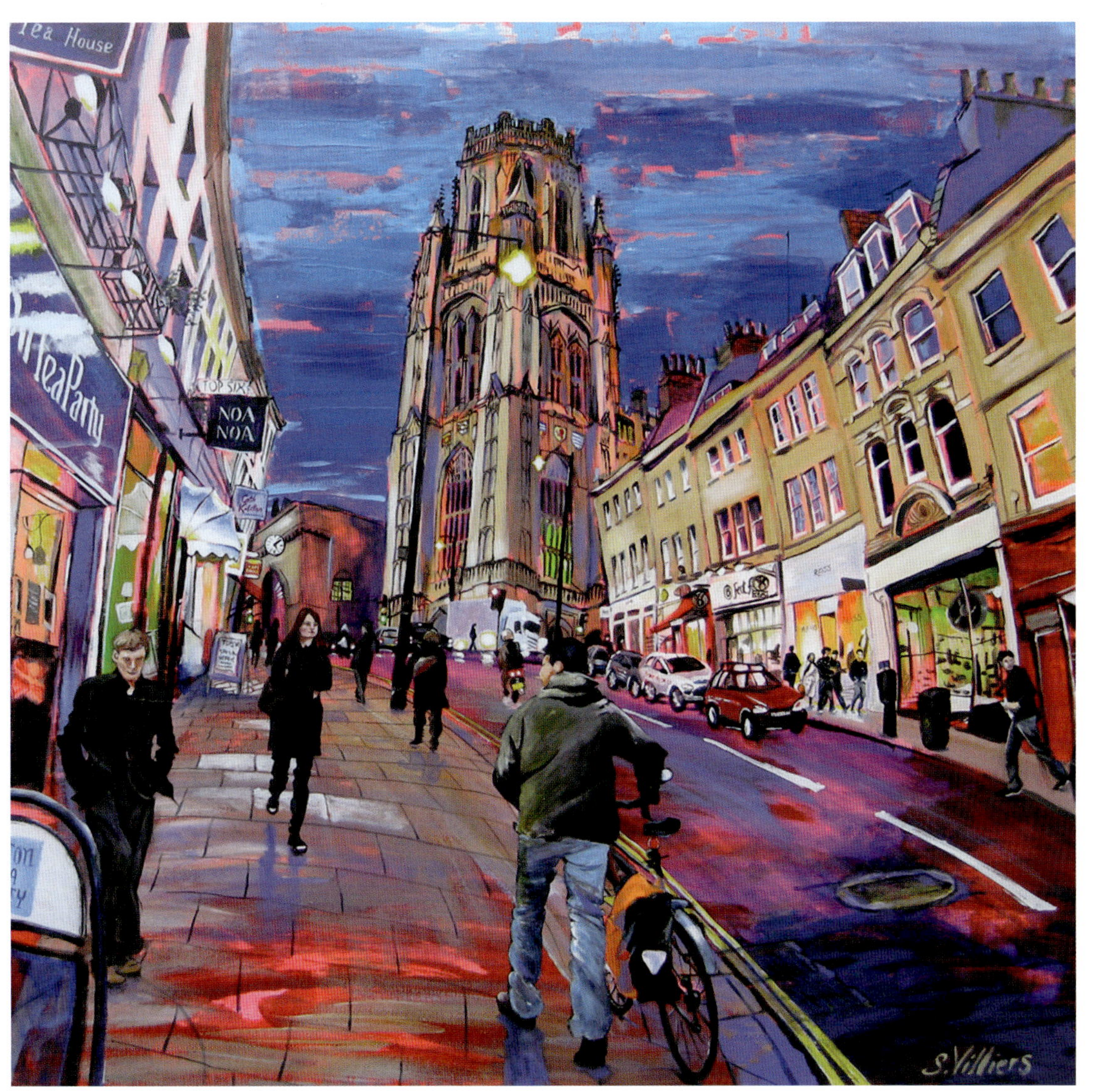

PARK STREET, SONIA VILLIERS

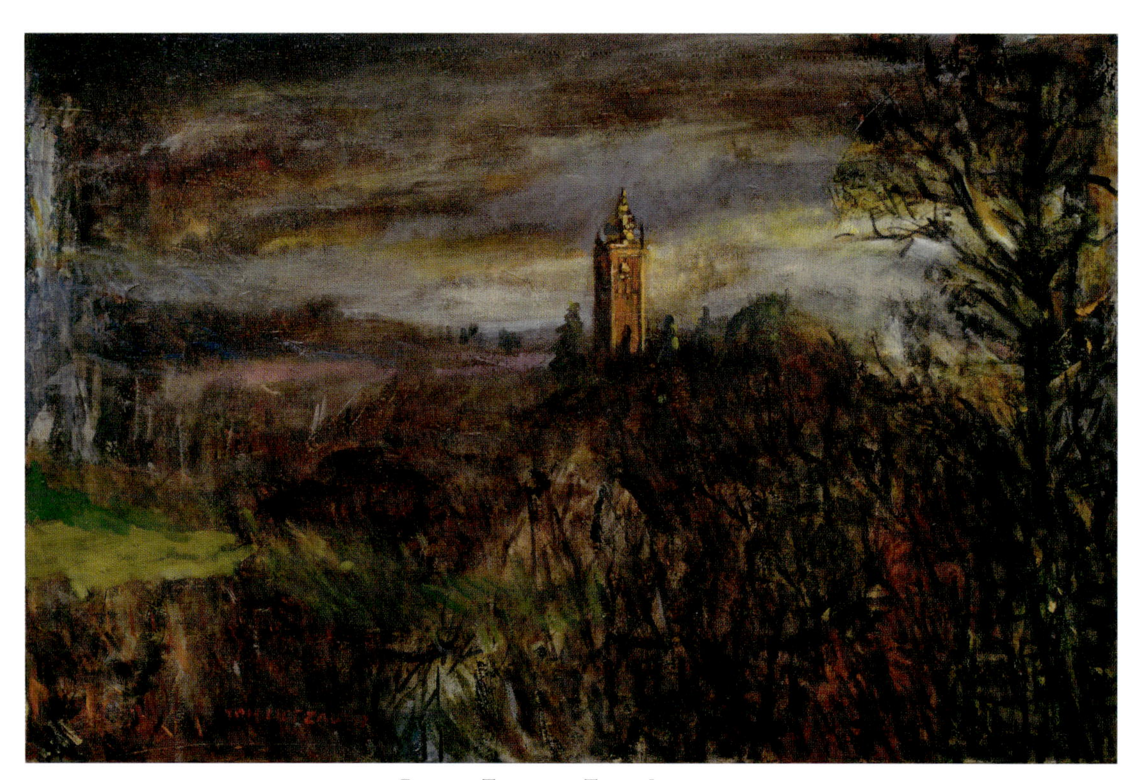

CABOT TOWER, TOM LIETZAU

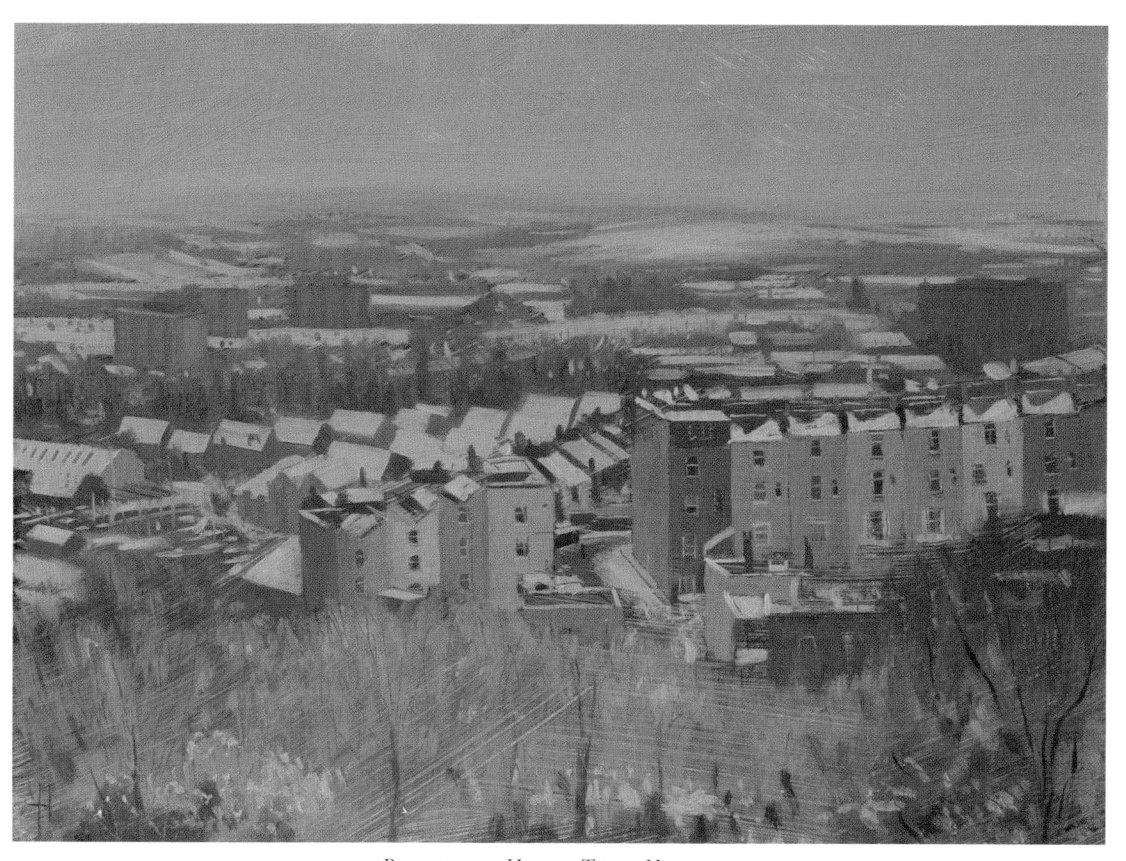

BRANDON HILL, TOM HUGHES

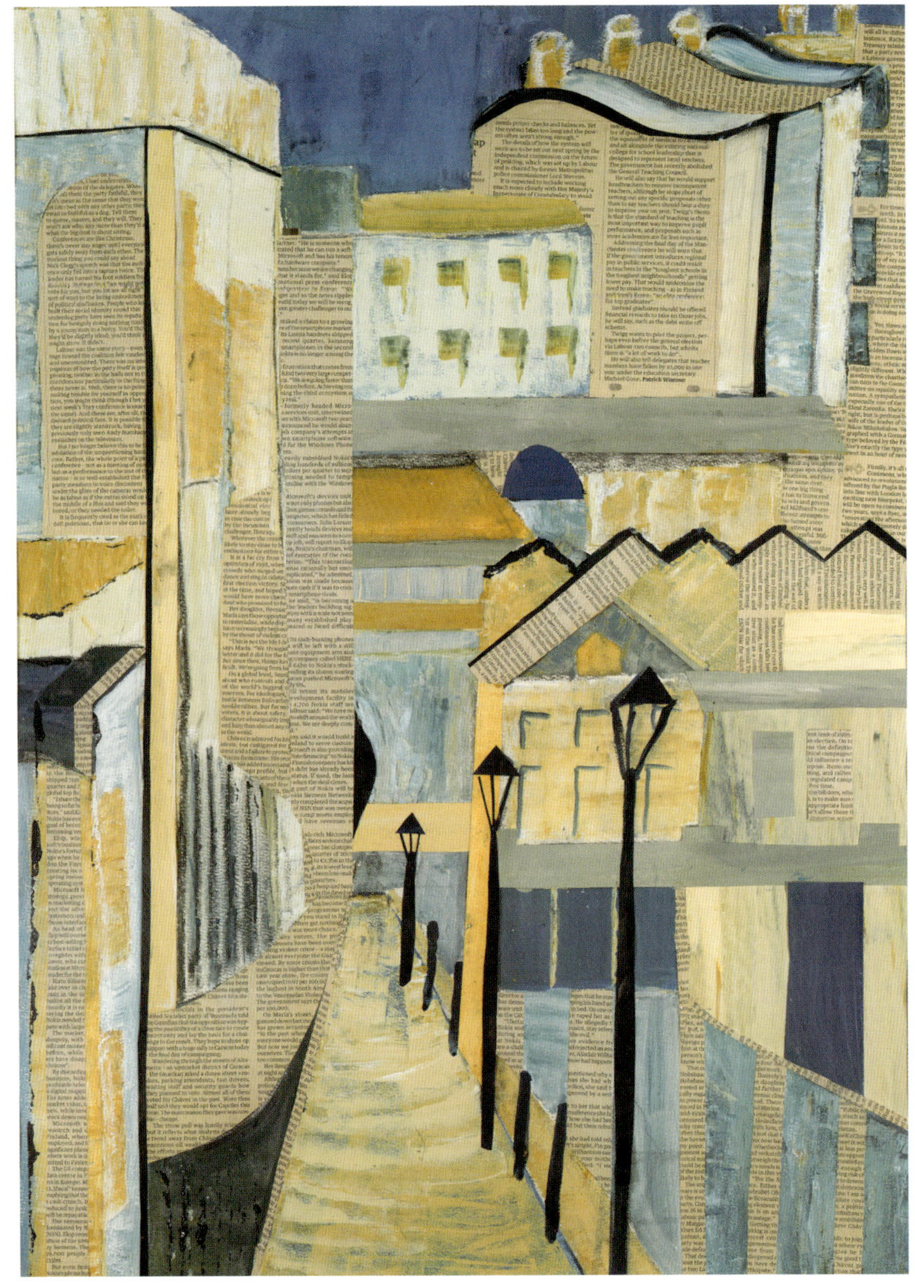

CHARLOTTE STREET, CARRIE POOLER

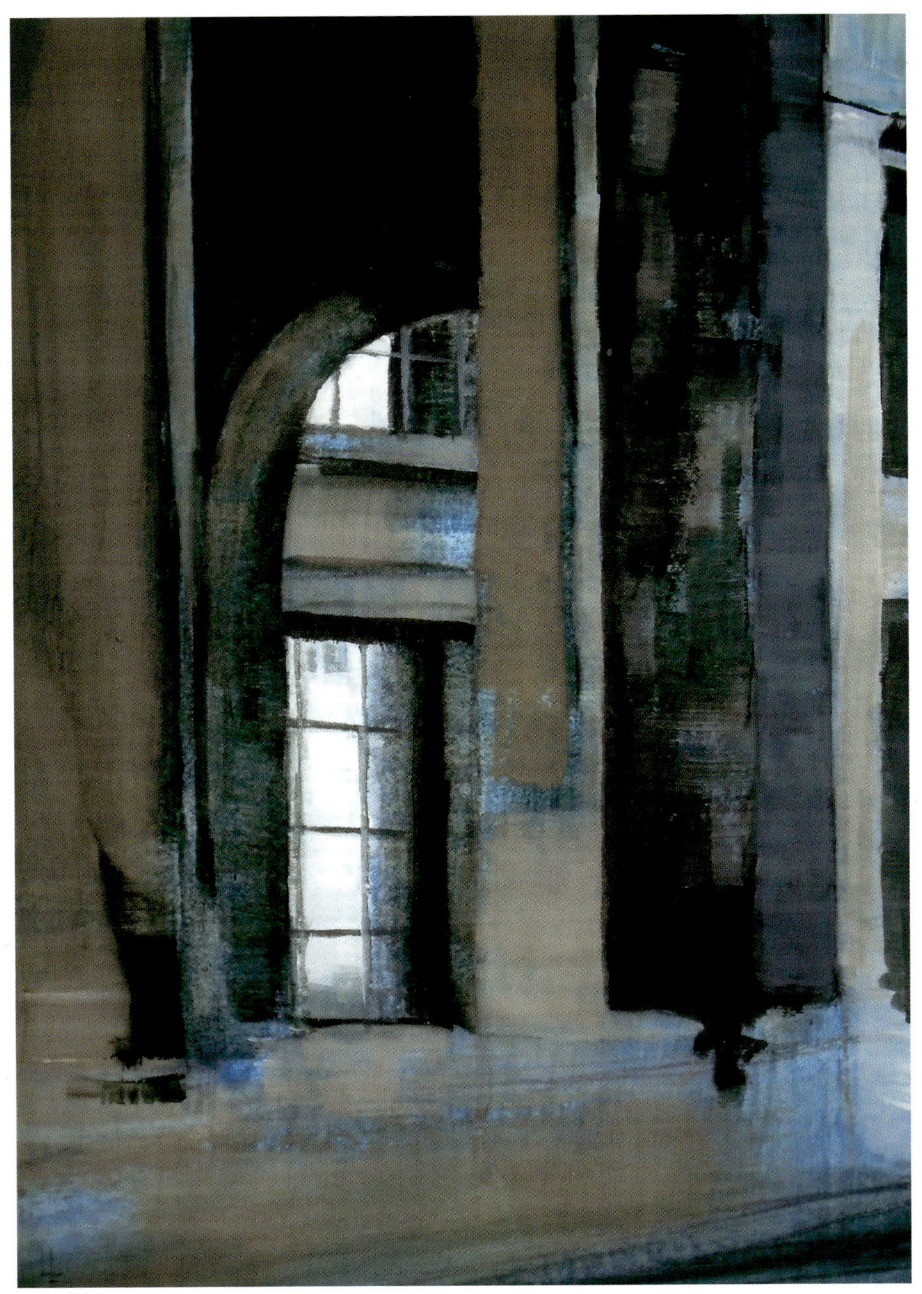

CITY HALL, LINDSEY LAVENDER

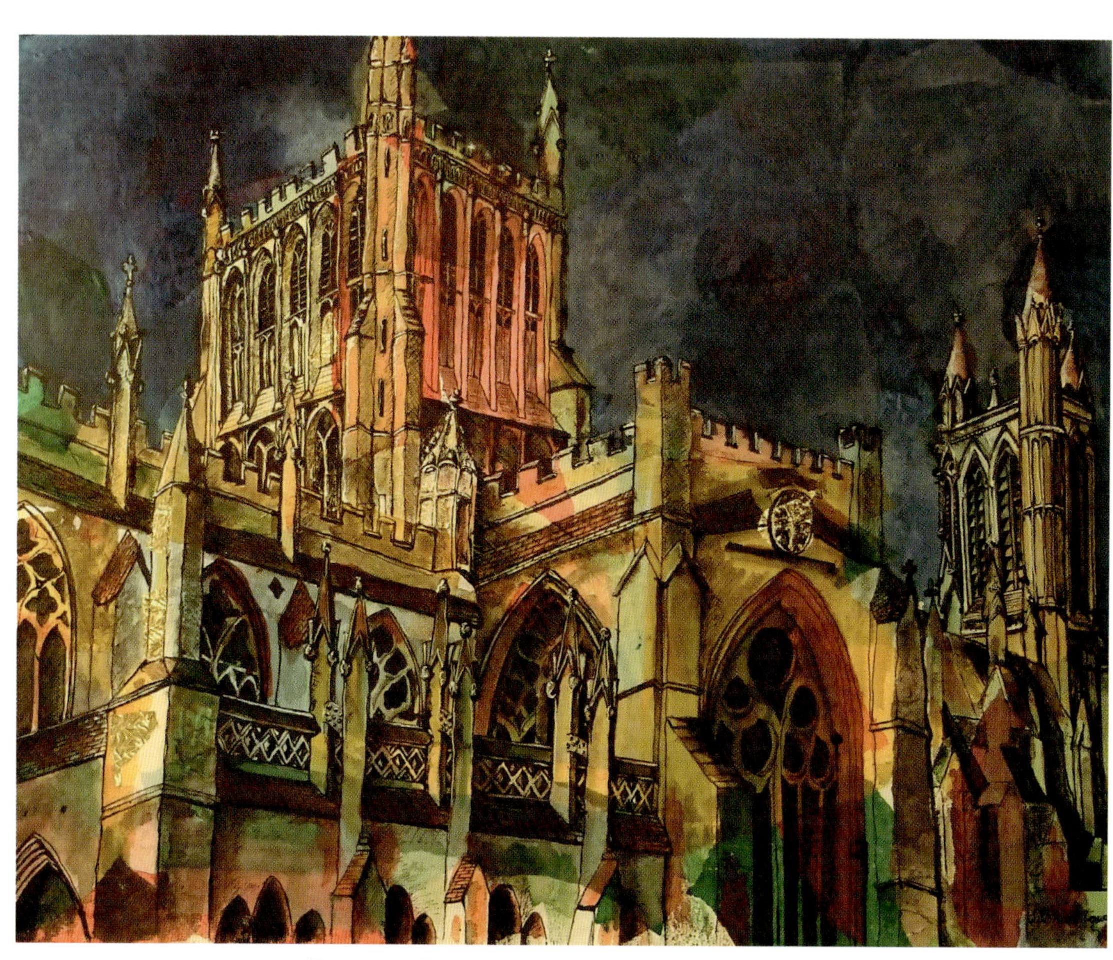

Bristol Cathedral, Juli-Anne Coward

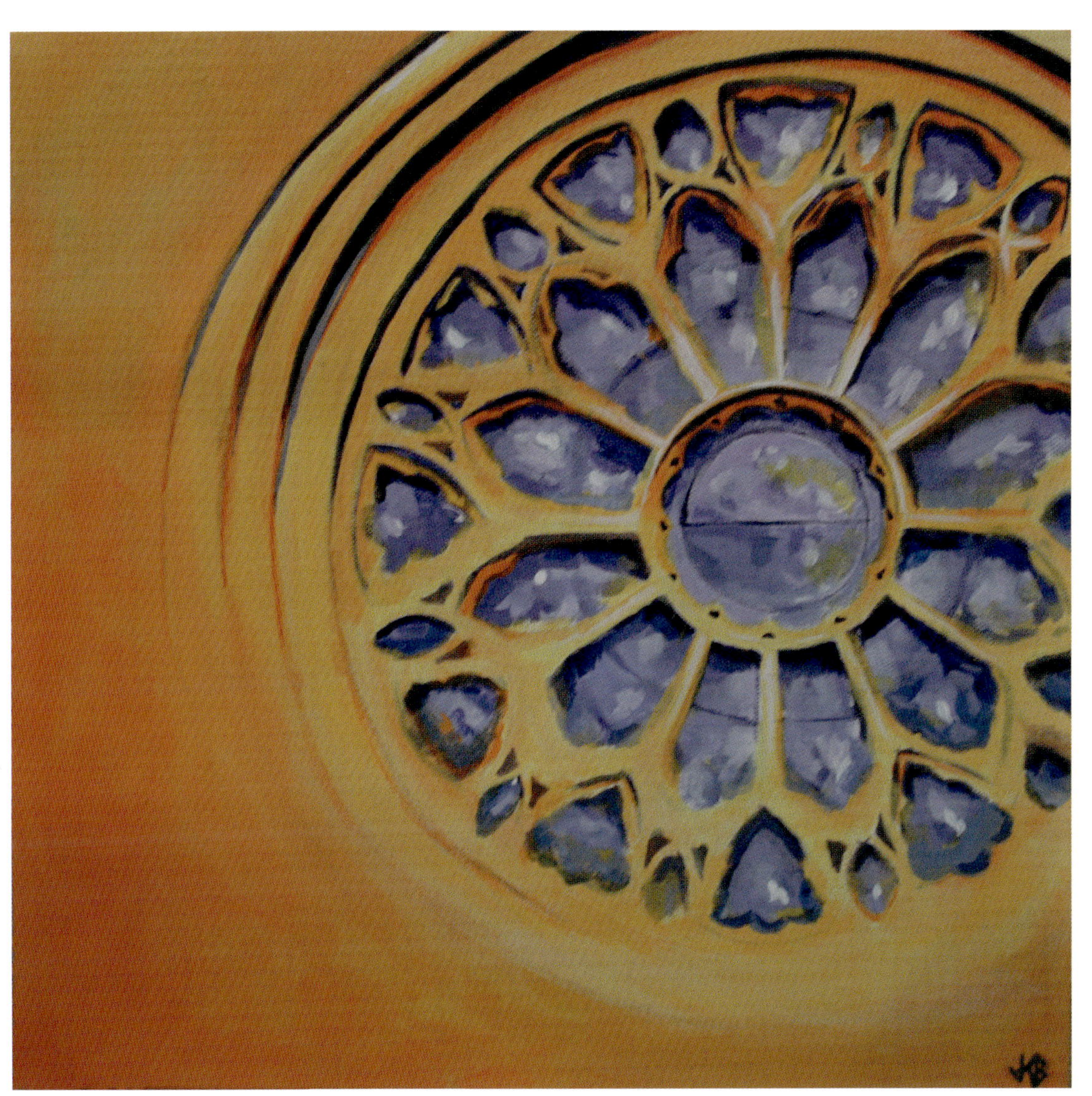

Bristol Cathedral Rose Window, Jennifer Keeney-Bleeg

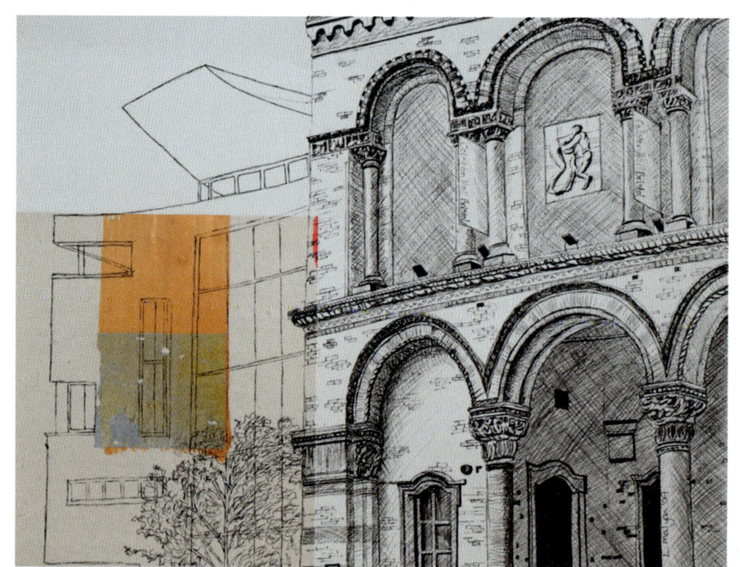

BRISTOL BEACON, OLD AND NEW, LISA MALYON

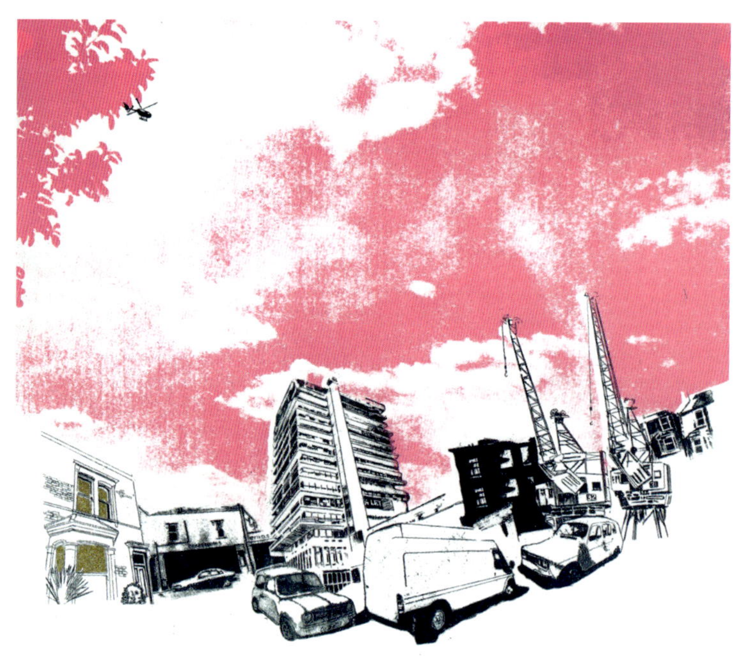

BEAUTIFUL BRISTOL, ANNA MARROW

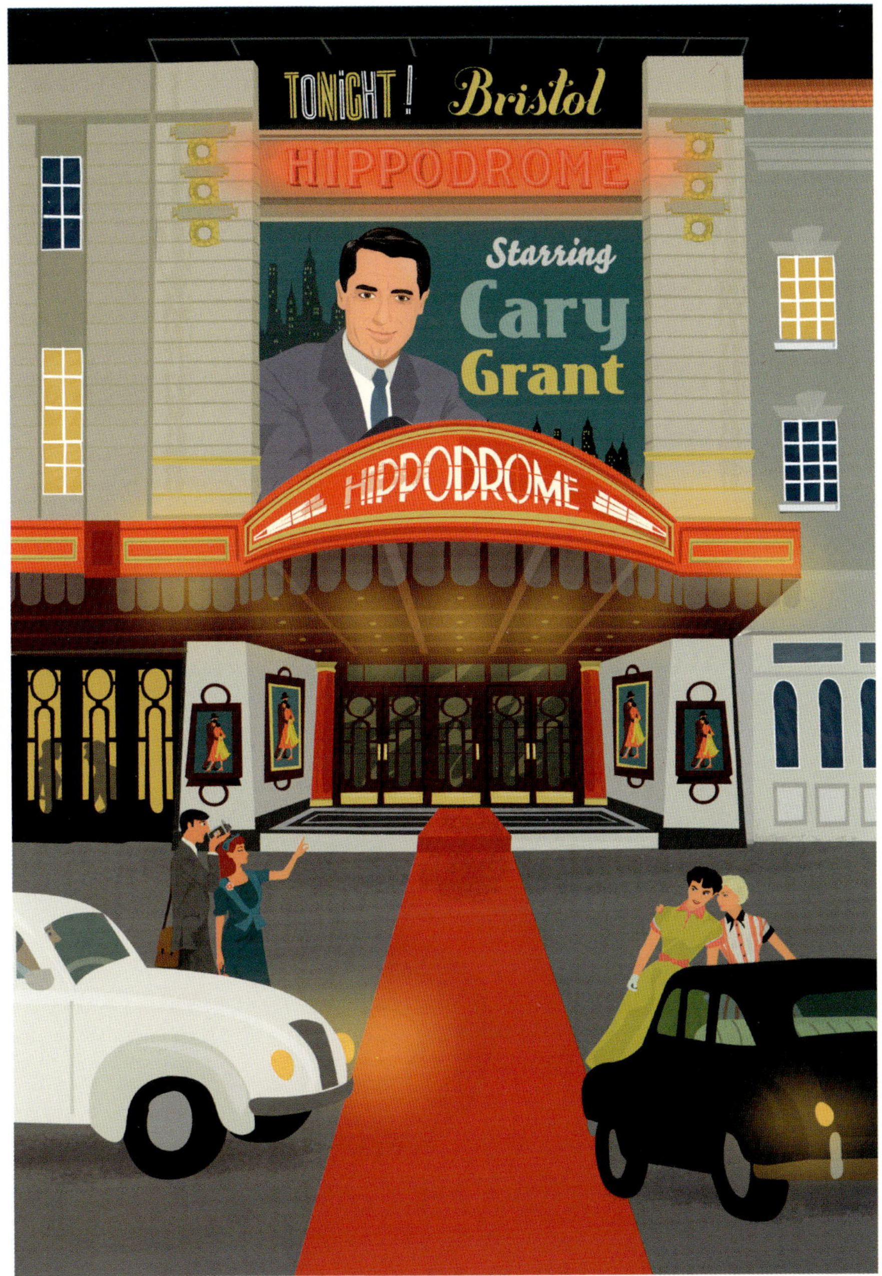

THE BRISTOL HIPPODROME, CLARE PHILLIPS

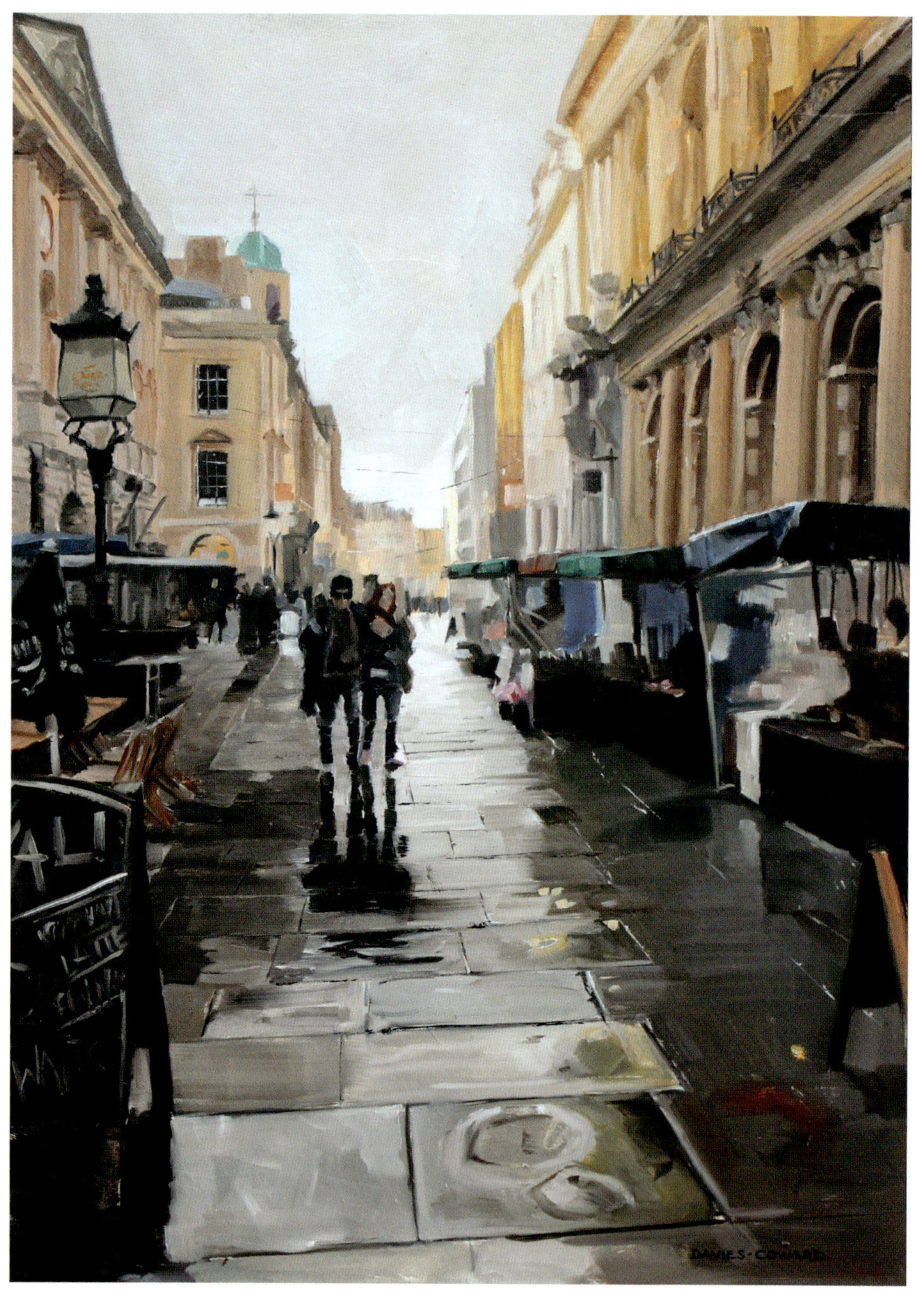

CORN STREET MARKET, ANDY DAVIES-COWARD

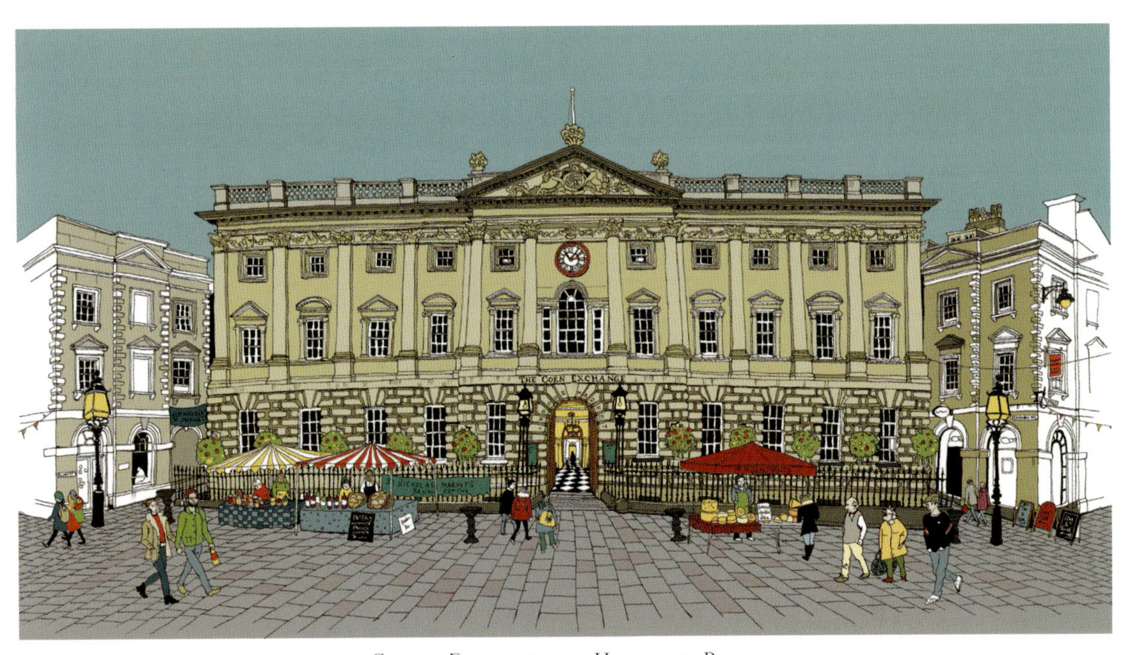

CORN EXCHANGE, HANNAH BUNN

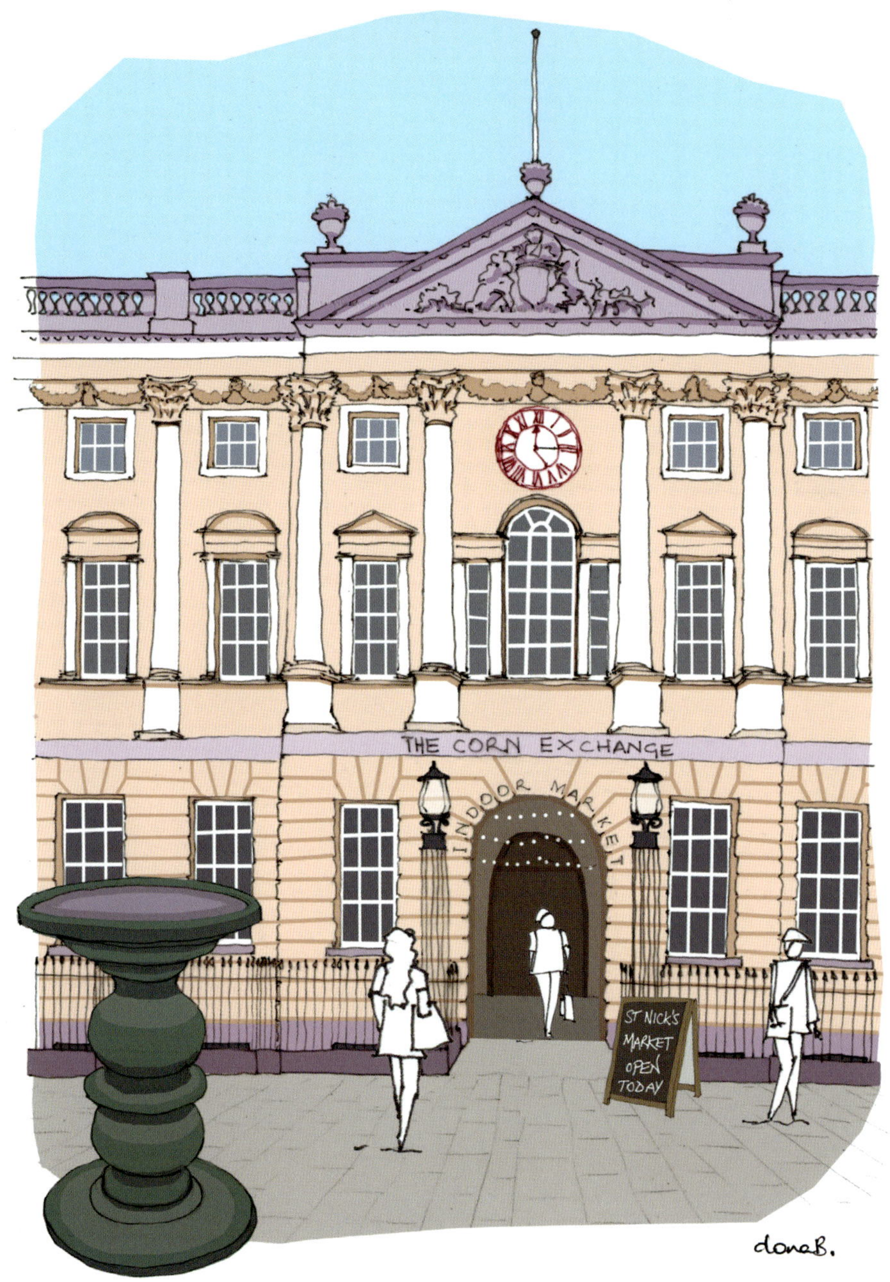


ST NICHOLAS MARKETS, DONA BRADLEY

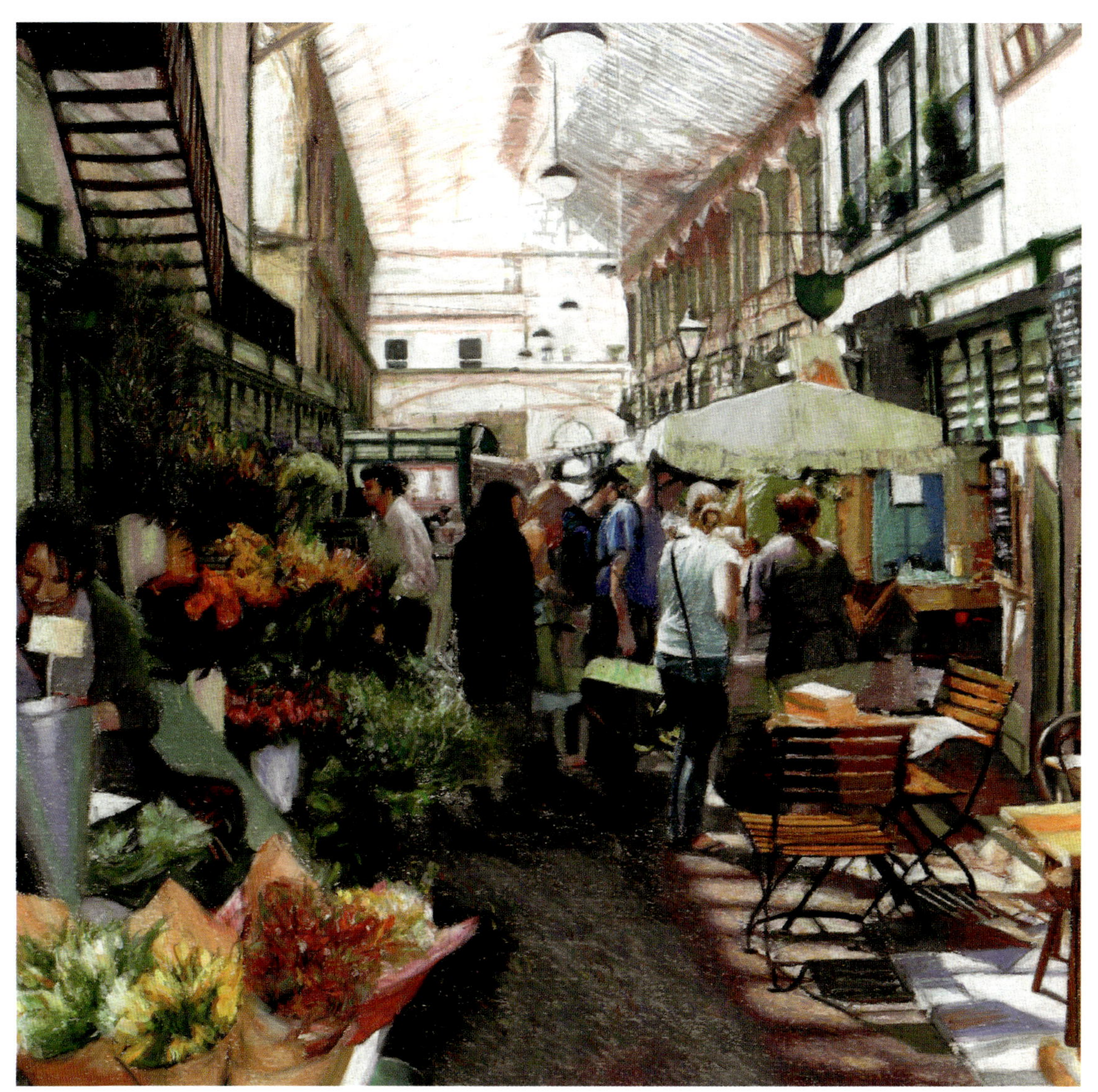

ST NICHOLAS MARKETS, ROBERT ANTELL

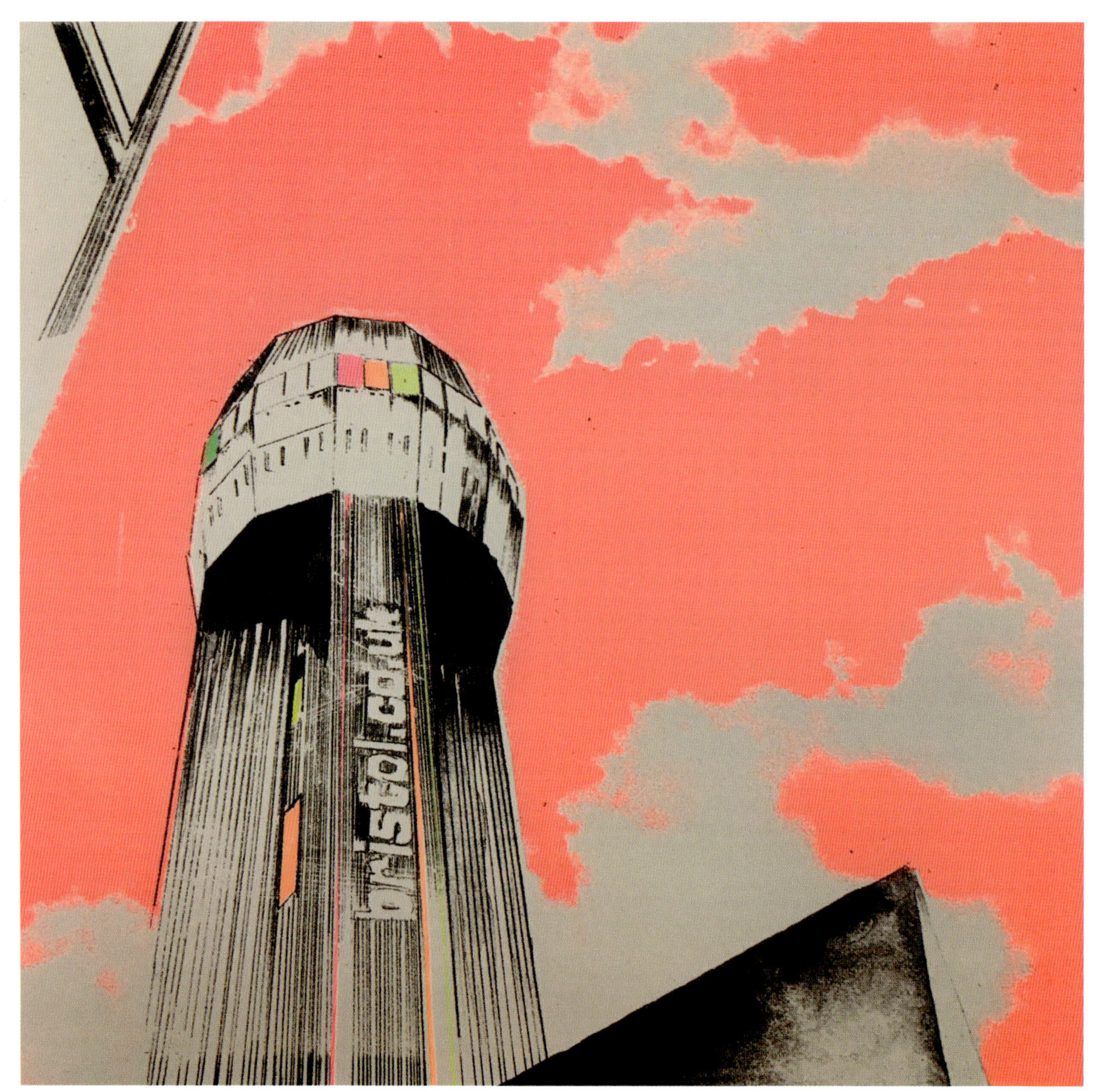



(Love) Bristol, Anna Marrow

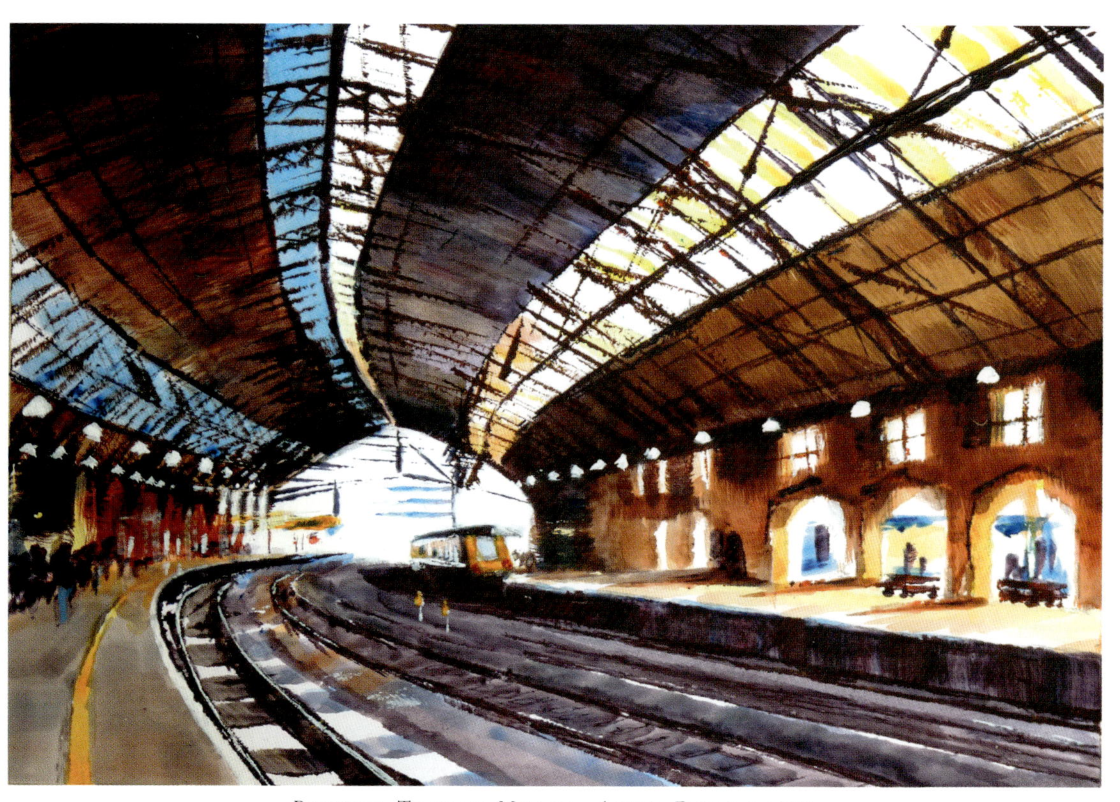

BRISTOL TEMPLE MEADS, ANNA DUCKWORTH

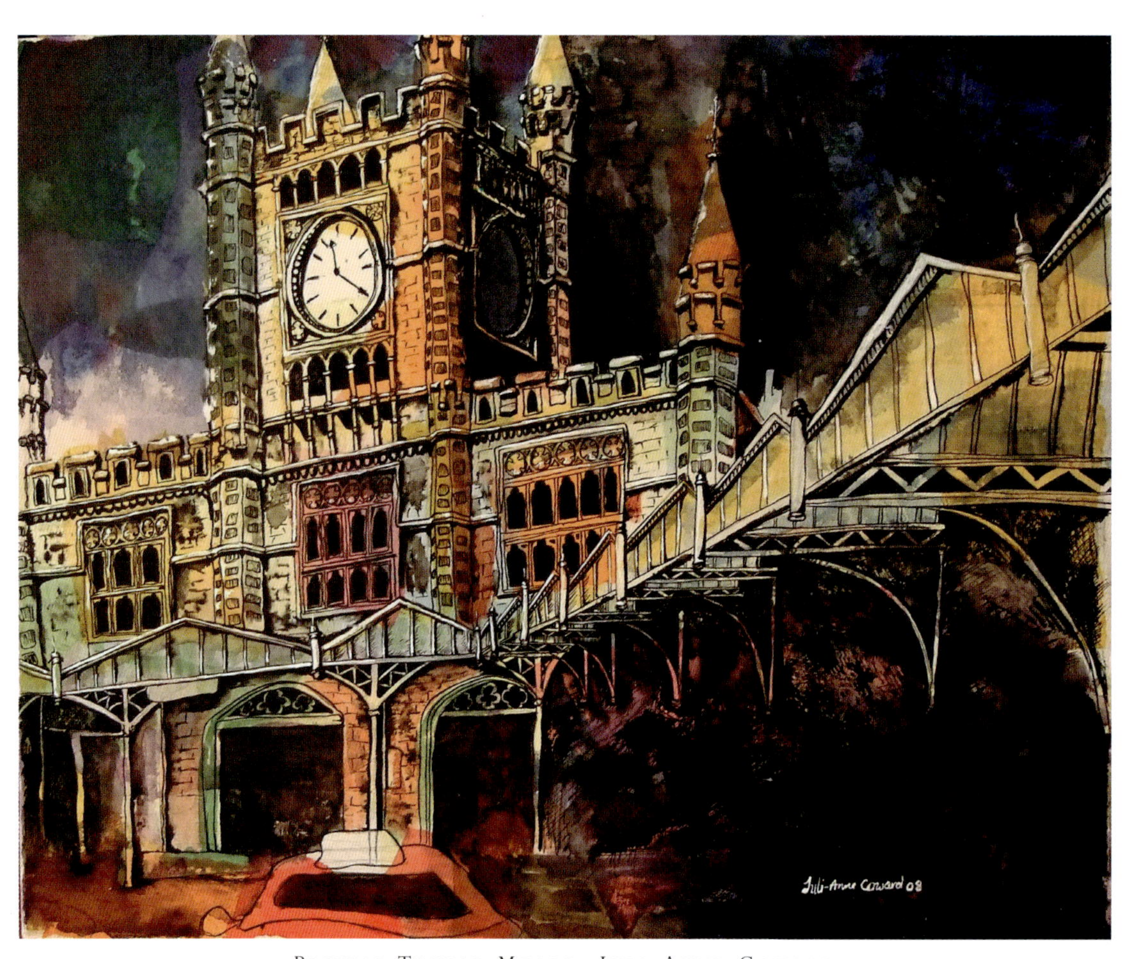

BRISTOL TEMPLE MEADS, JULI-ANNE COWARD

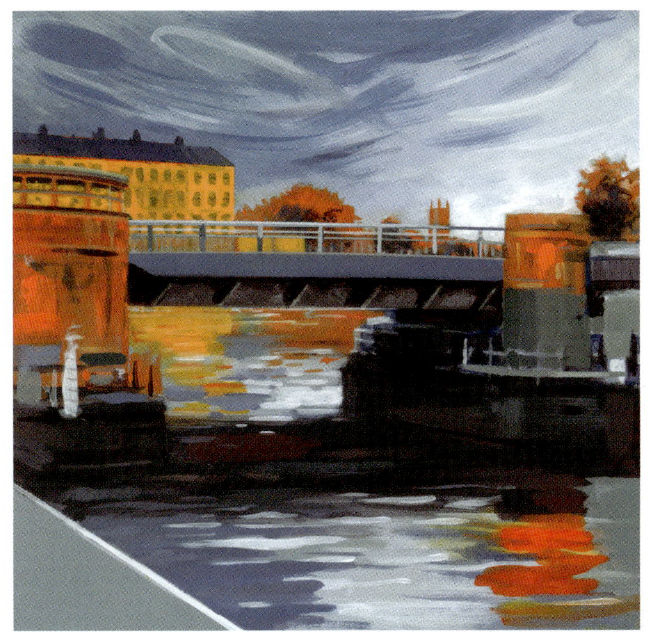

Redcliffe Bascule Bridge, Nick Gerolemou

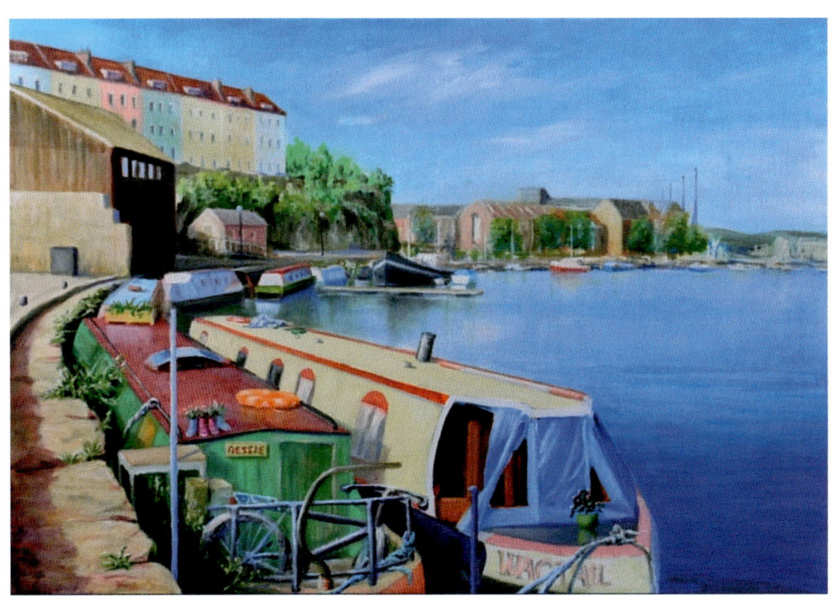

Redcliffe Wharf, Kathy Luders

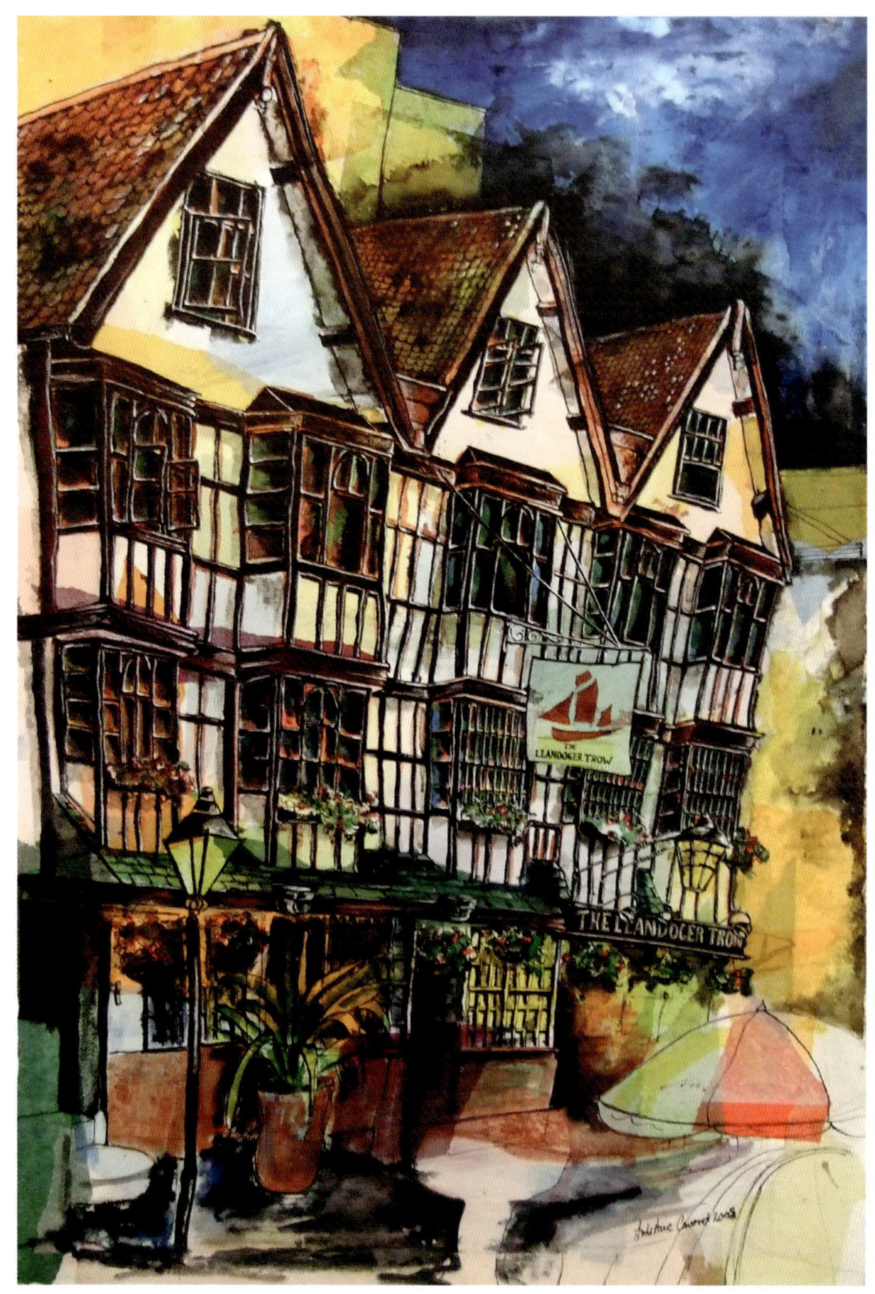



LLANDOGER TROW, JULI-ANNE COWARD

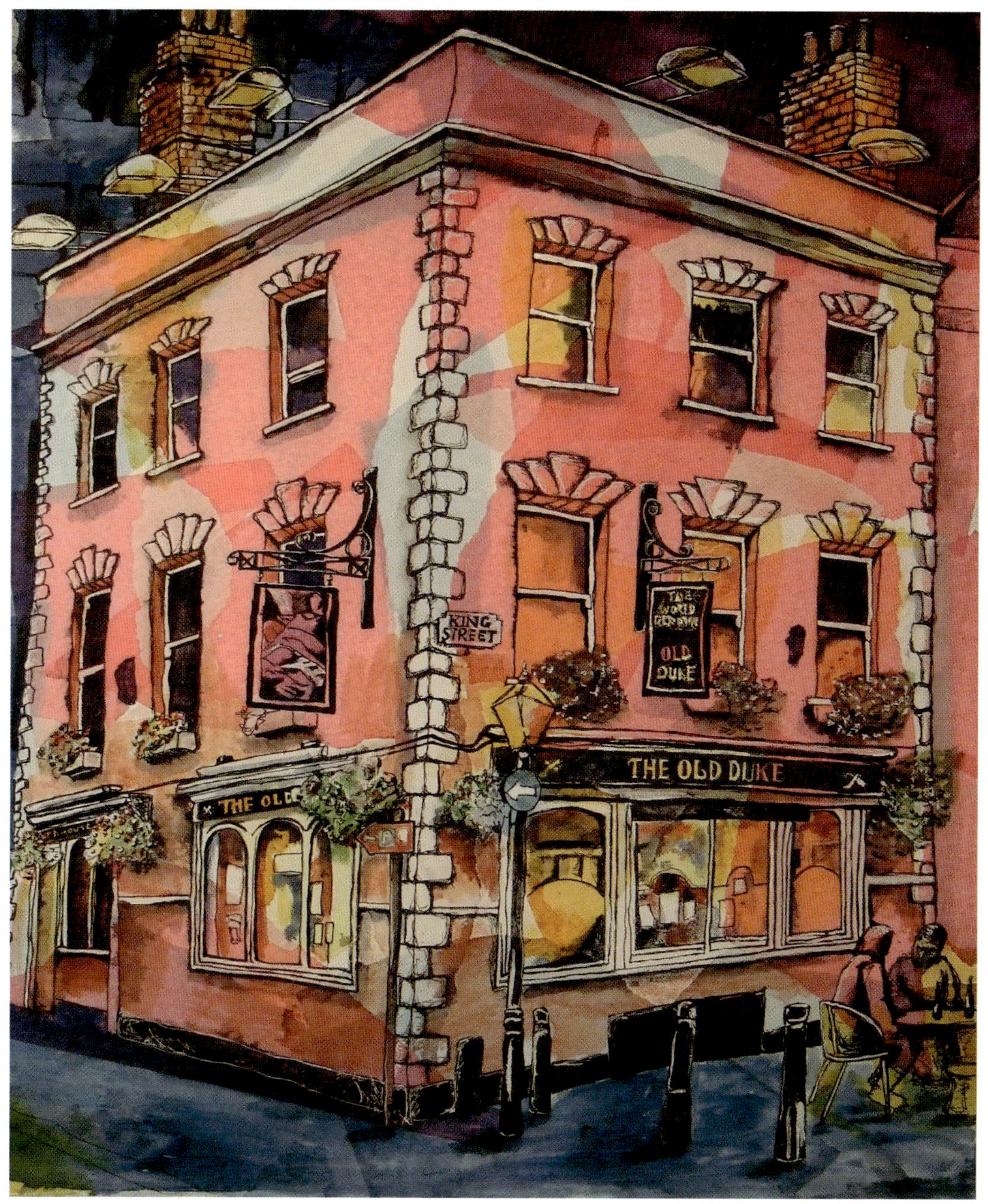


THE OLD DUKE, JULI-ANNE COWARD

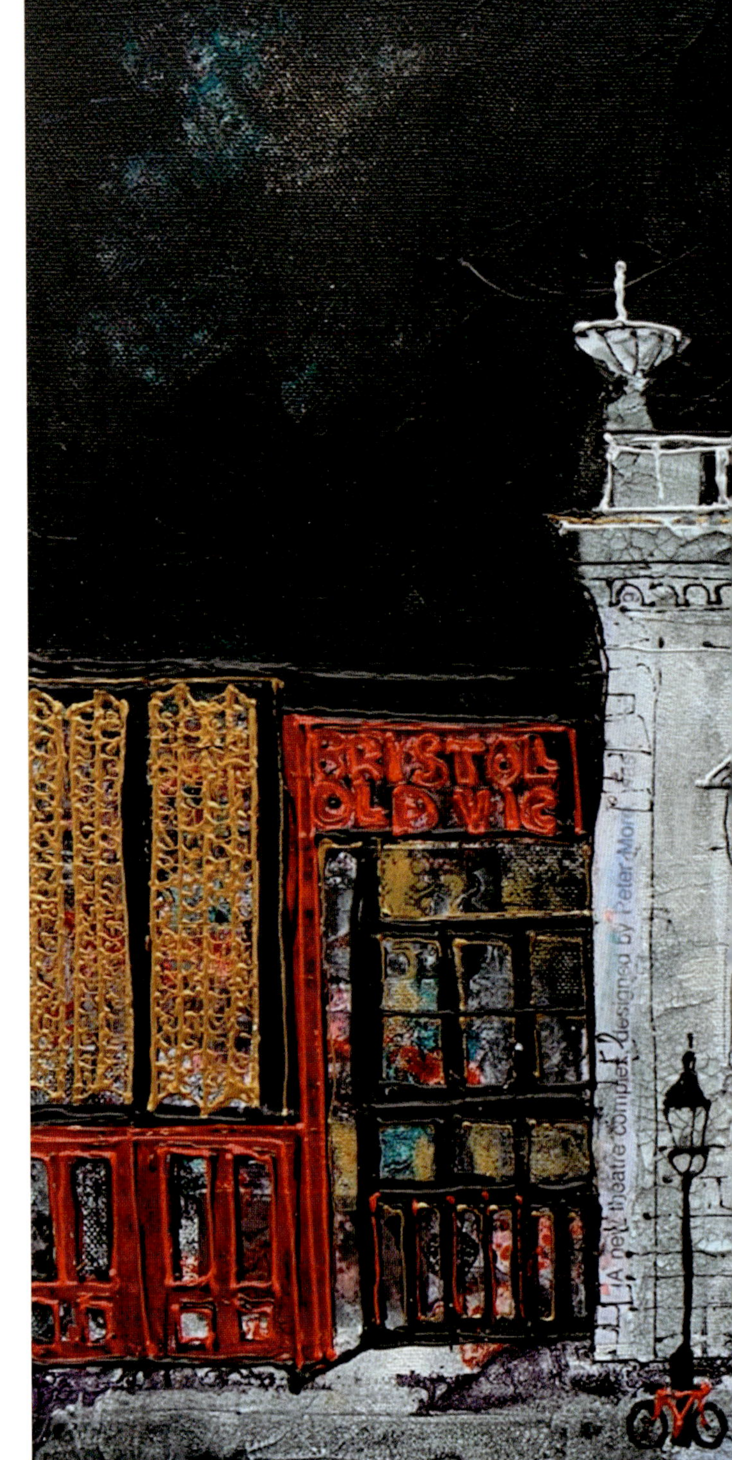



BRISTOL OLD VIC,
KATHARINE DOVE

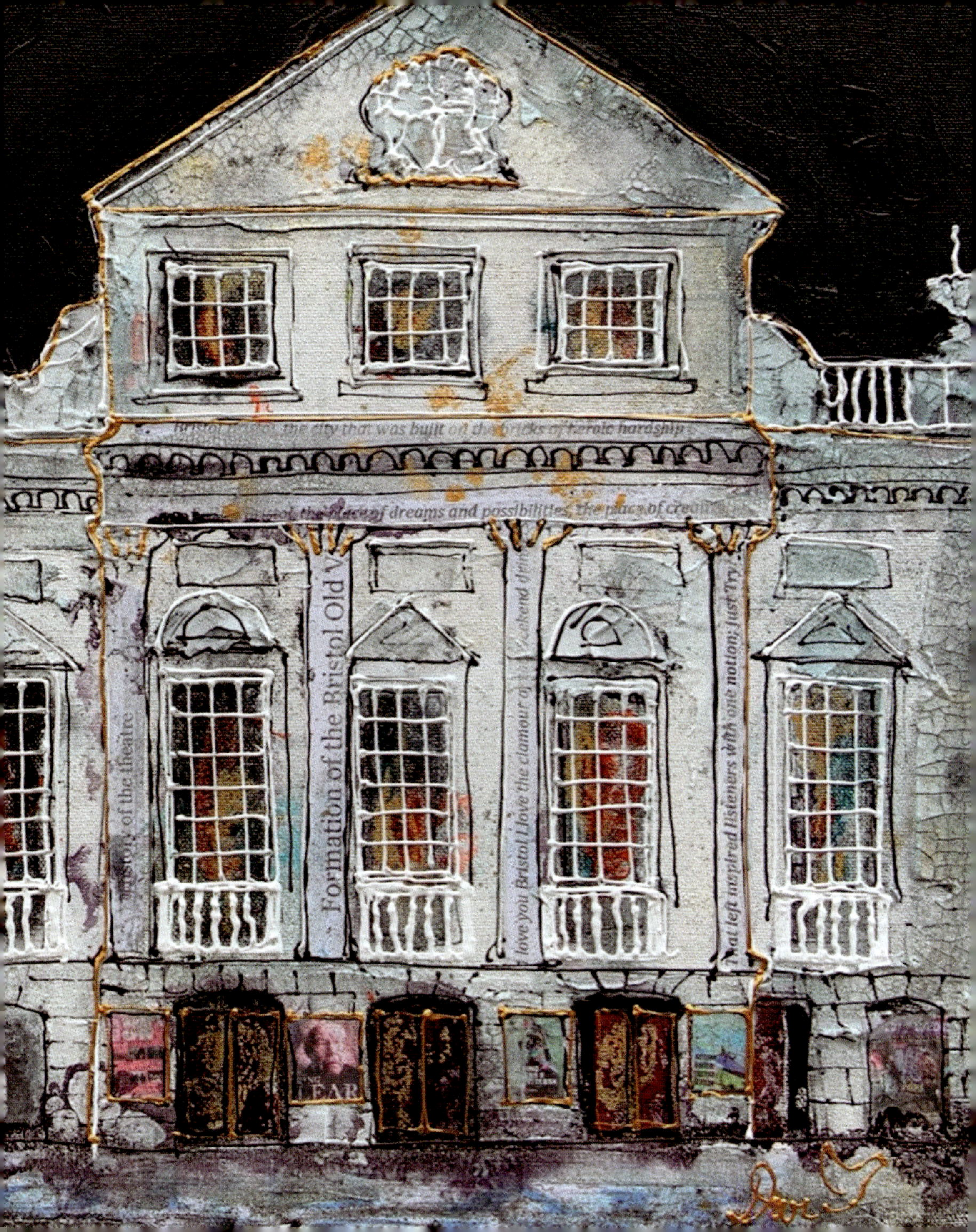
Bristol Bristol the city that was built on the bricks of heroic hardship
the place of dreams and possibilities, the place of crea
Formation of the Bristol Old V
ation of the theatre
love you Bristol I love the clamour o
weekend
at left inspired listeners with one notion; Just try
LEAR

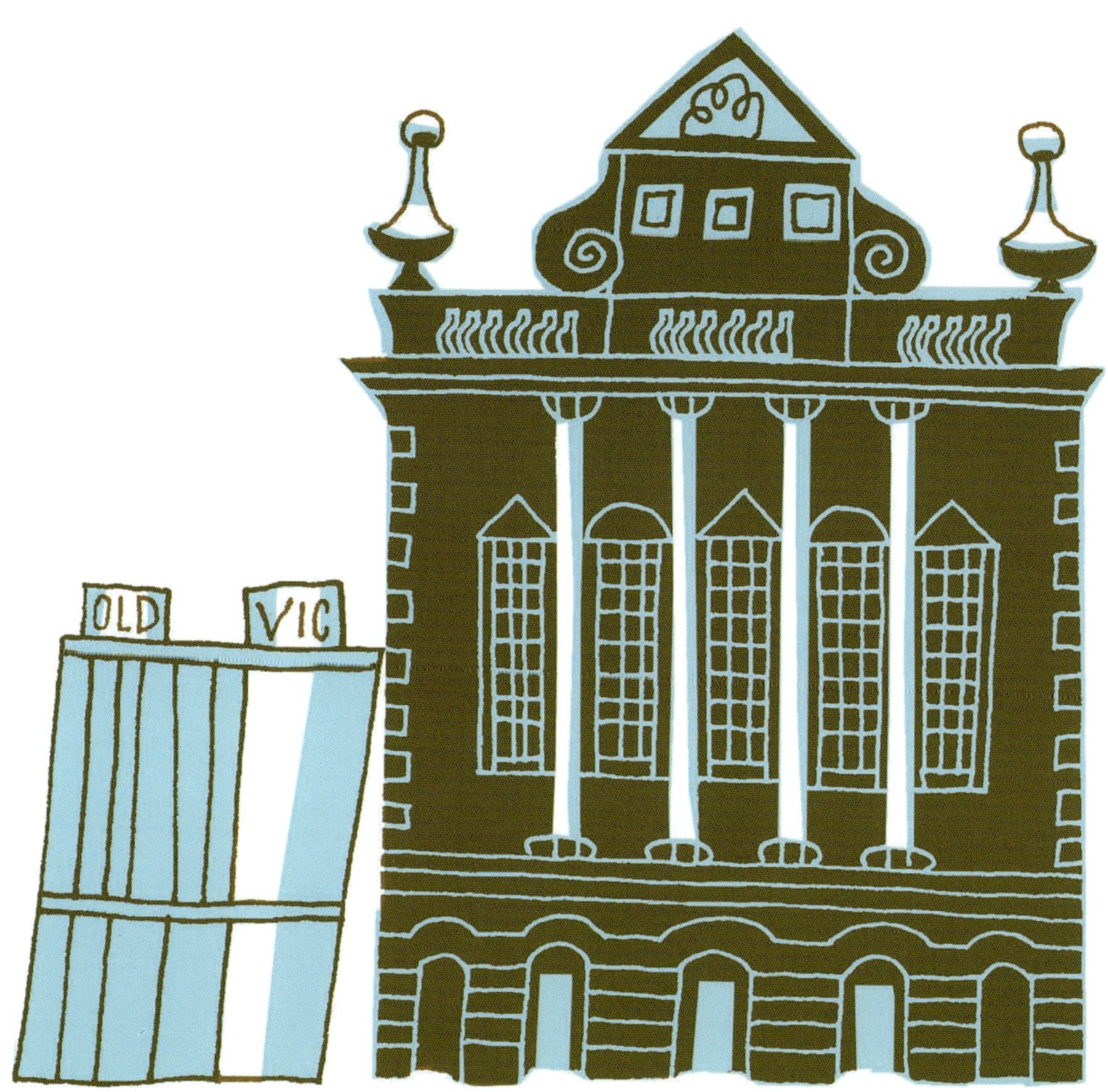



BRISTOL OLD VIC, SIMON TOZER

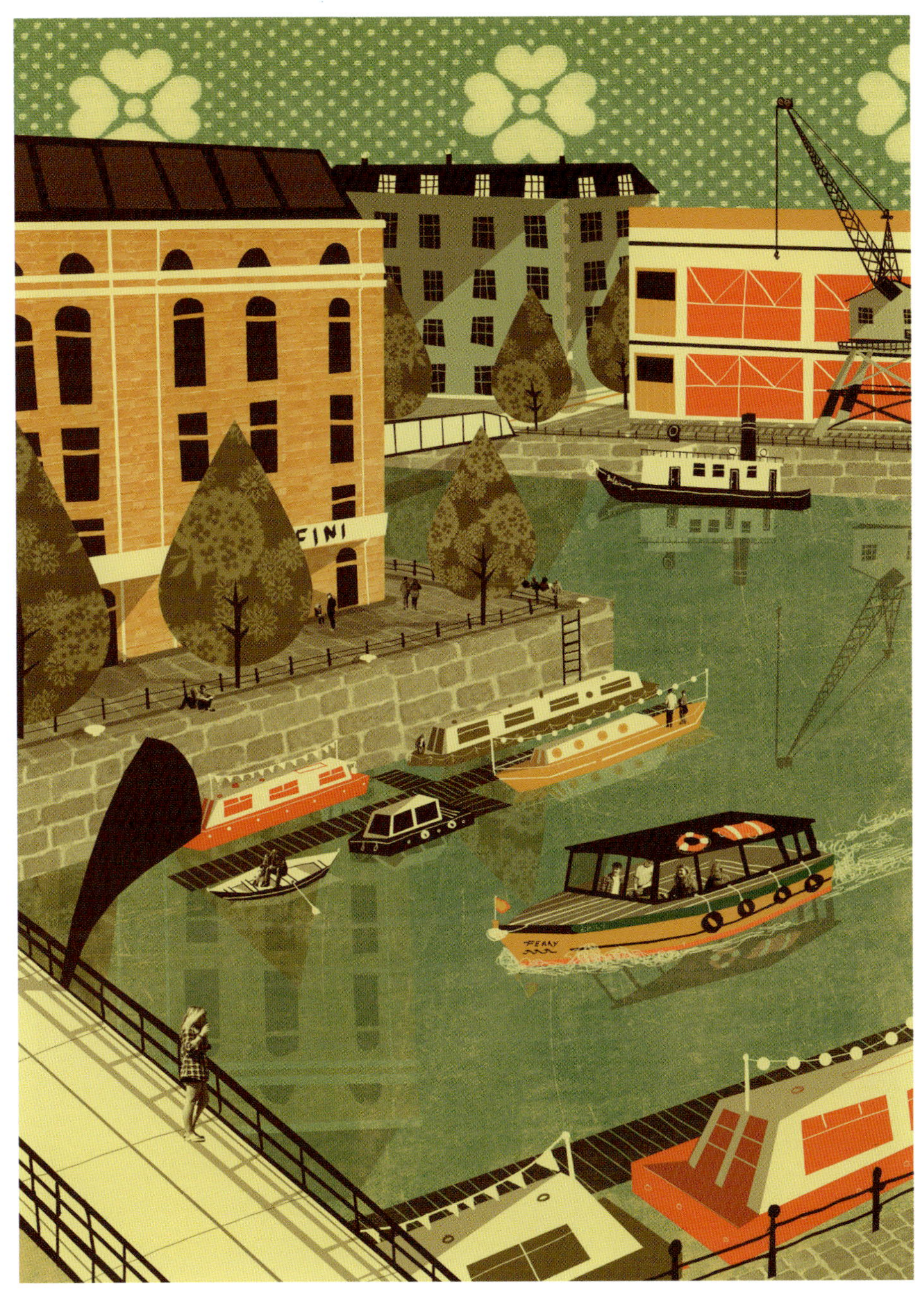



ARNOLFINI, EMY LOU HOLMES

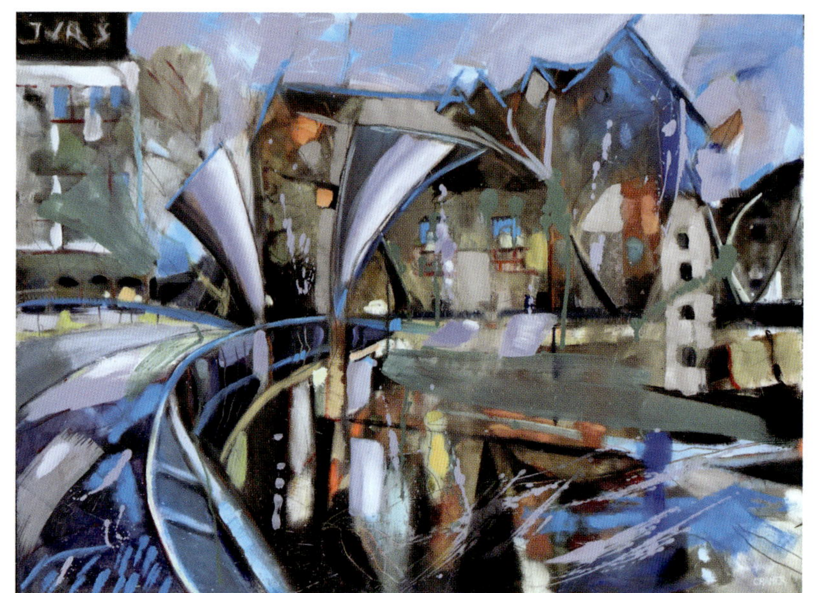

PERO'S BRIDGE, LAURA CRAMER

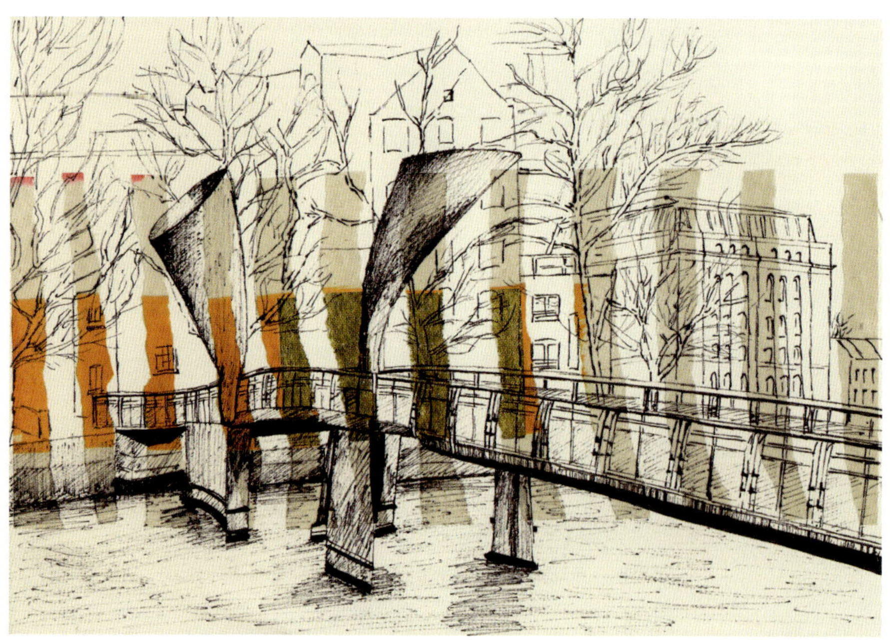

PERO'S BRIDGE, LISA MALYON

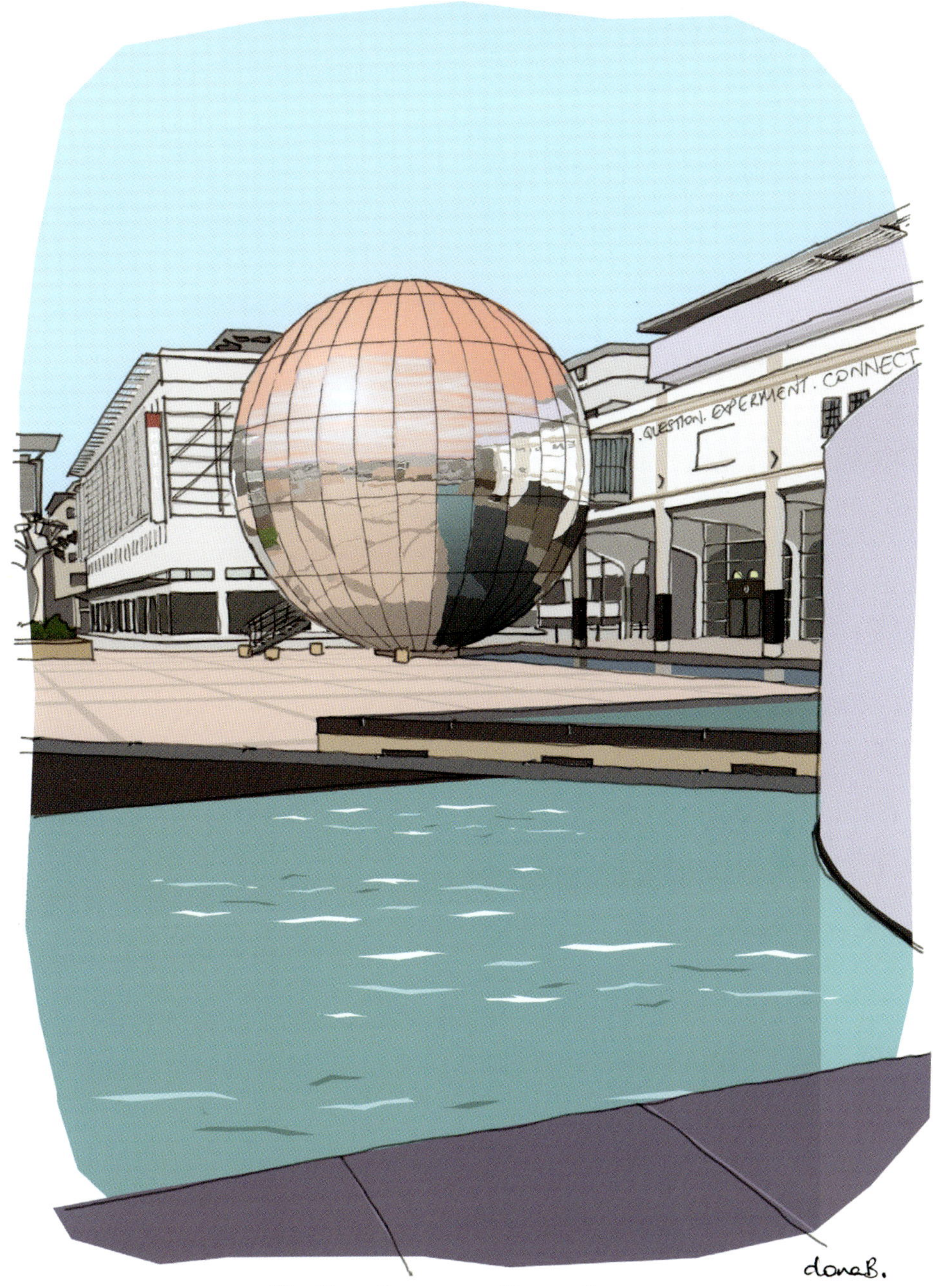



We The Curious, Dona Bradley

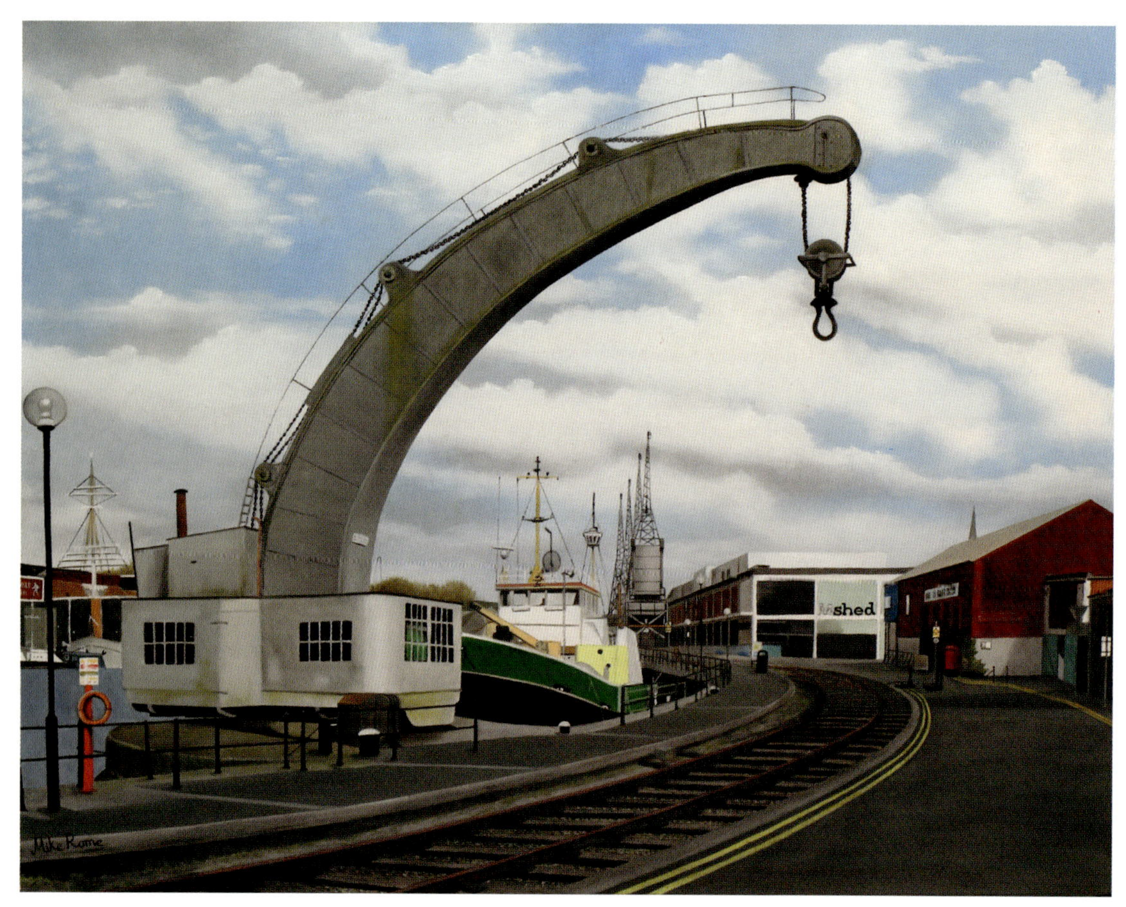

BRISTOL'S STEAM CRANE, MIKE ROME

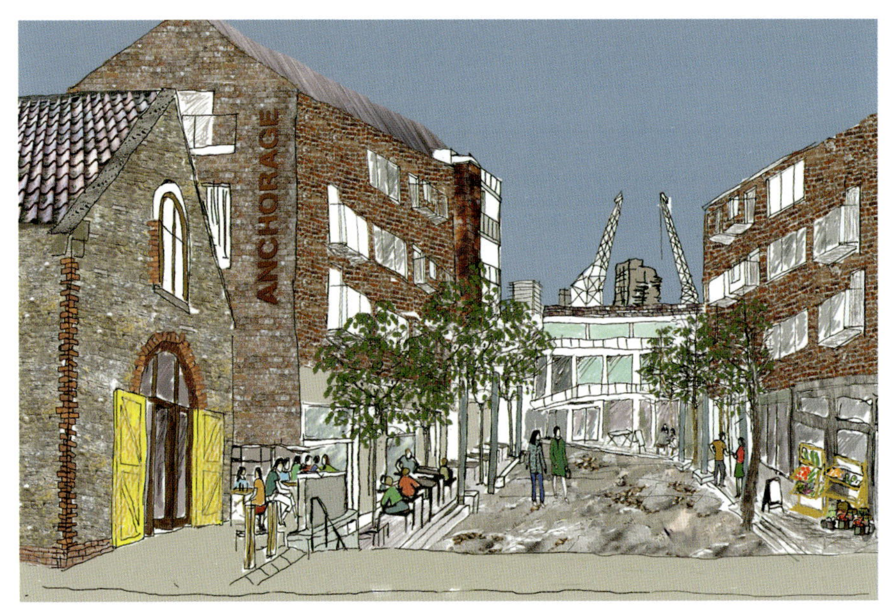


Wapping Wharf, Emmeline Simpson

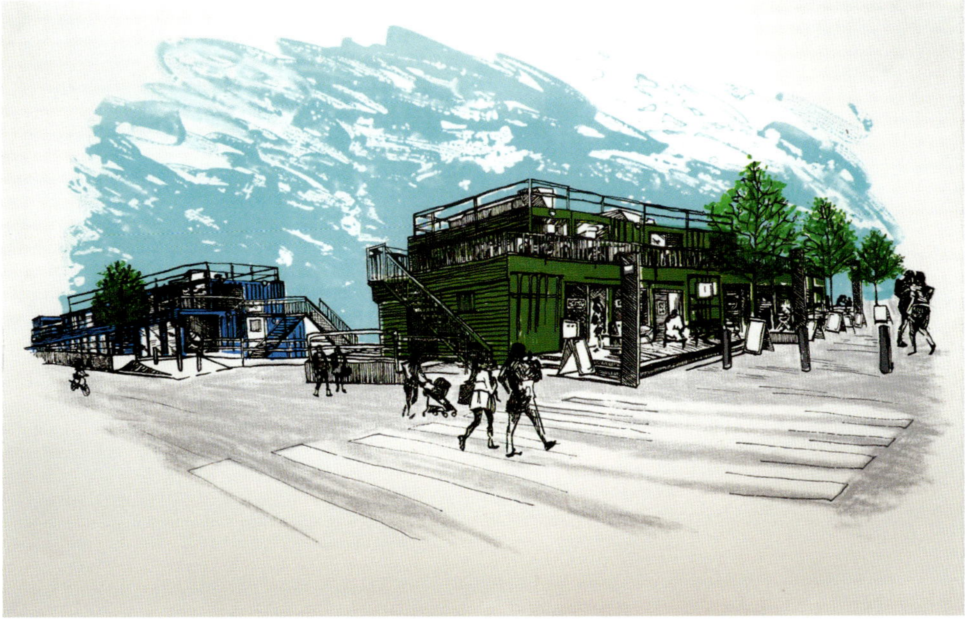

Cargo, Wapping Wharf, Amy Hutchings

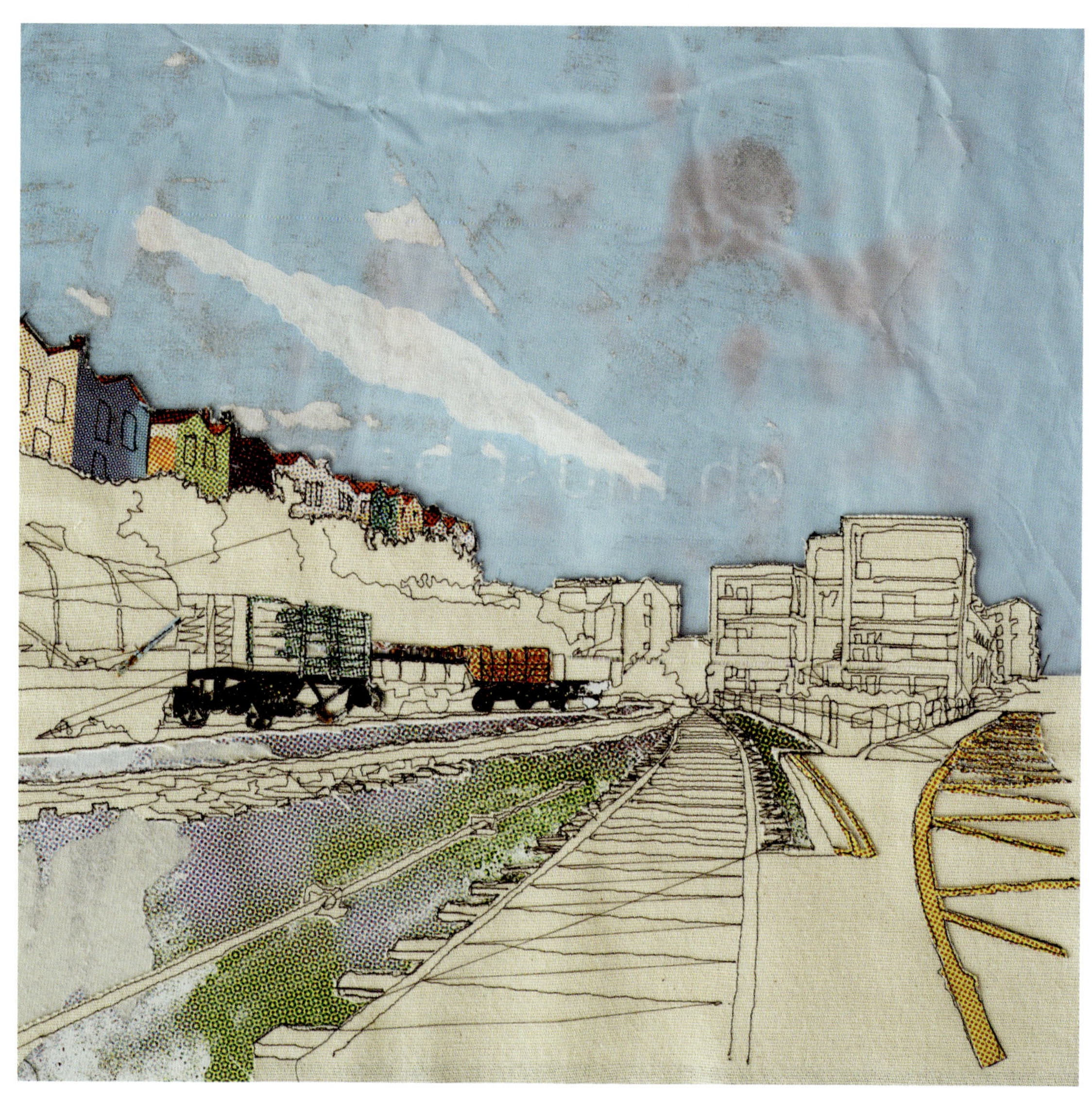

TRAIN TRACKS, HARBOURSIDE, ZOE BILLBOARD GIBBONS

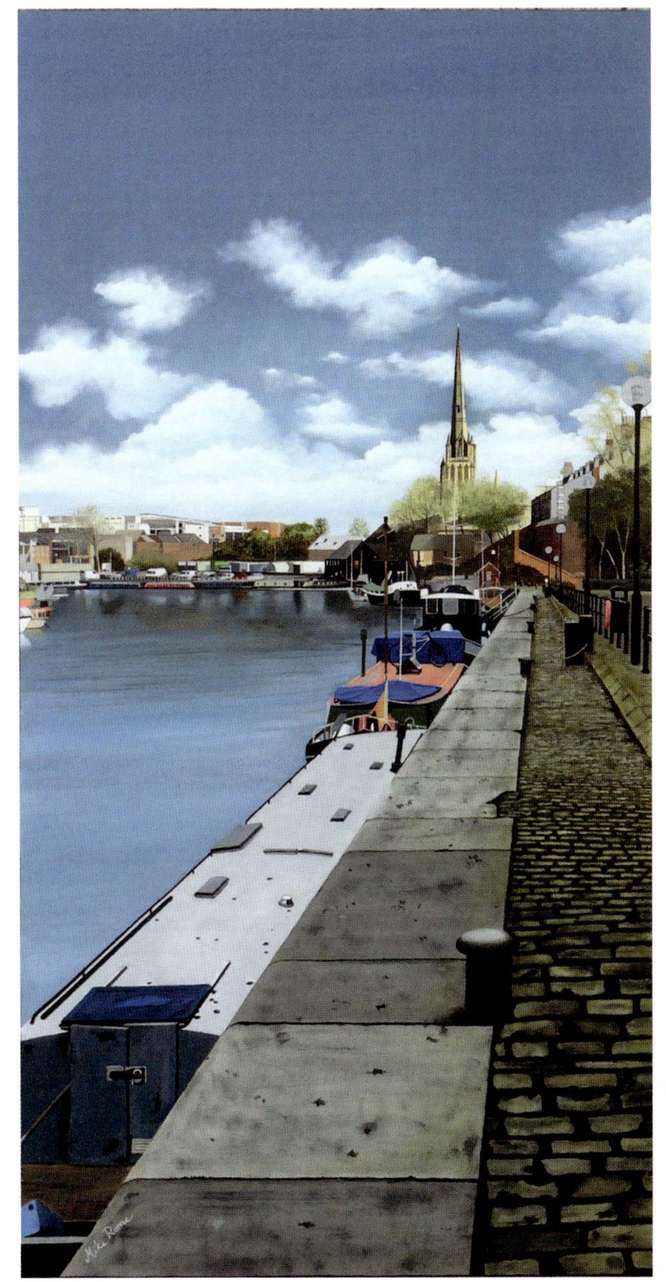

HARBOURSIDE, MIKE ROME

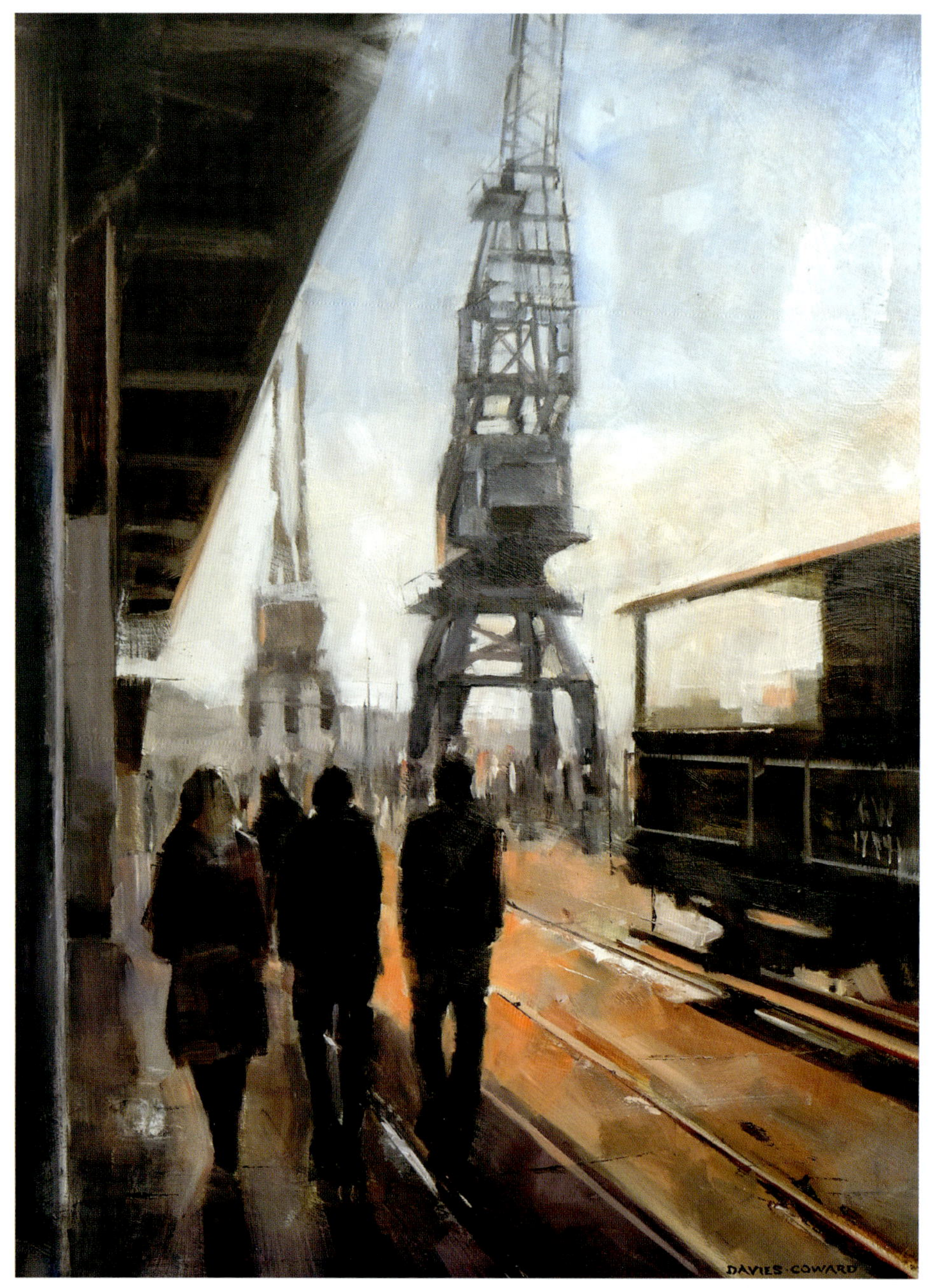

M-SHED CRANES, ANDY DAVIES-COWARD

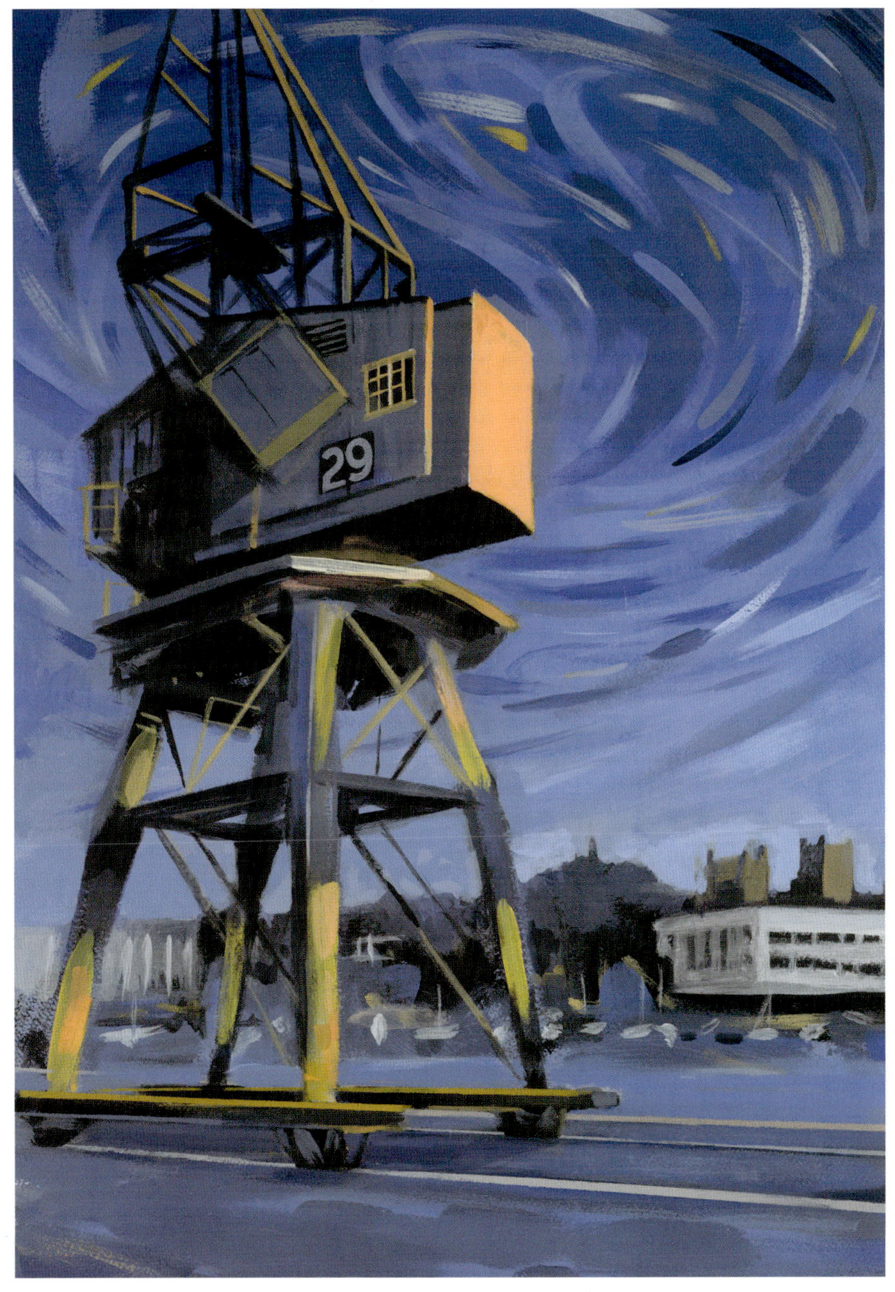

CRANE 29, HARBOURSIDE, NICK GEROLEMOU

43

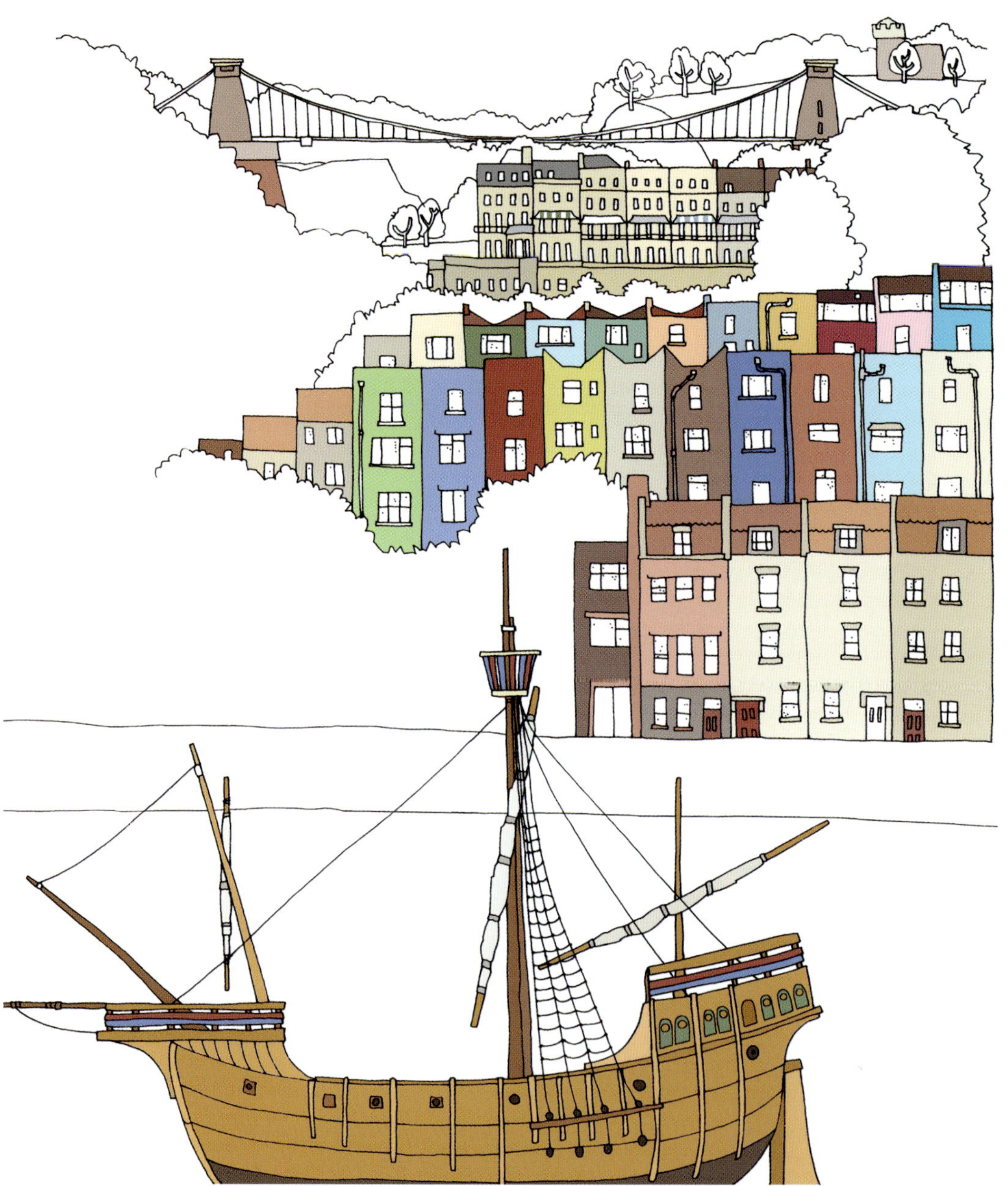

THE MATTHEW IN FRONT OF CLIFTON SUSPENSION BRIDGE, EMILY KETTERINGHAM

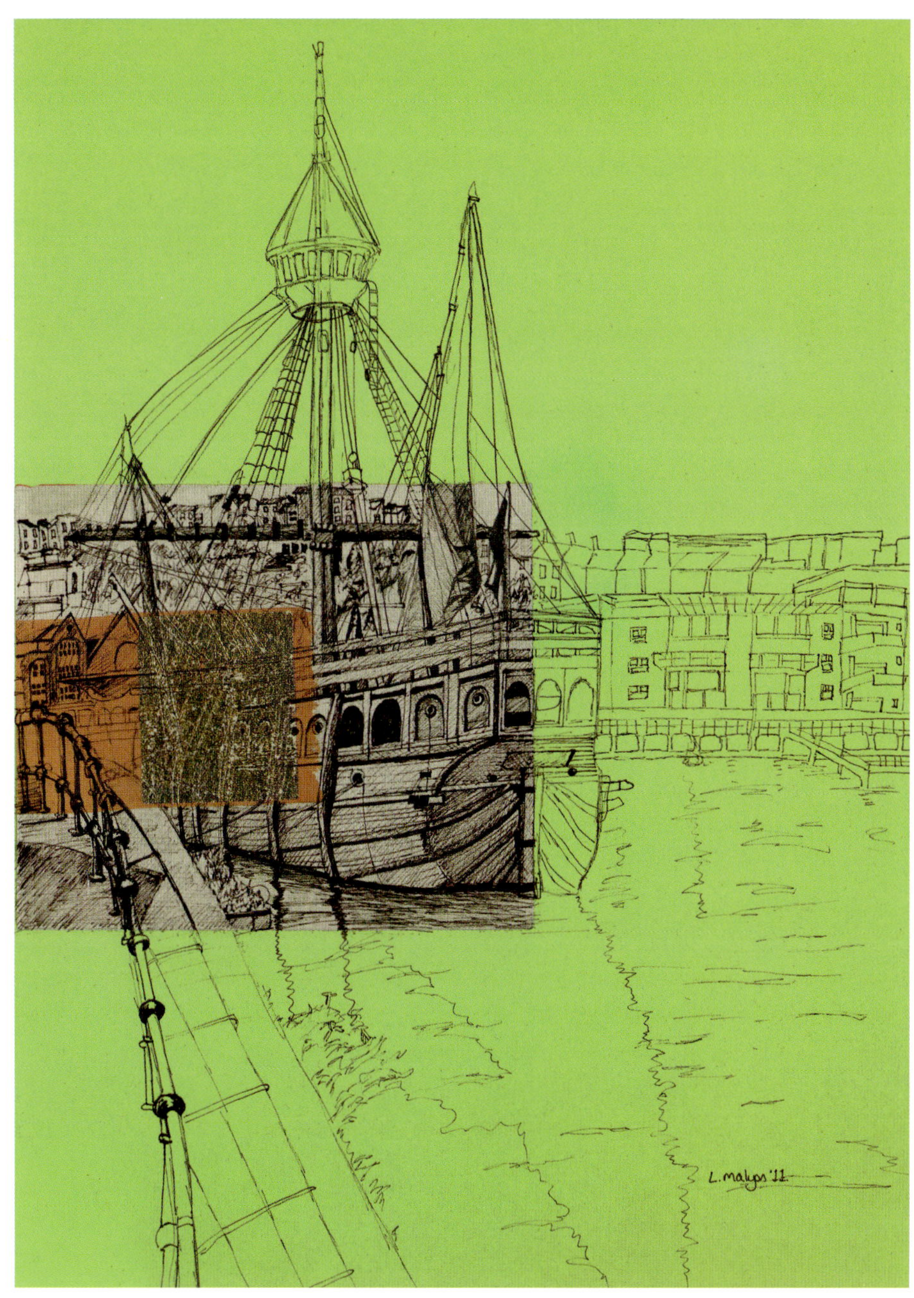

The Matthew, Lisa Malyon

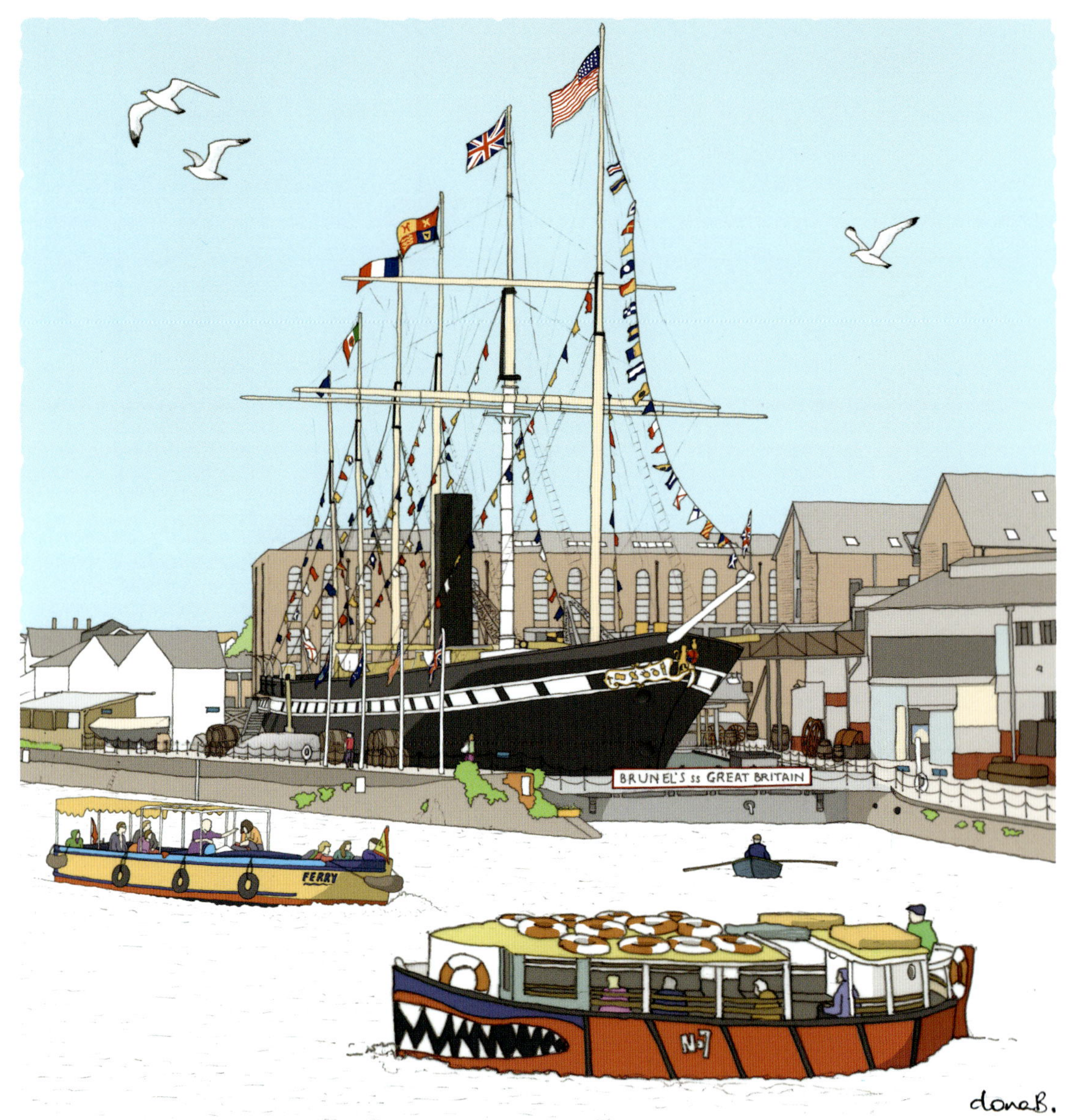

Brunel's SS Great Britain, Dona Bradley

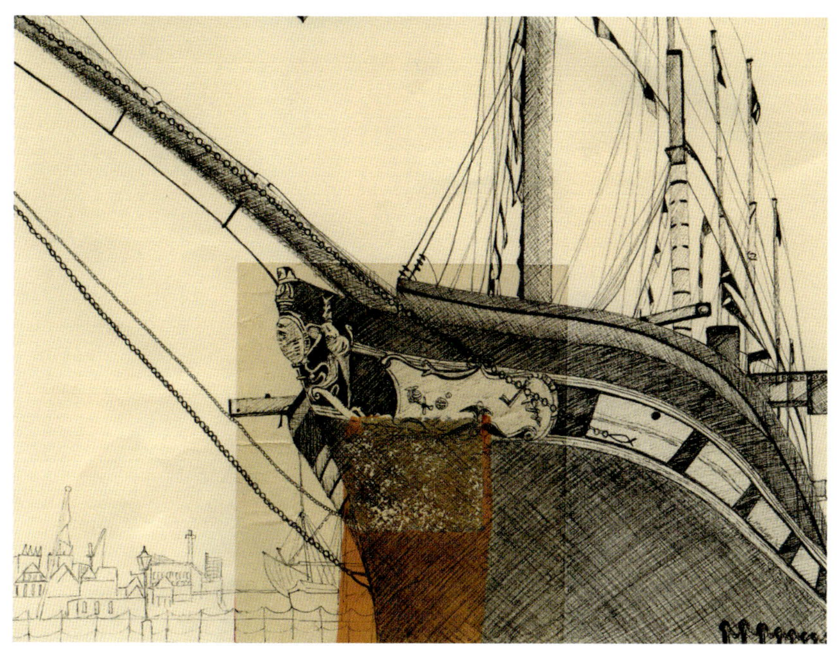

Brunel's SS Great Britain, Lisa Malyon

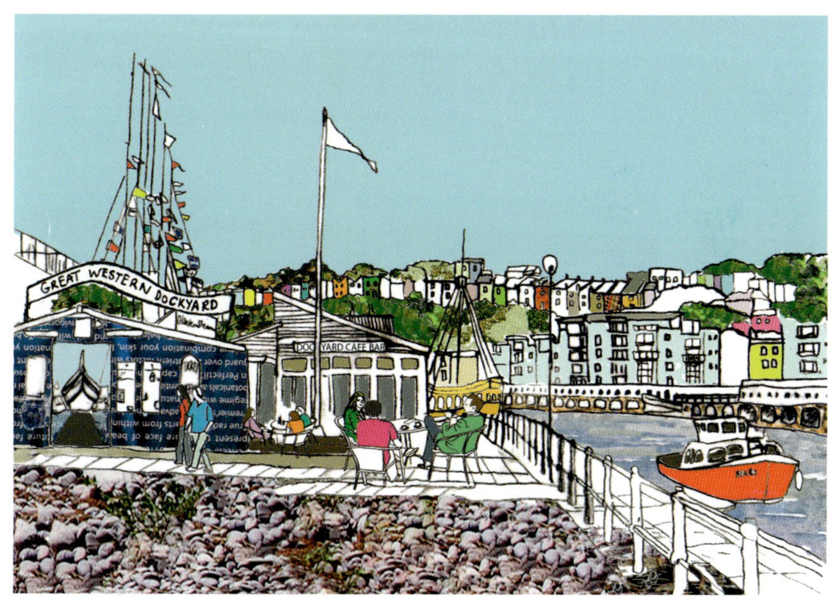


Dockyard Cafe, Emmeline Simpson

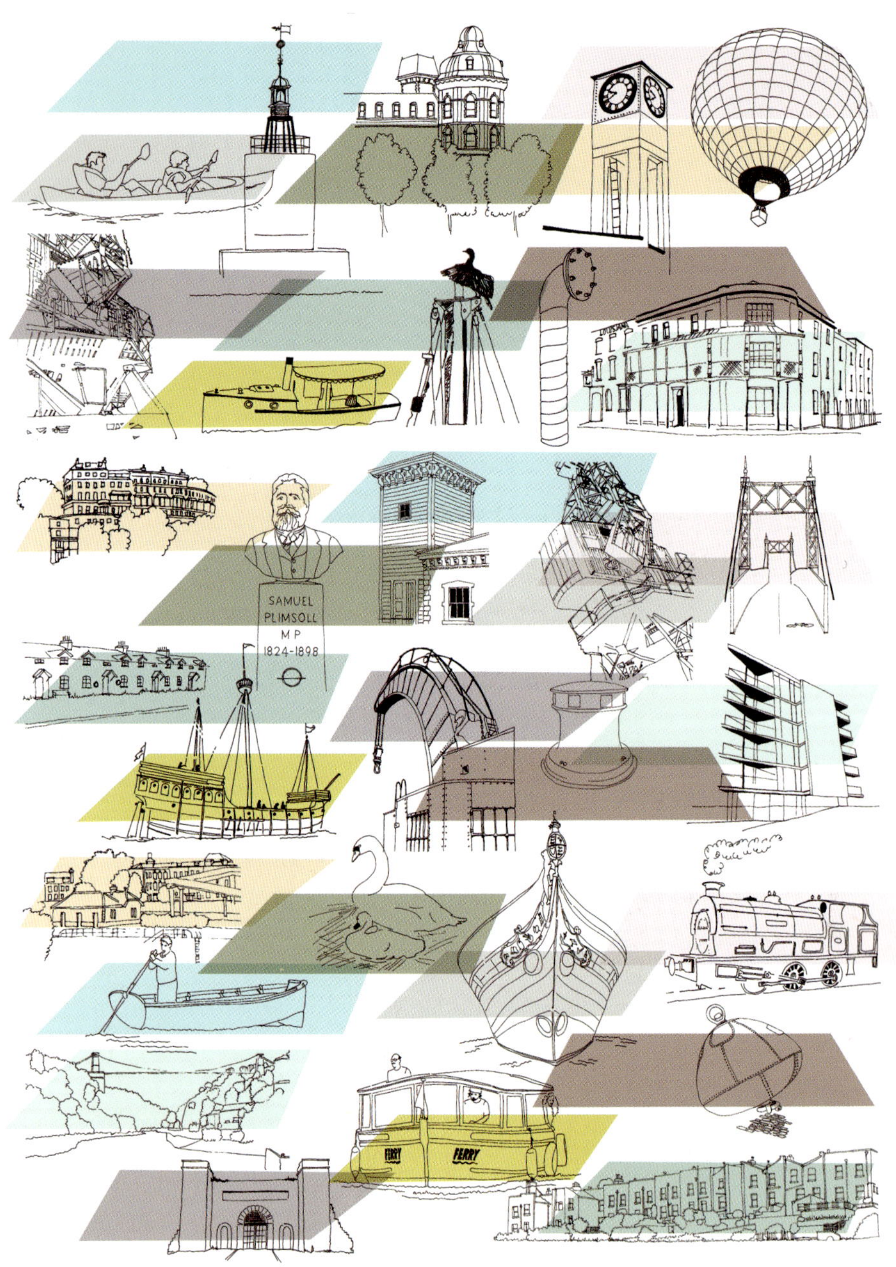


A WALK AROUND BRISTOL, SUE PORTER

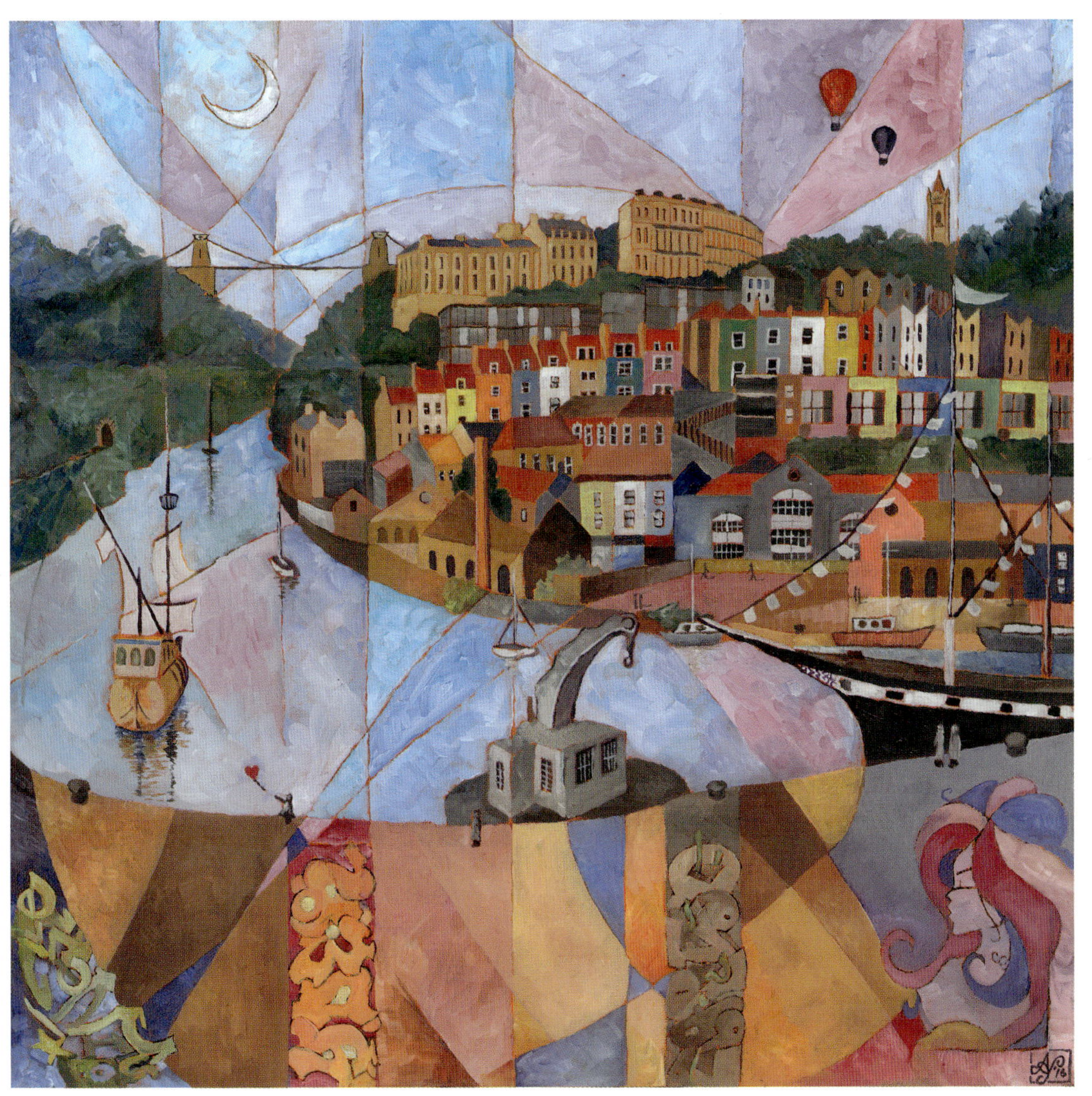

BRISTOL HARBOUR, AMY YATES

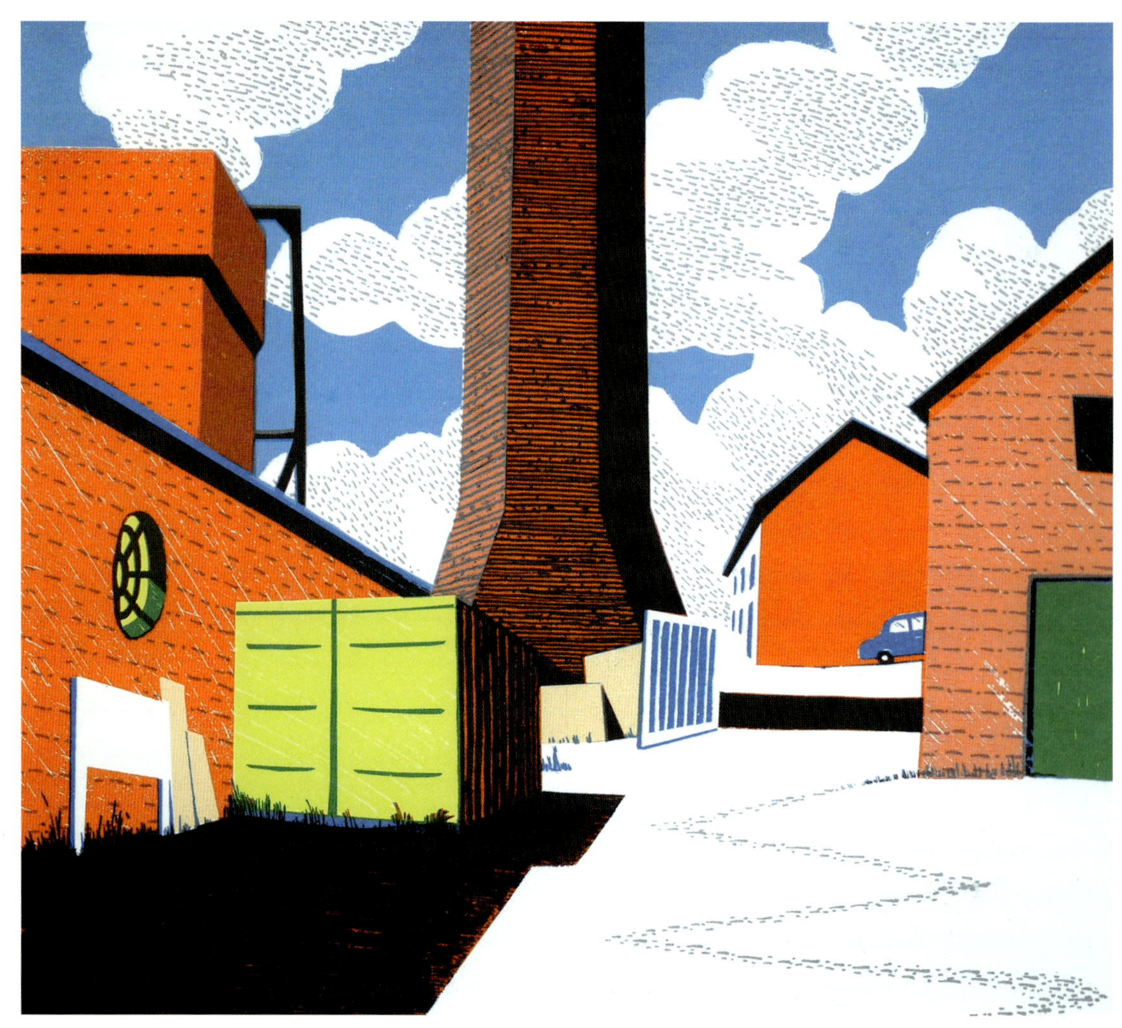

Underfall Yard Pumping Station, Simon Tozer

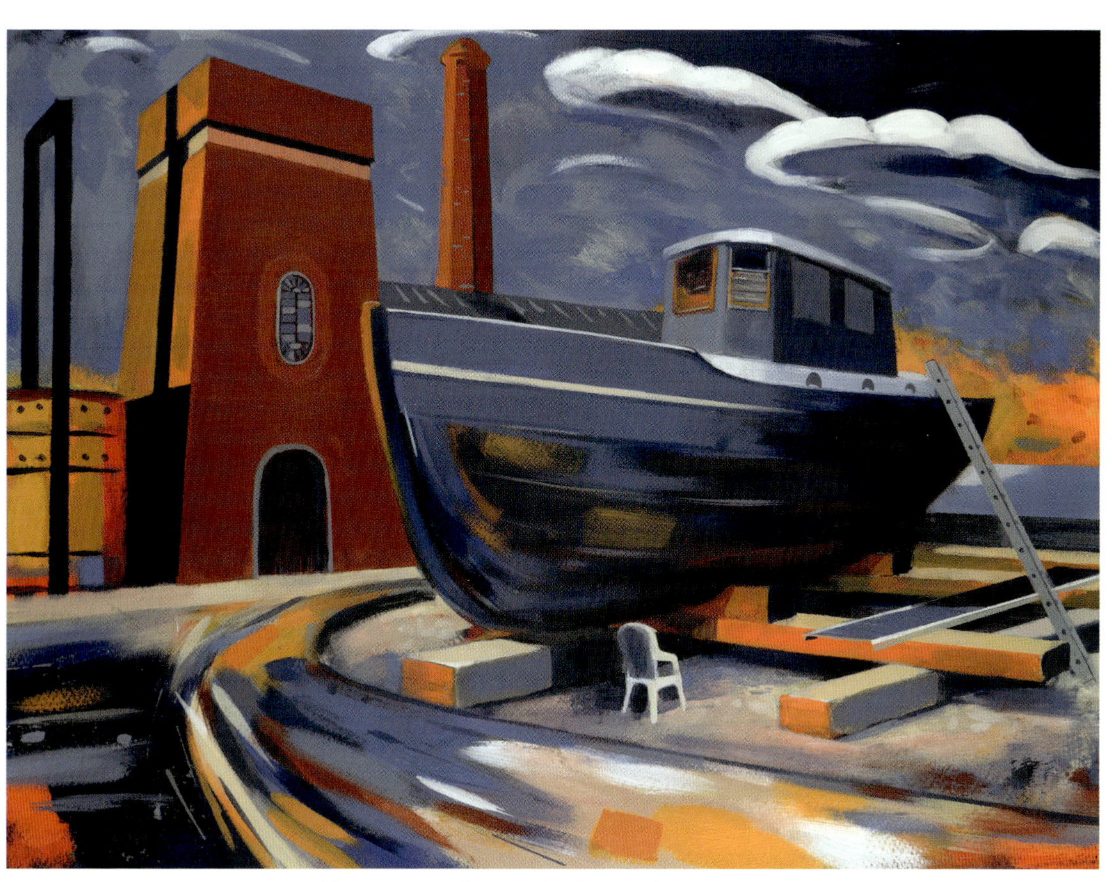

UNDERFALL YARD 1, NICK GEROLEMOU

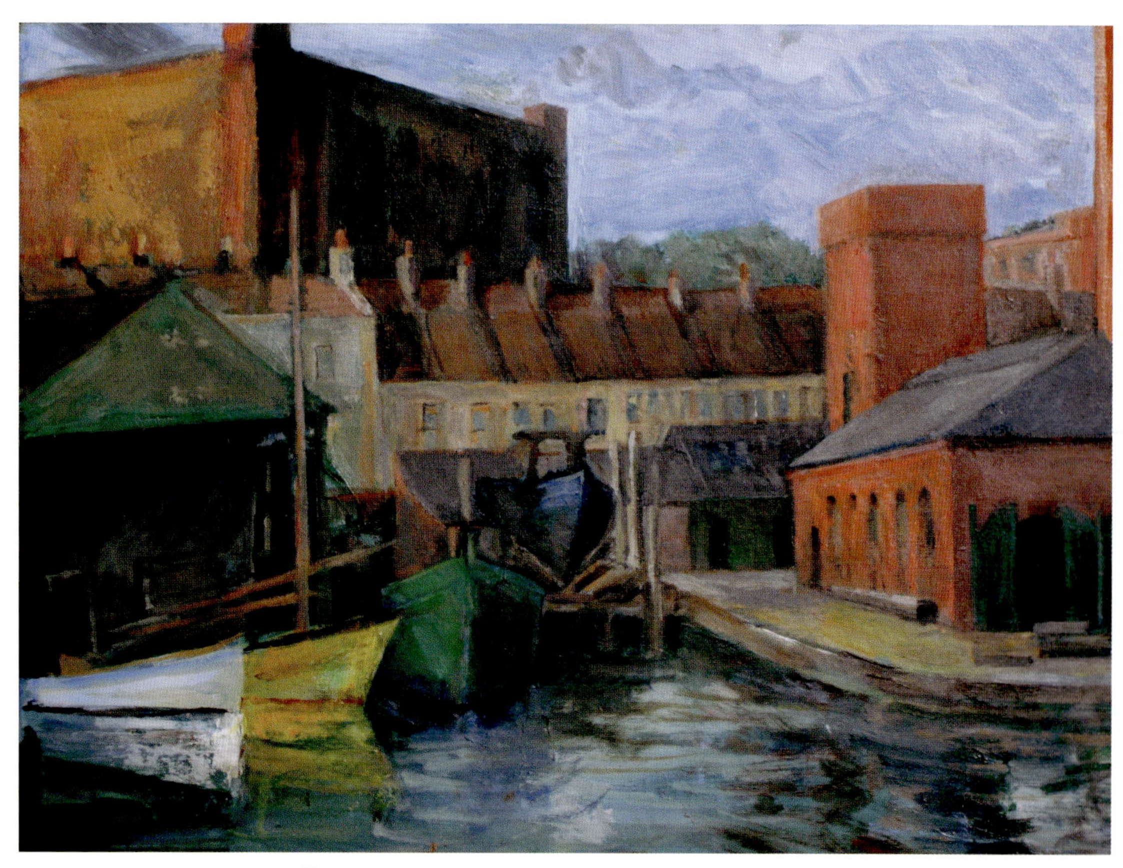

UNDERFALL BOATYARD, JULIET CARMICHAEL

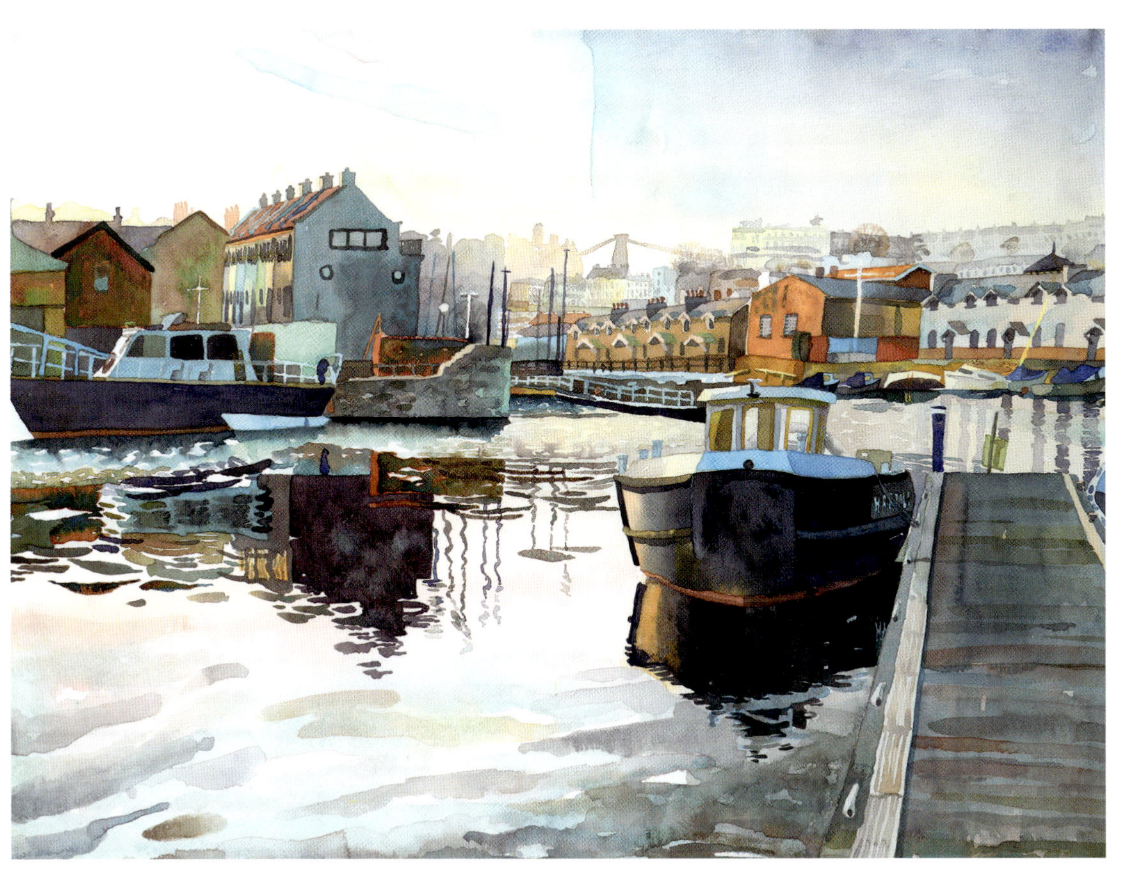

HARBOUR MASTER, ABIGAIL McDOUGALL

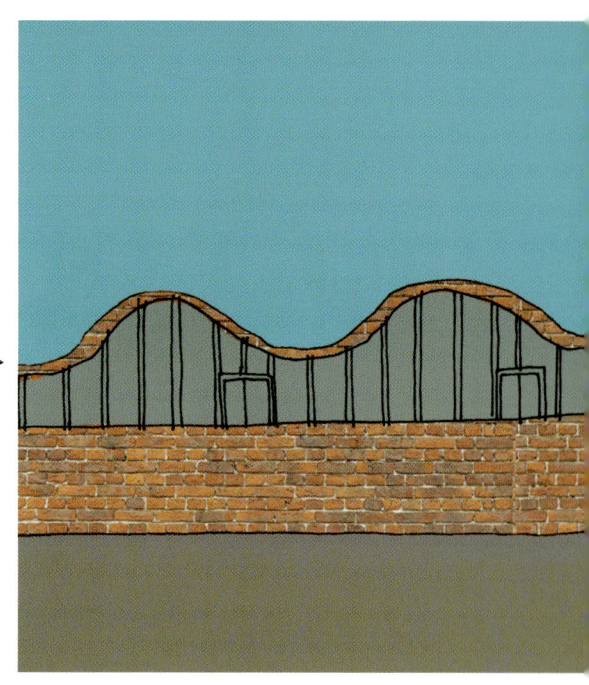

SPIKE ISLAND, HANNAH BROADWAY

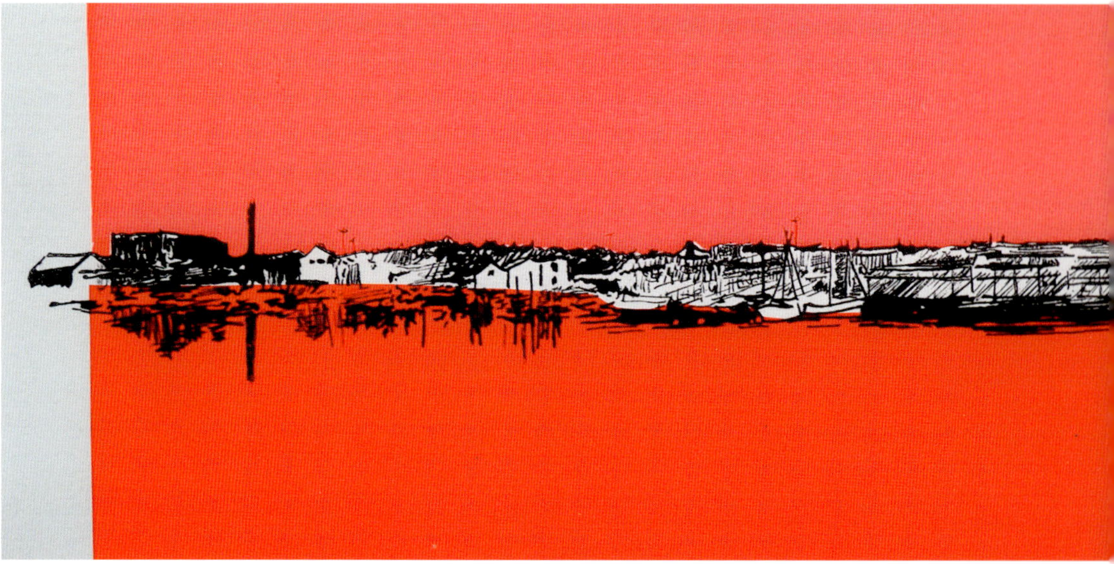

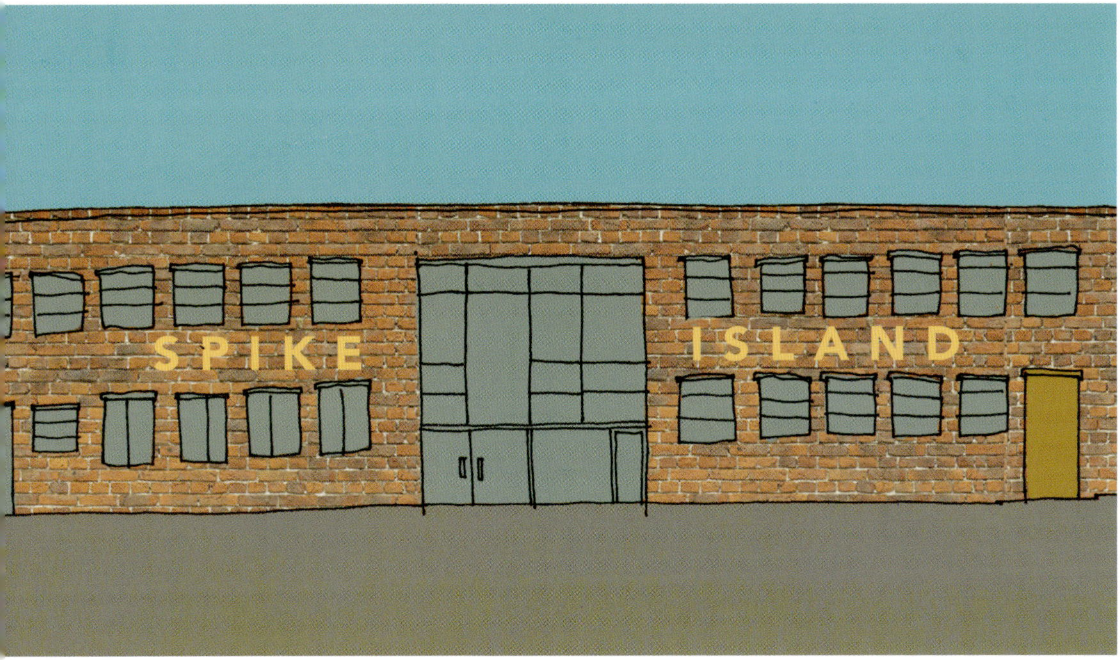

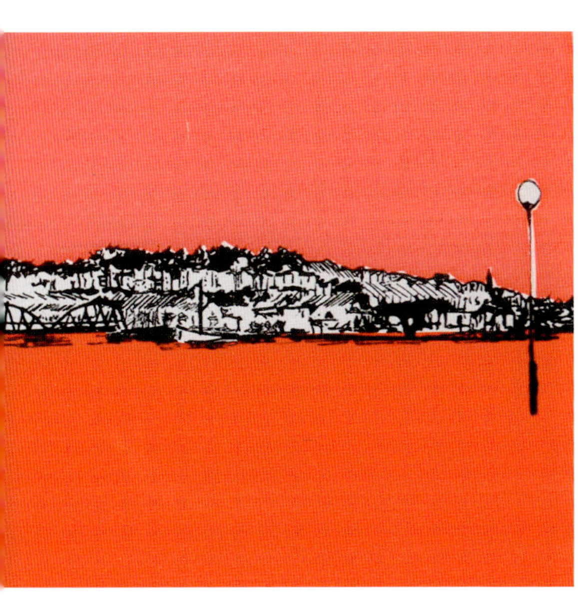

BRISTOL HARBOUR, AMY HUTCHINGS

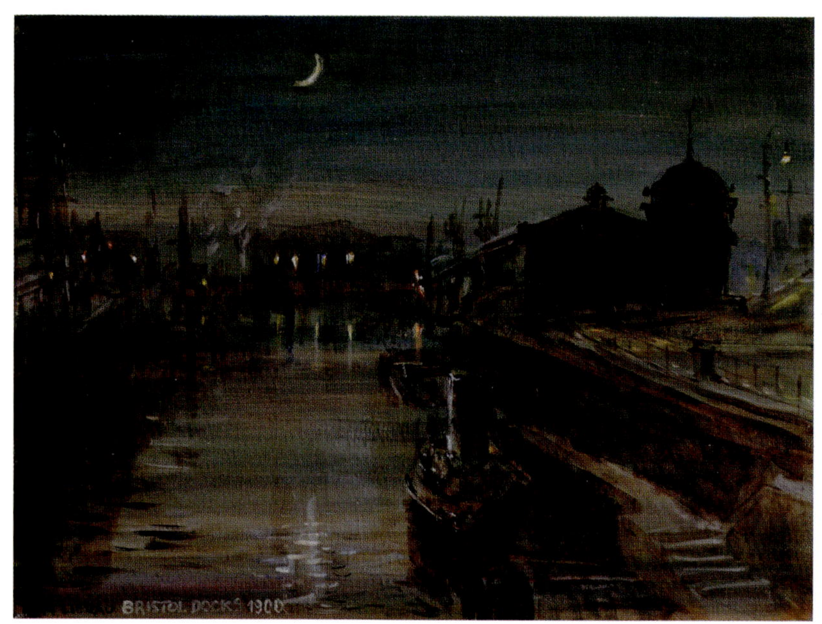

OLD HARBOUR, TOM LIETZAU

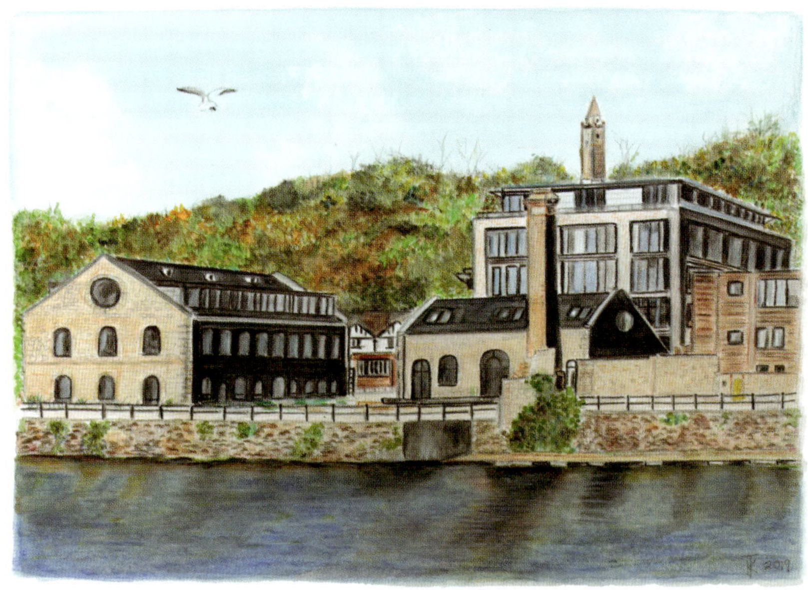

HARBOURSIDE, KATHERINE THORNTON

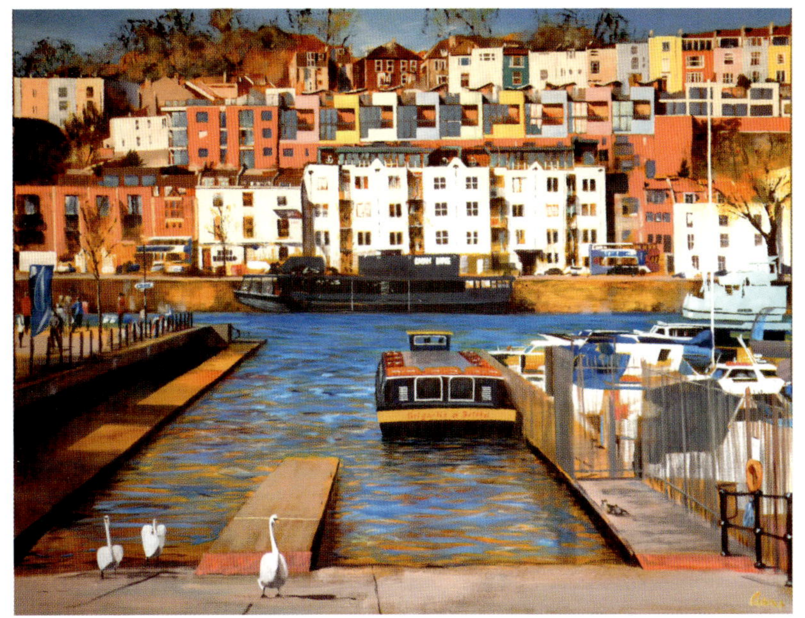

VIBRANT BRISTOL, ANNA DUCKWORTH

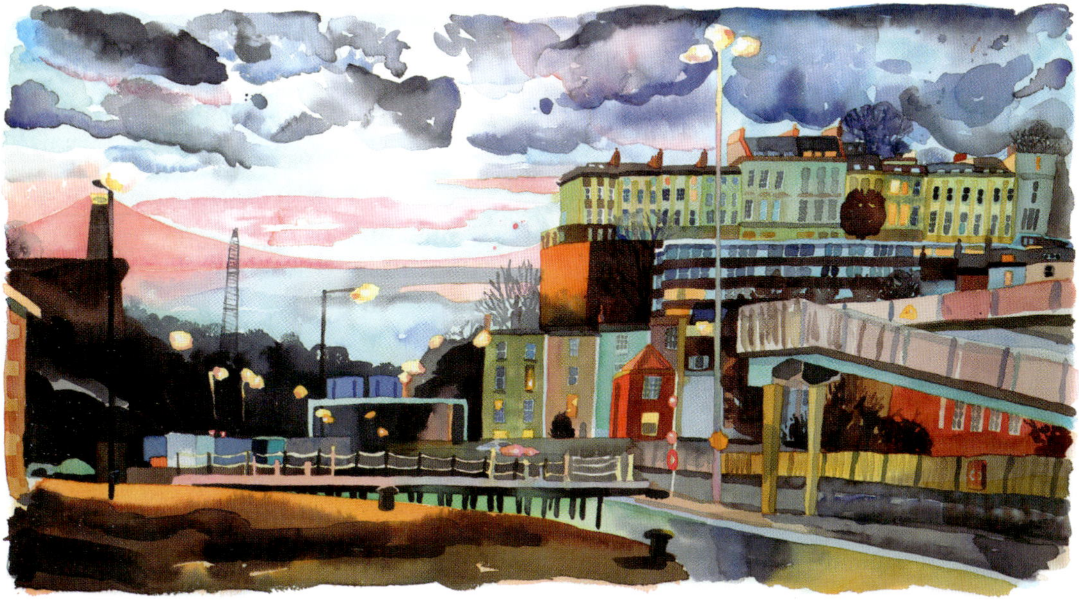

CLIFTON SUSPENSION BRIDGE AT DUSK, ABIGAIL MCDOUGALL

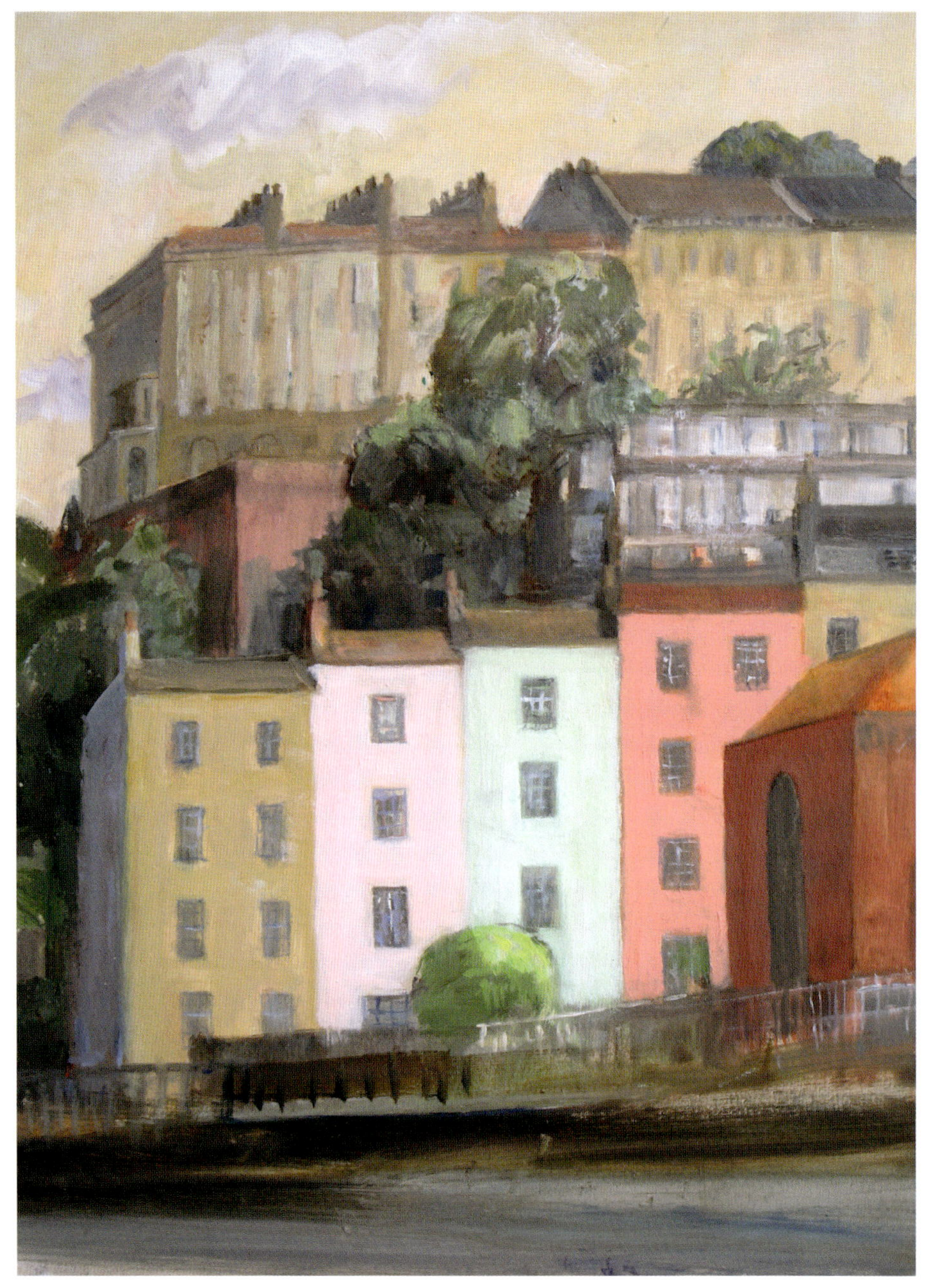

CLIFTON HOUSES, JULIET CARMICHAEL

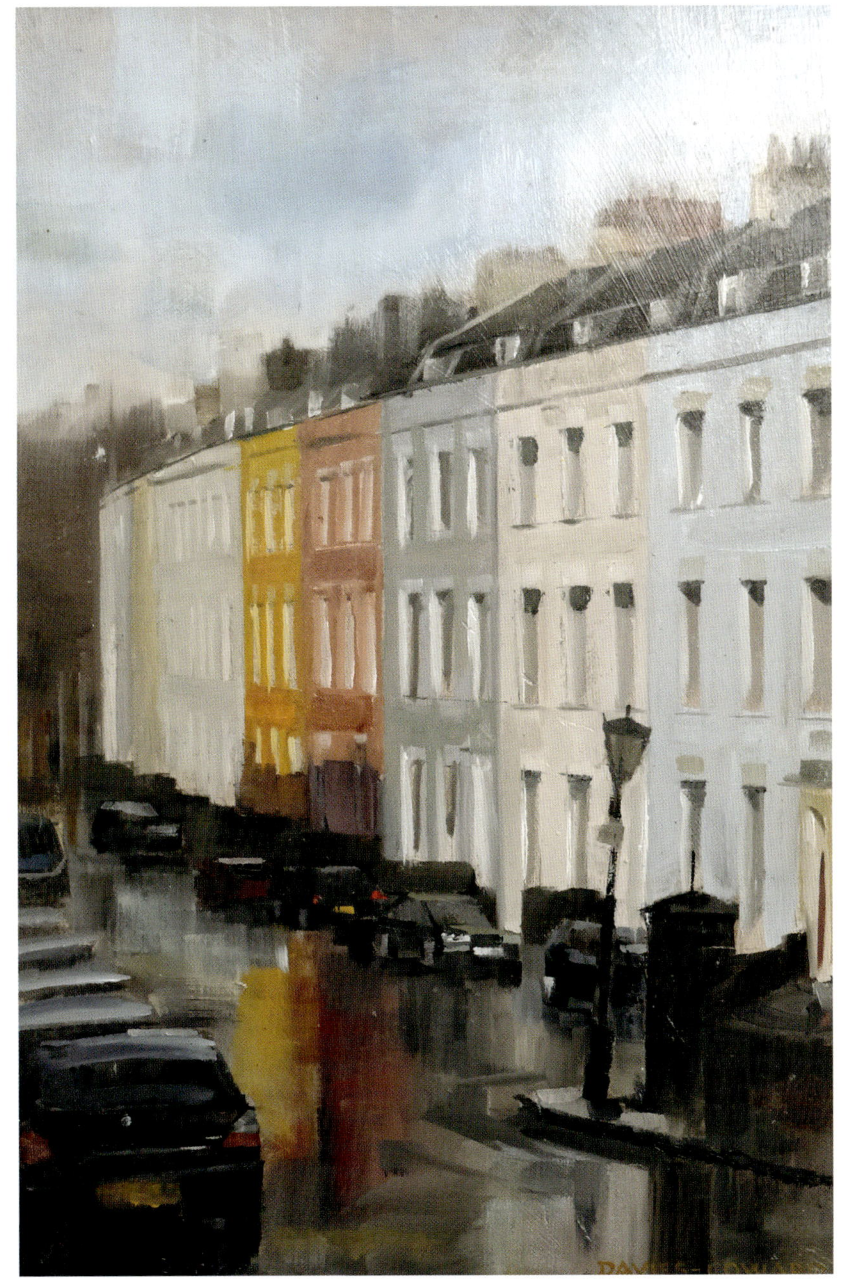



CORNWALLIS CRESCENT, ANDY DAVIES-COWARD

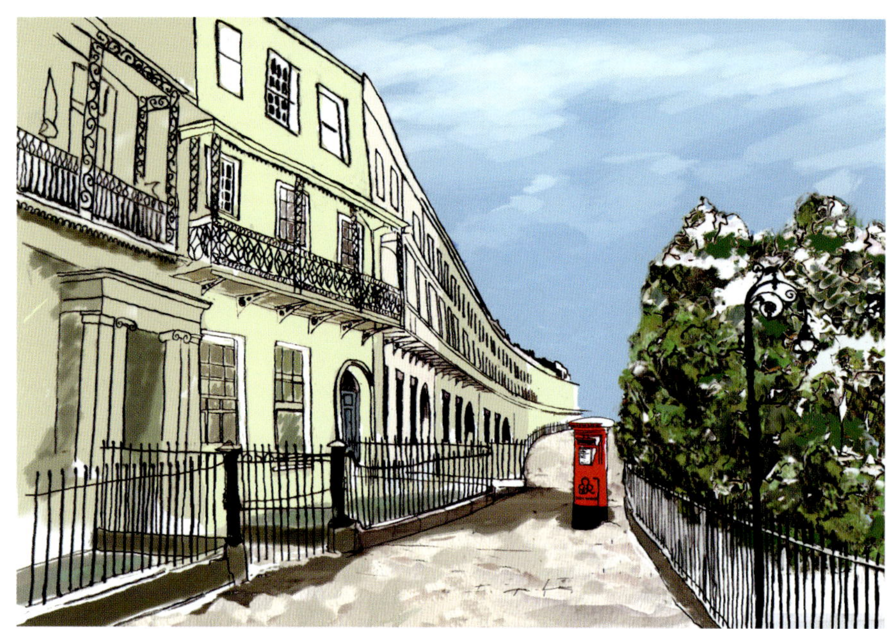

ROYAL YORK CRESCENT, EMMELINE SIMPSON

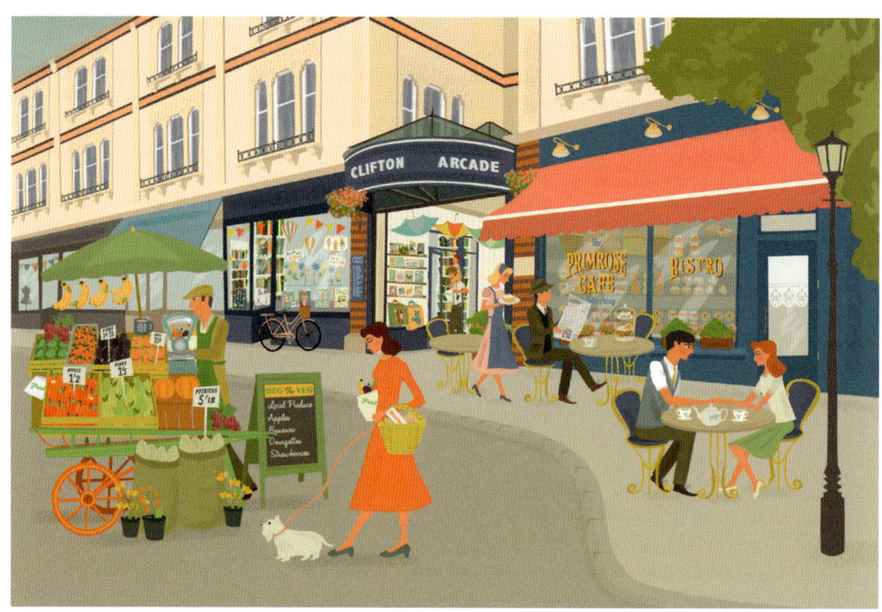



CLIFTON VILLAGE, CLARE PHILLIPS

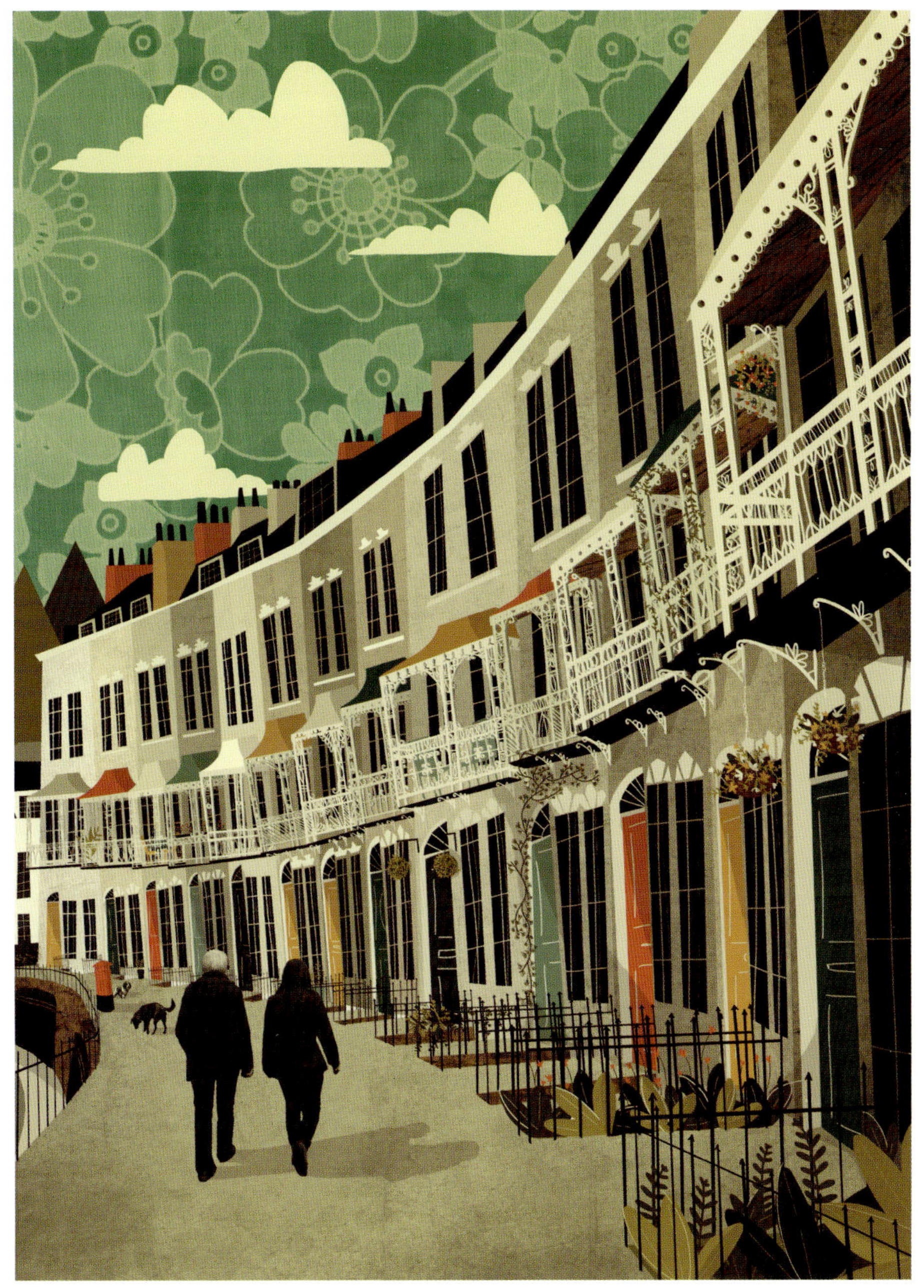

ROYAL YORK CRESCENT, EMY LOU HOLMES

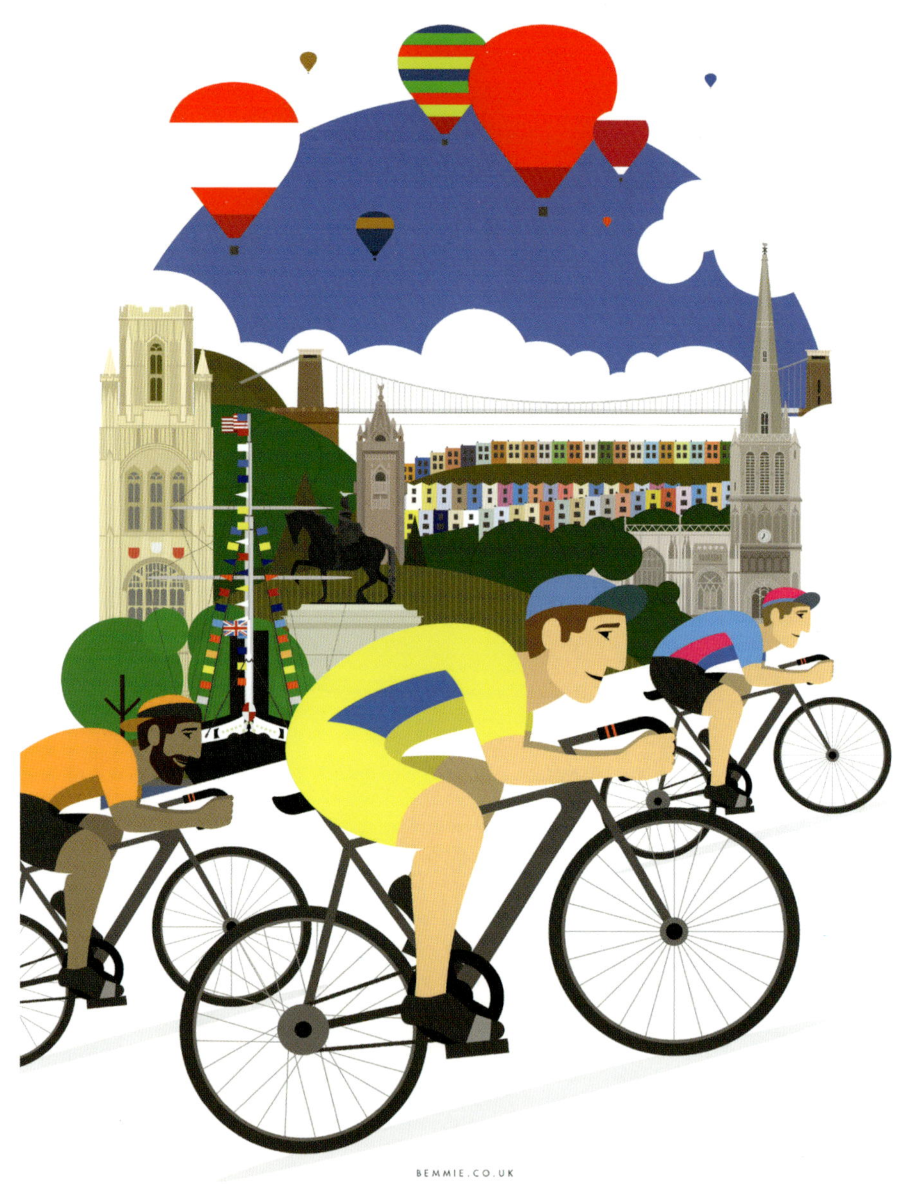



BRISTOL MAN CYCLING, ROBIN RICHARDS

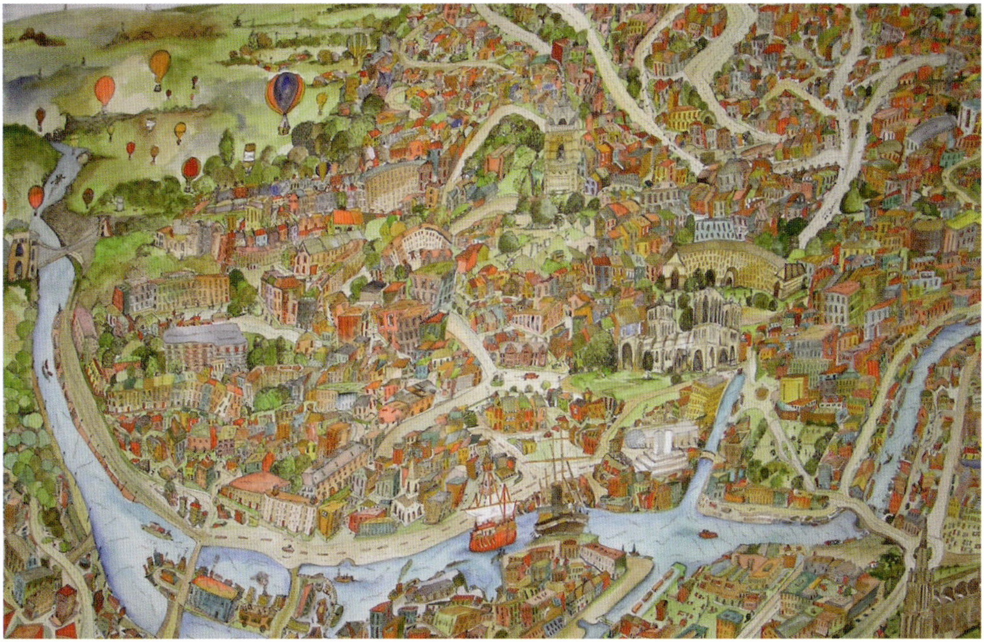

CLIFTON, ADRIAN GREEN

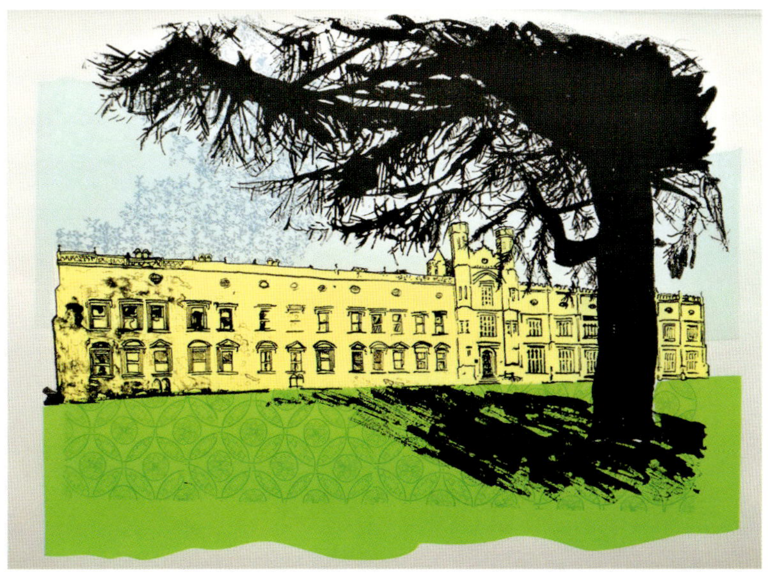

ASHTON COURT MANSION, AMY HUTCHINGS

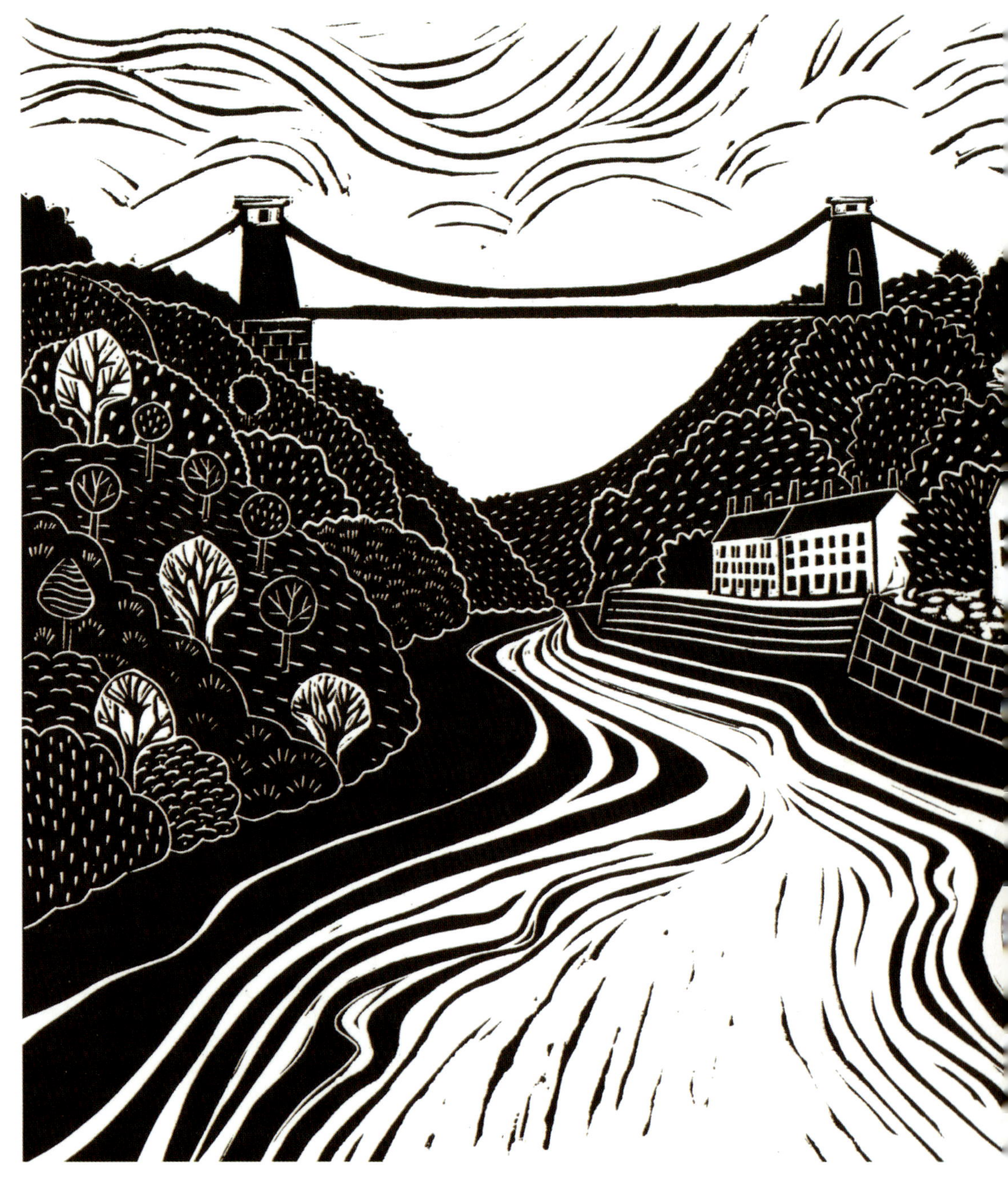

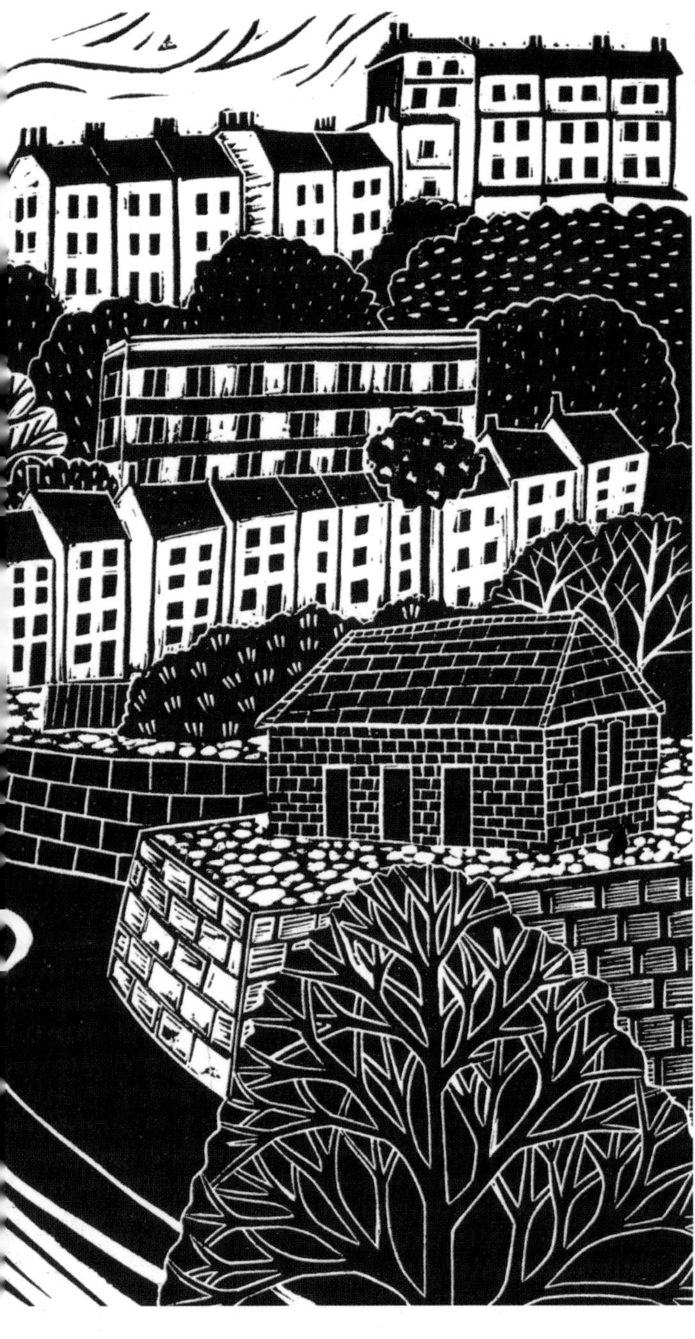

CLIFTON SUSPENSION BRIDGE,
LAURA ROBERTSON

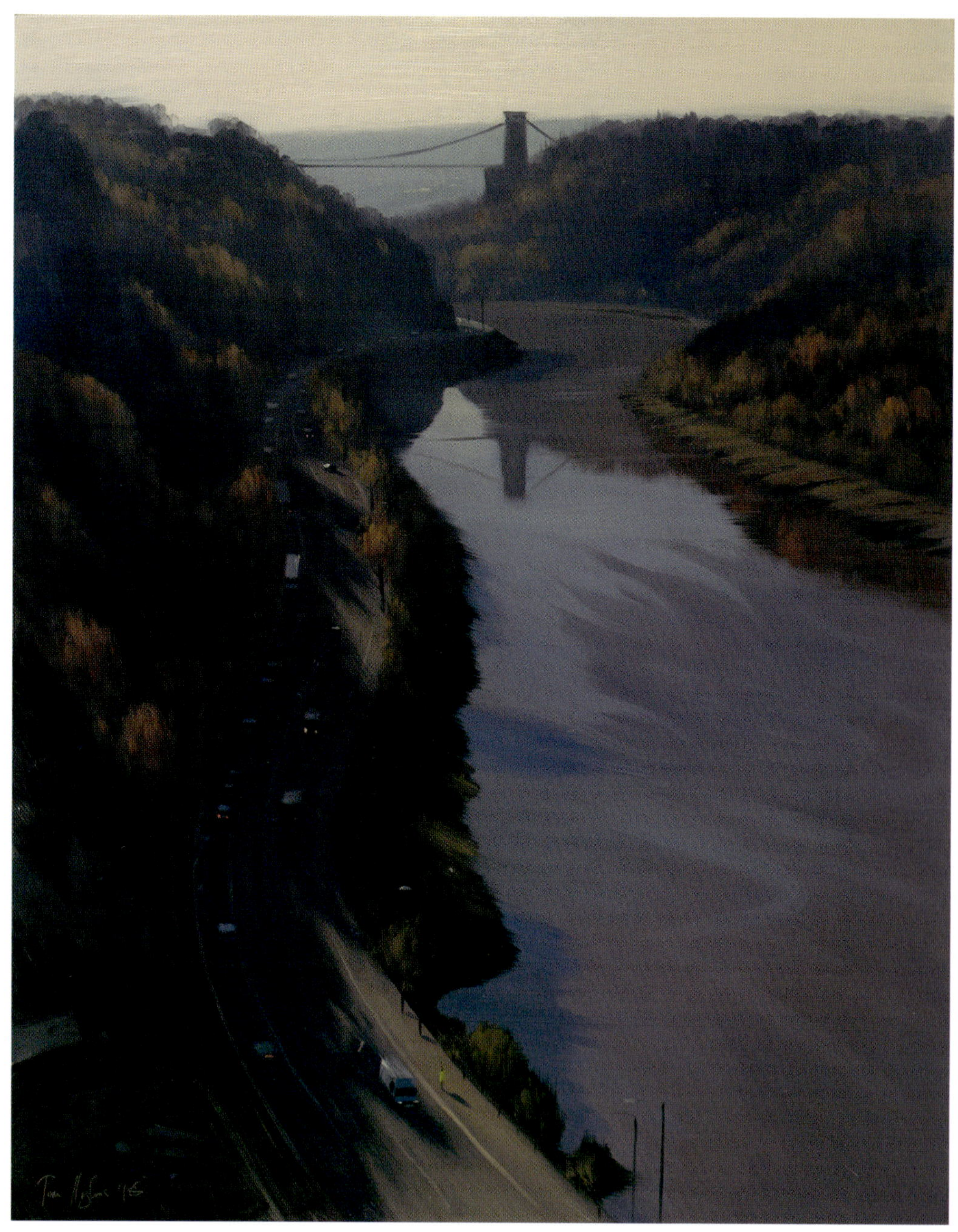

AVON GORGE, TOM HUGHES

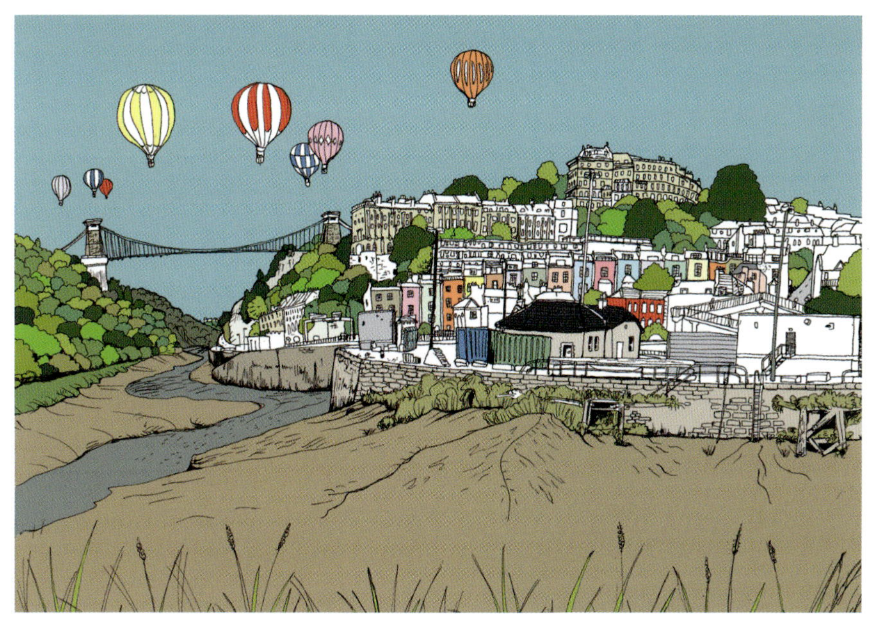

CLIFTON SUSPENSION BRIDGE, HANNAH BUNN

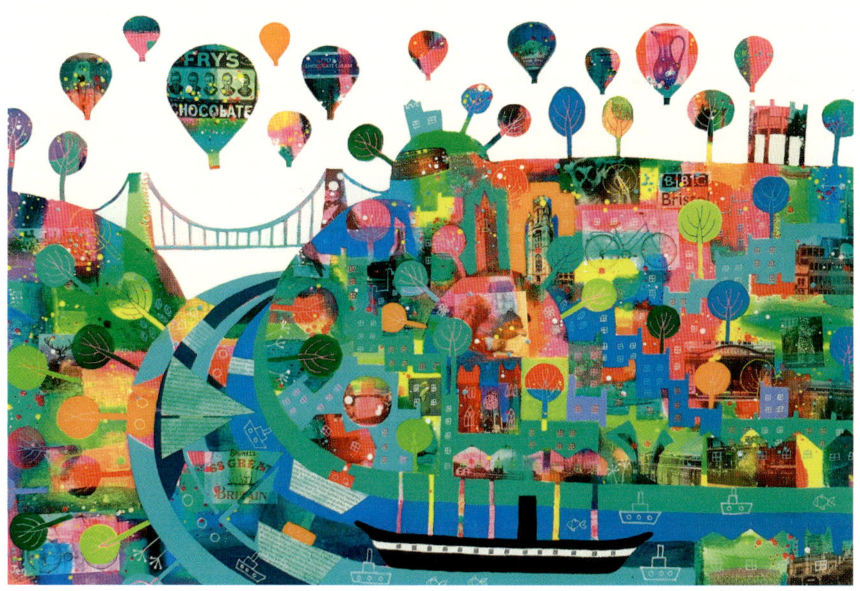

BRISTOL, JENNY URQUHART

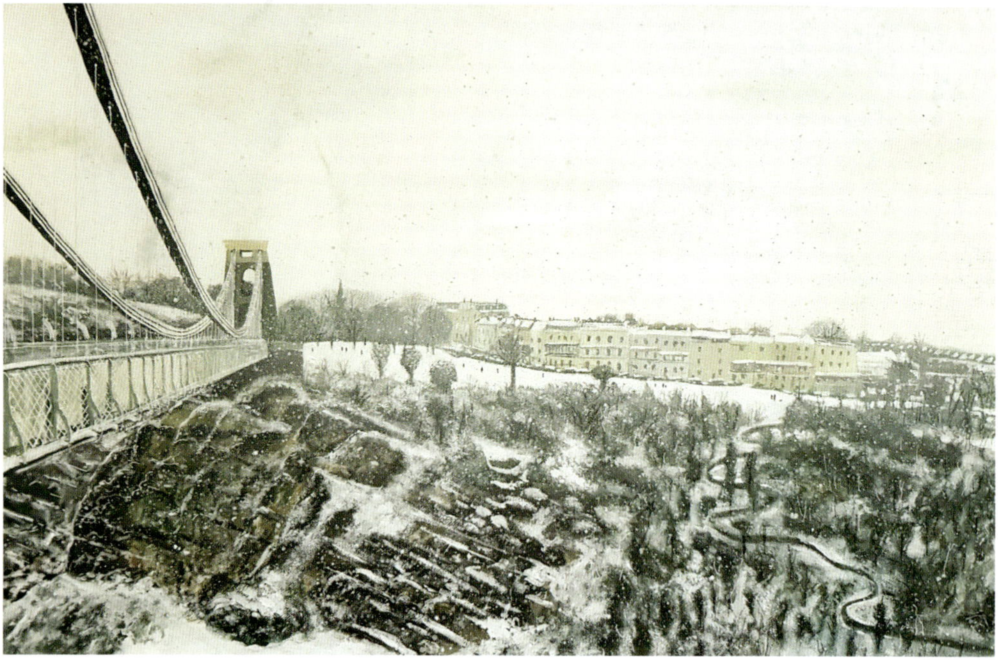

AVON GORGE, JENNY URQUHART

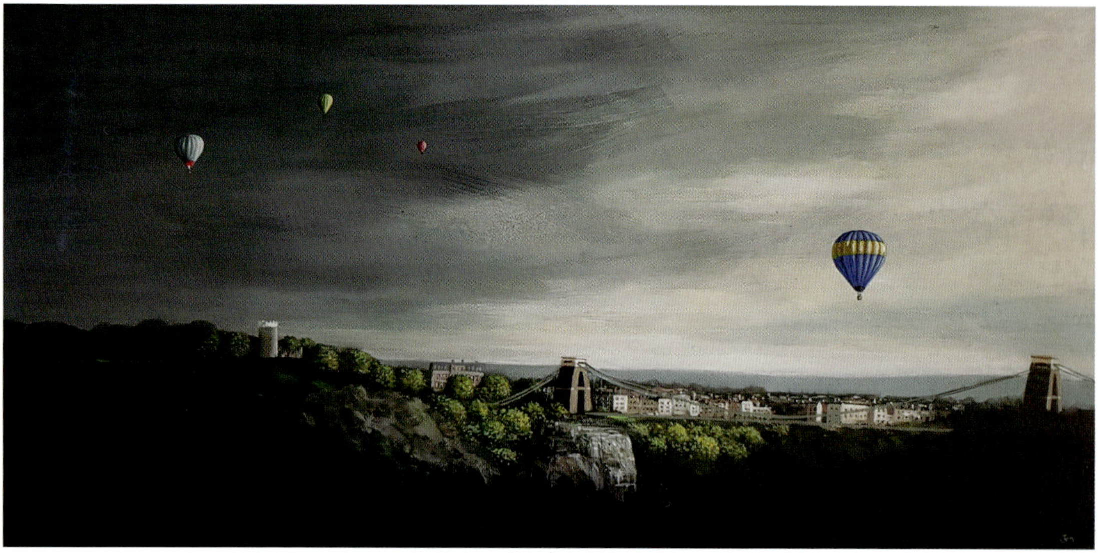

CLIFTON SUSPENSION BRIDGE FROM LEIGH WOODS, JENNY URQUHART

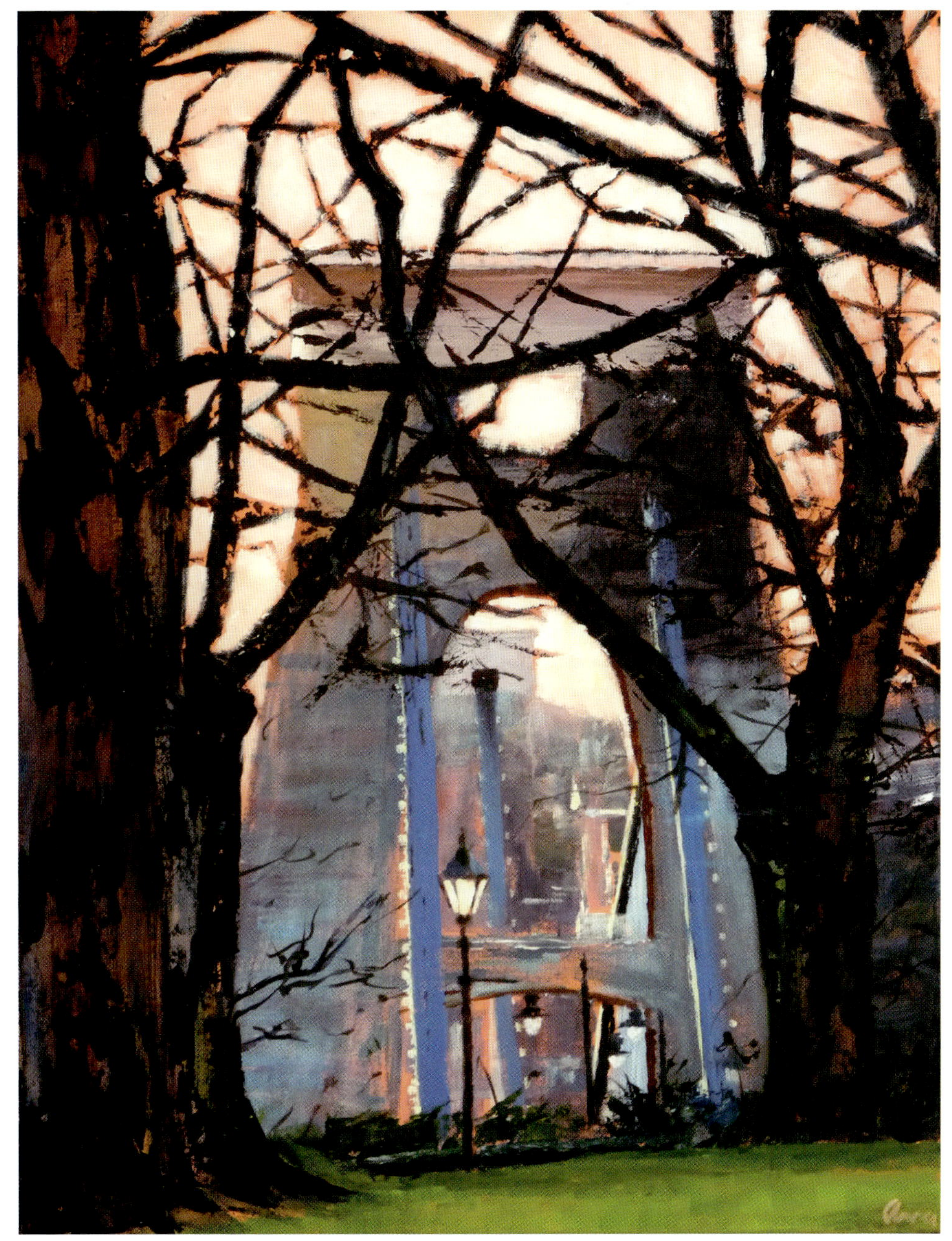

IN SUSPENSE, ANNA DUCKWORTH

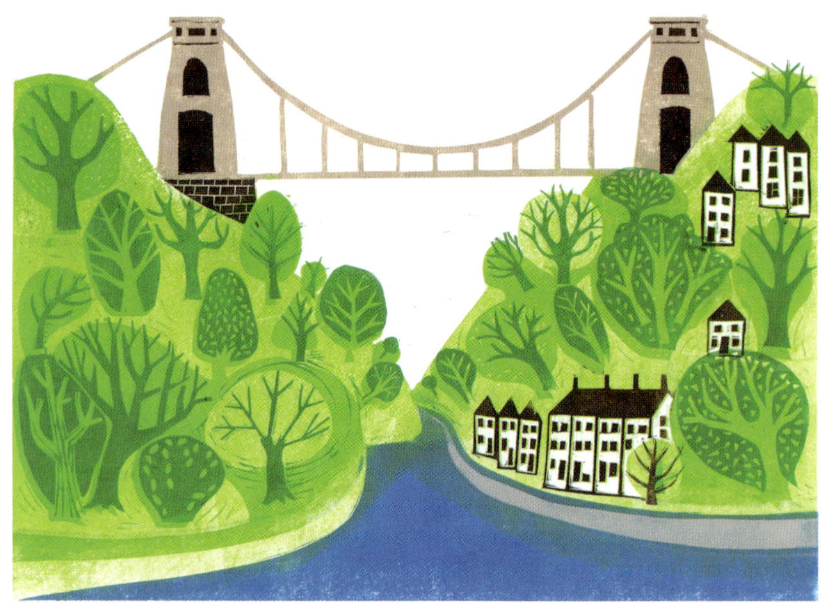

CLIFTON SUSPENSION BRIDGE, LAURA ROBERTSON

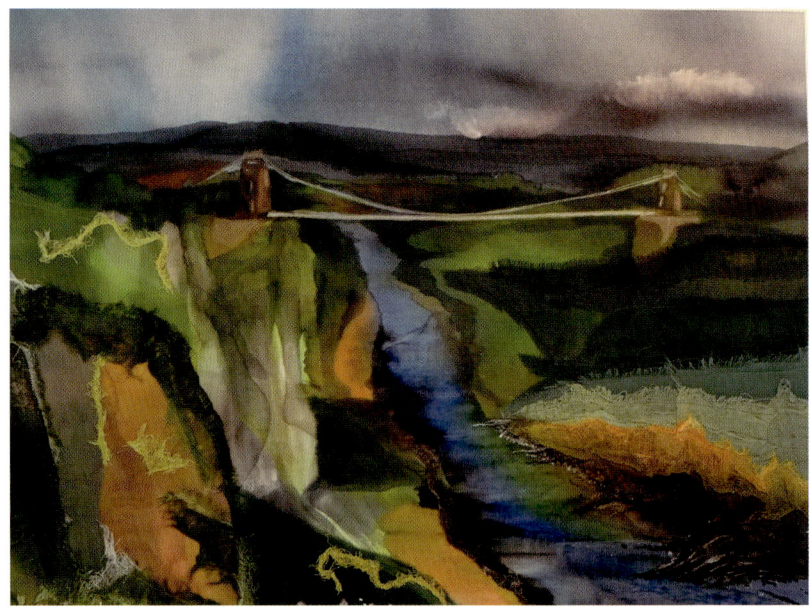

AVON GORGE, SU WILLIAMS

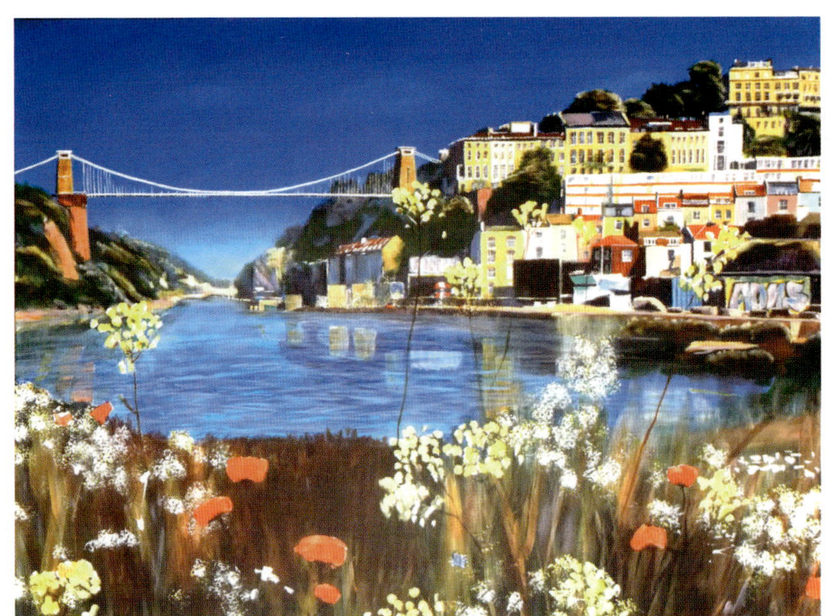

BRISTOL CONTRASTS, ANNA DUCKWORTH

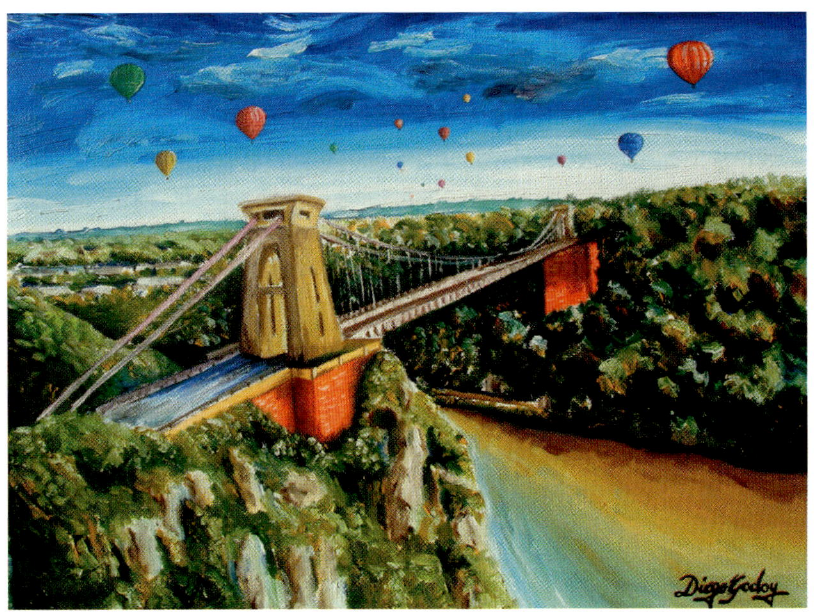

CLIFTON SUSPENSION BRIDGE, DIEGO GODOY

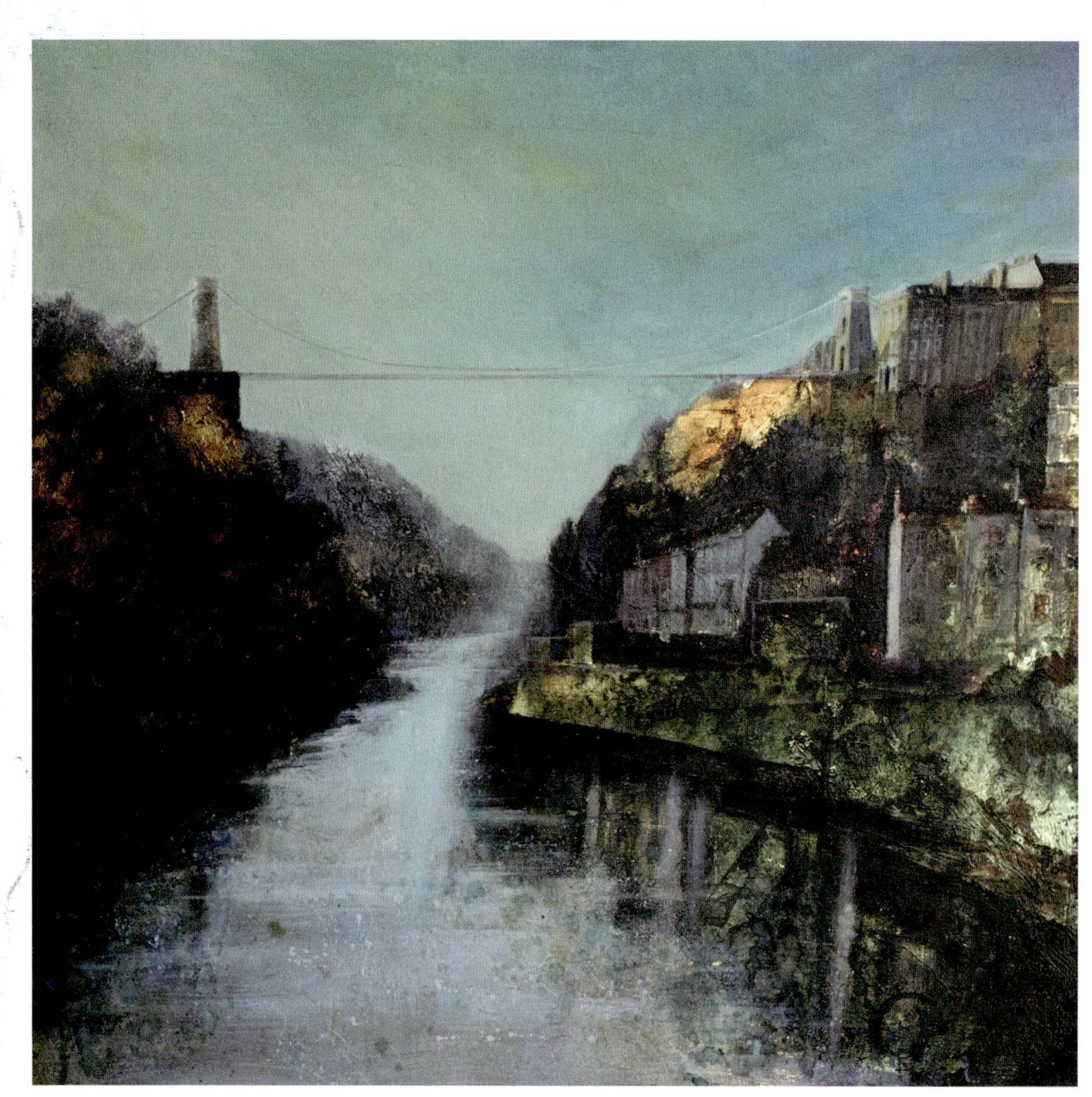

CLIFTON SUSPENSION BRIDGE, ELAINE SHAW

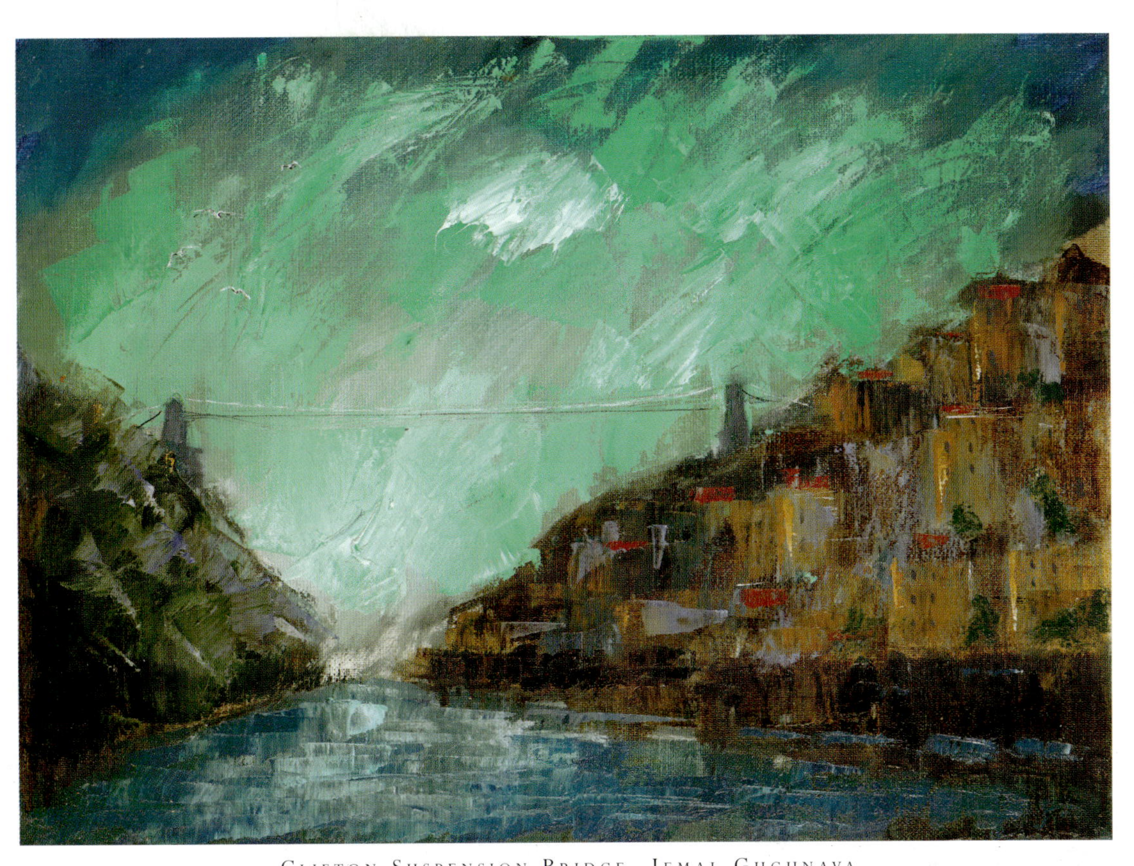

CLIFTON SUSPENSION BRIDGE, JEMAL GUGUNAVA

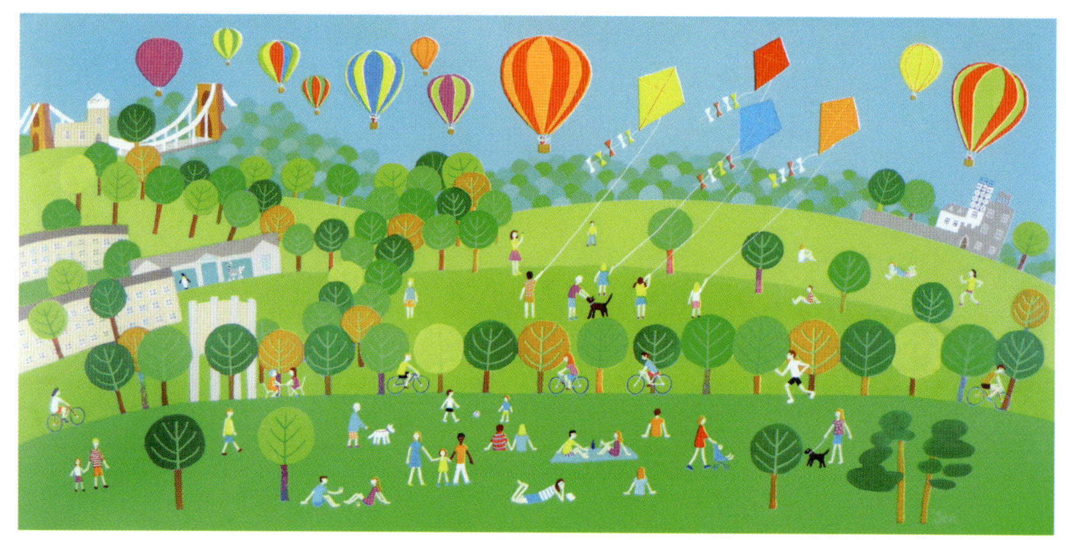

DURDHAM DOWNS, JENNY URQUHART

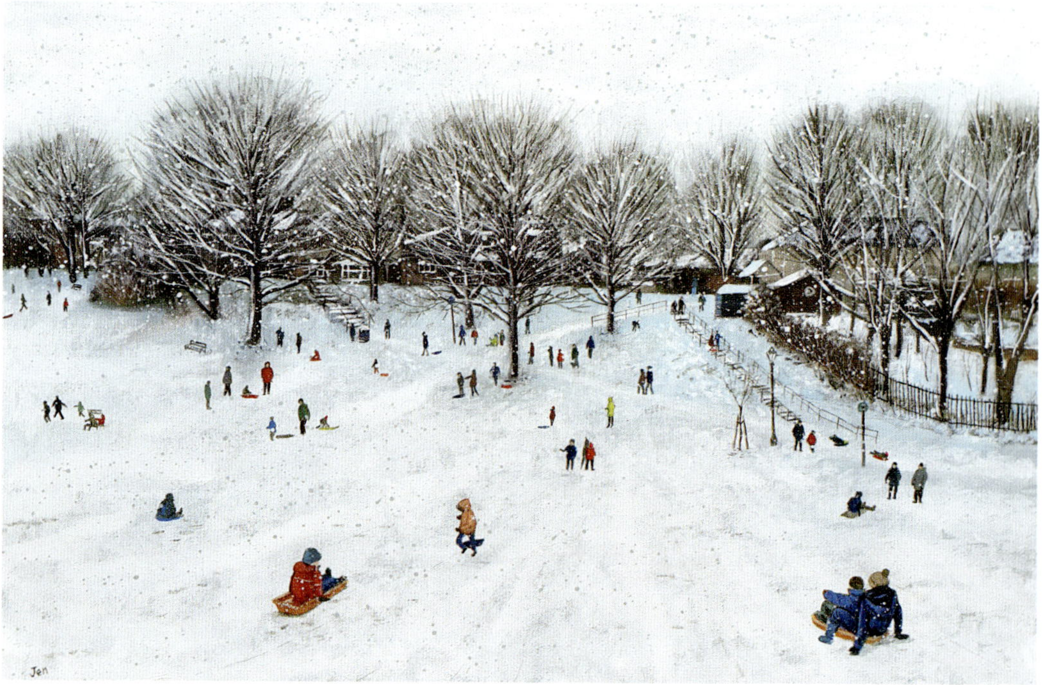

REDLAND GREEN PARK, JENNY URQUHART

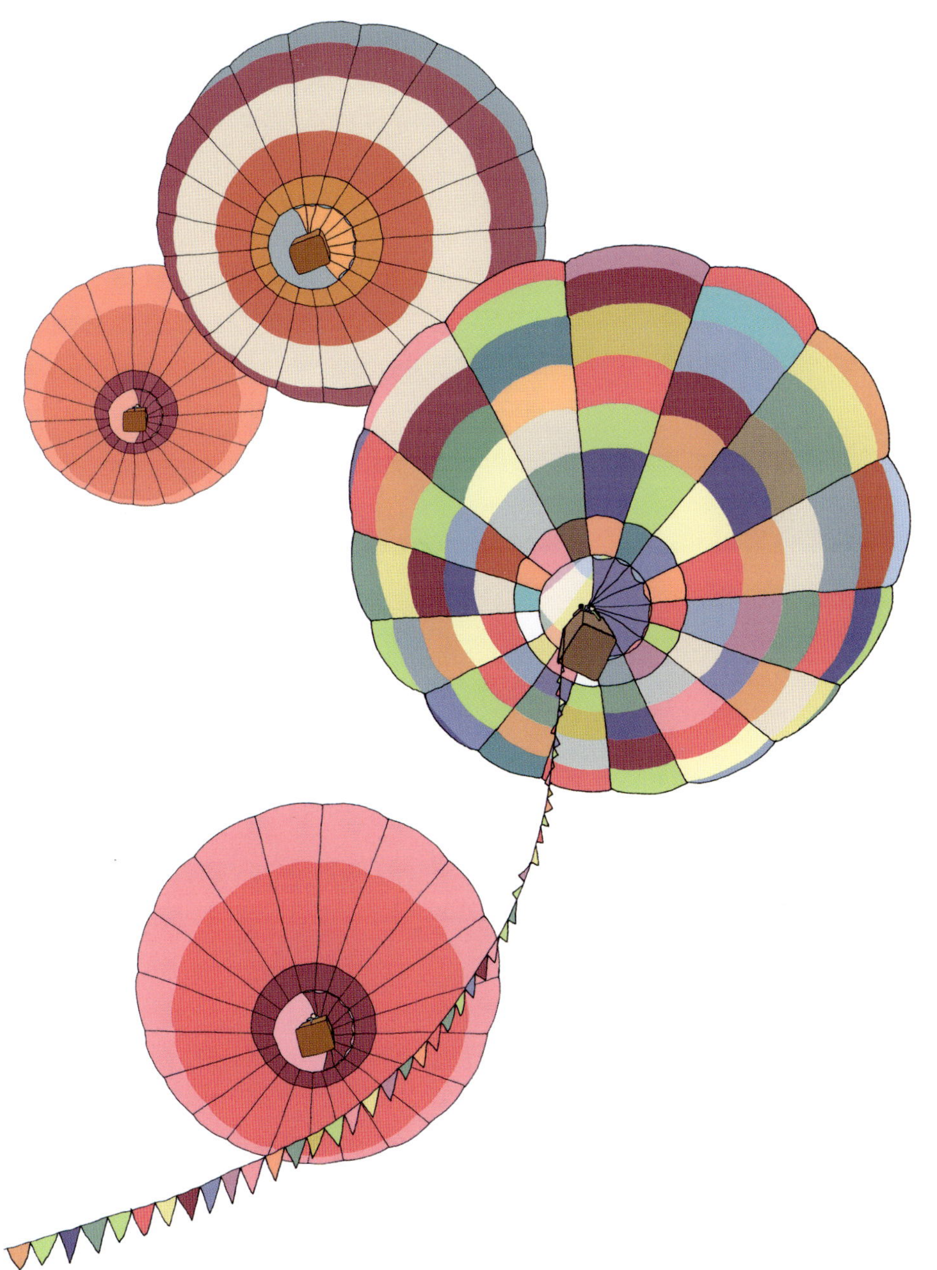

BALLOONS BRISTOL, EMILY KETTERINGHAM

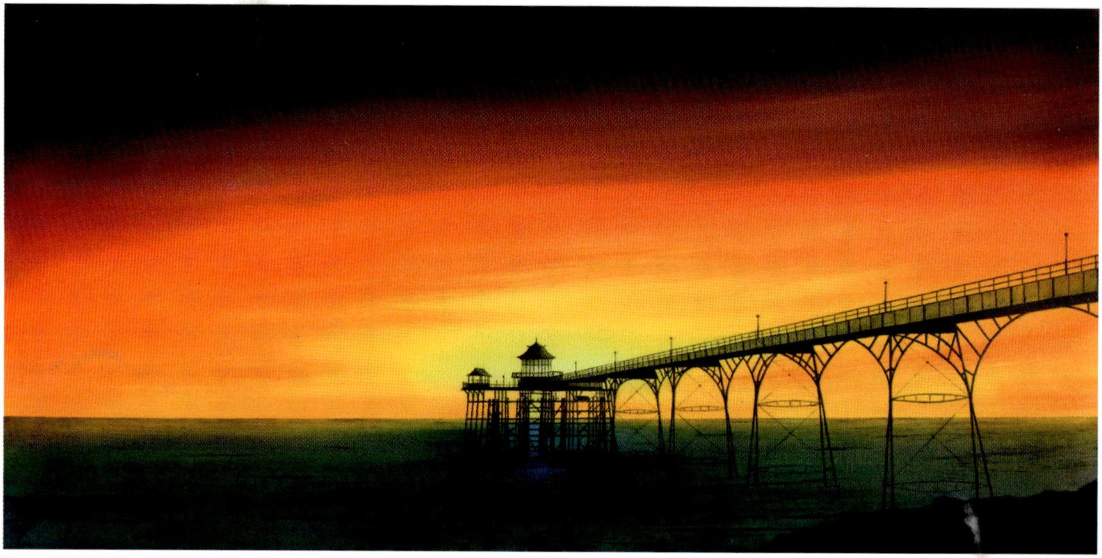

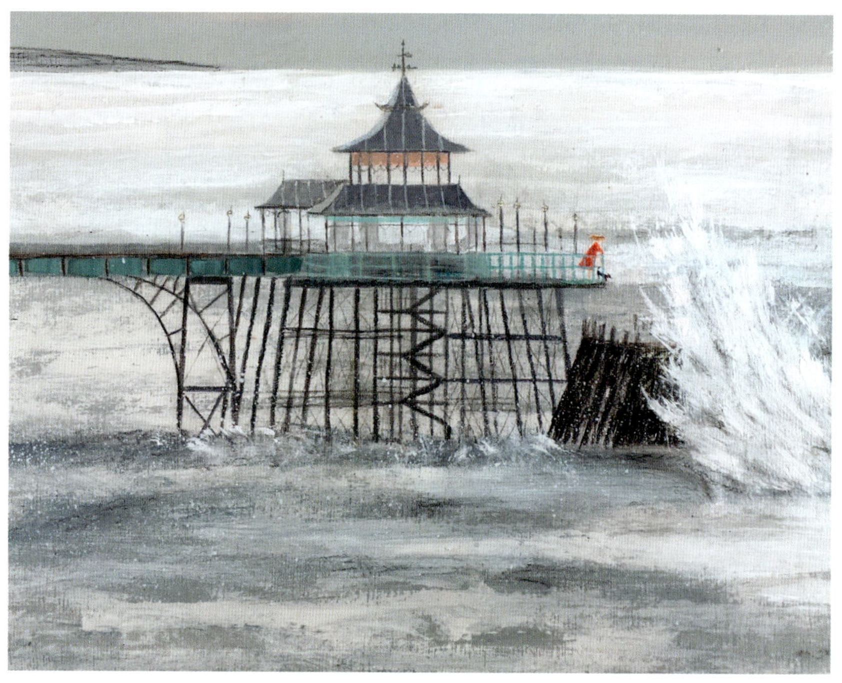

CLEVEDON PIER, MIKE ROME

CLEVEDON PIER, BARBARA PEIRSON

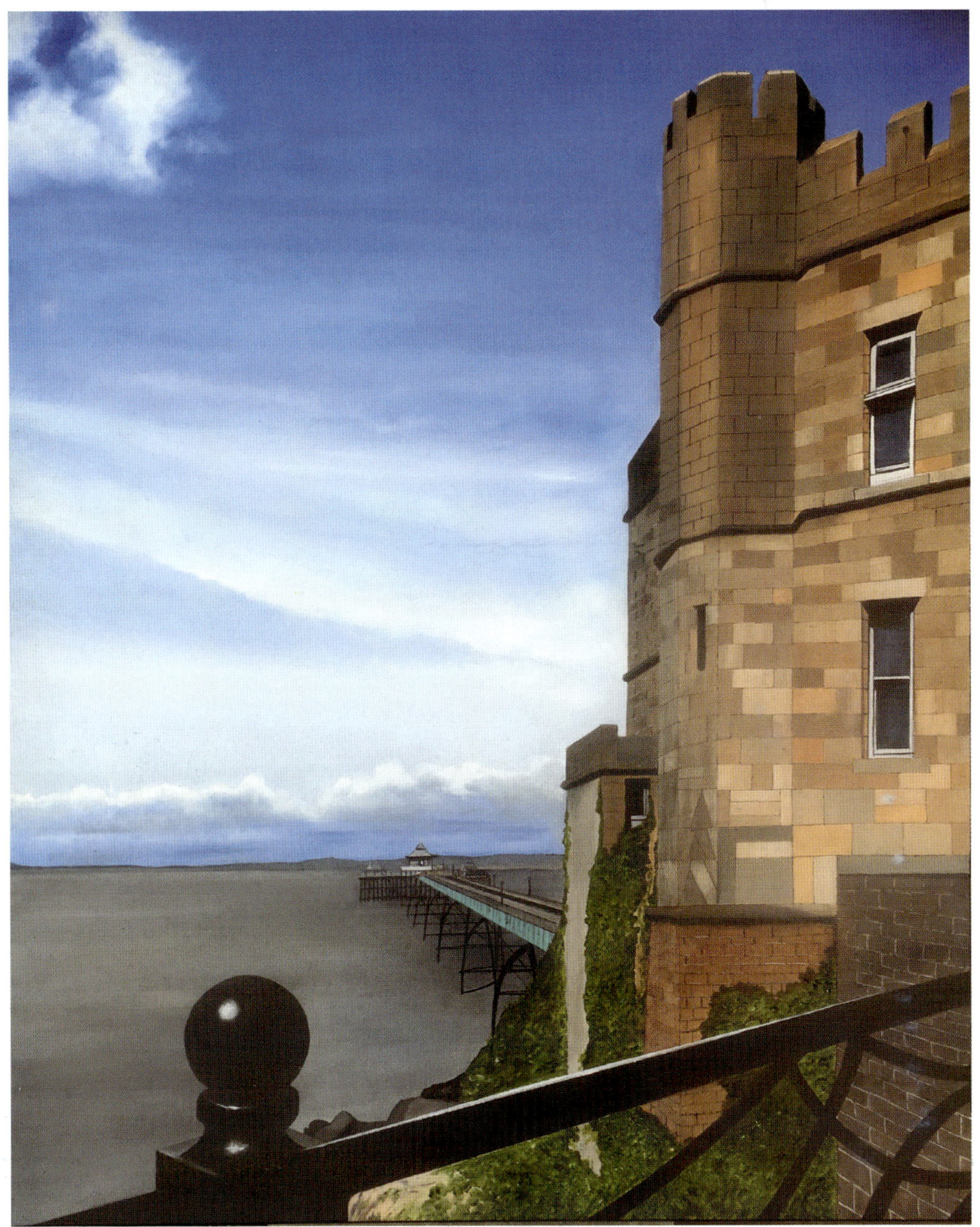

CLEVEDON PIER, MIKE ROME

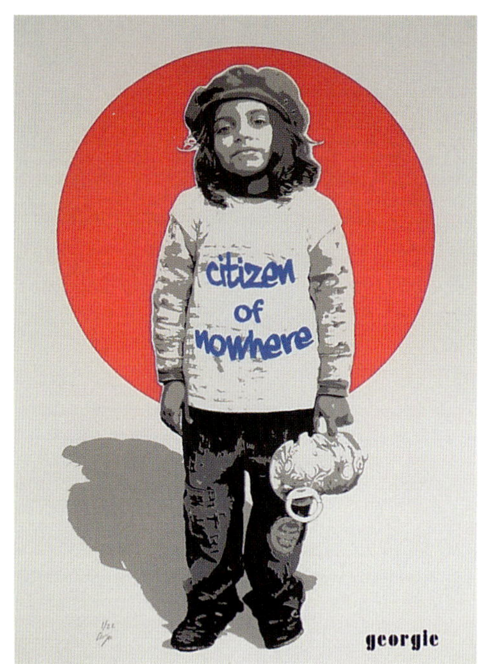


CITIZEN OF NOWHERE, GEORGIE

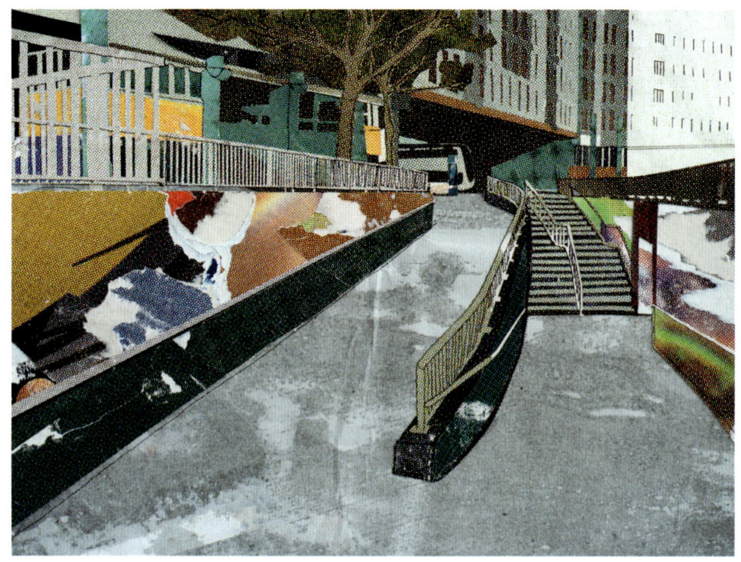

BEARPIT, ZOE BILLBOARD GIBBONS

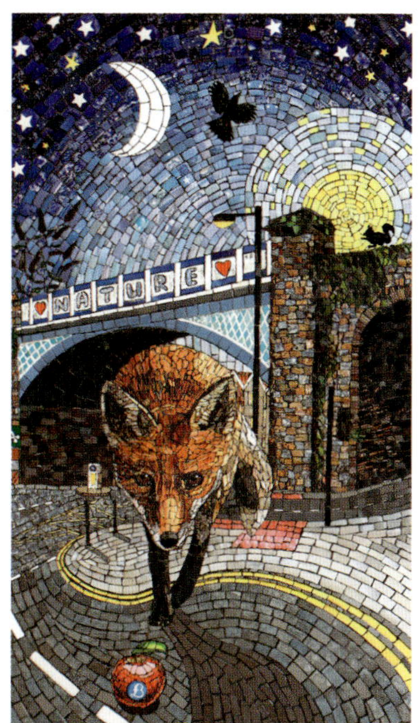



THE ARCHES, GLOUCESTER ROAD, TONI BURROWS

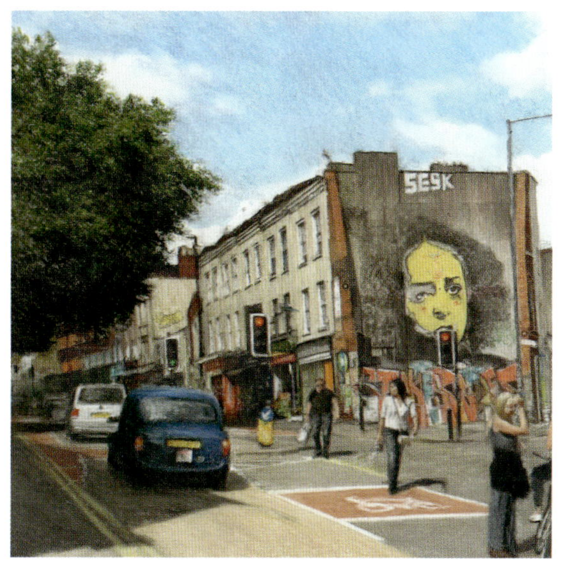



STOKES CROFT, ROBERT ANTELL

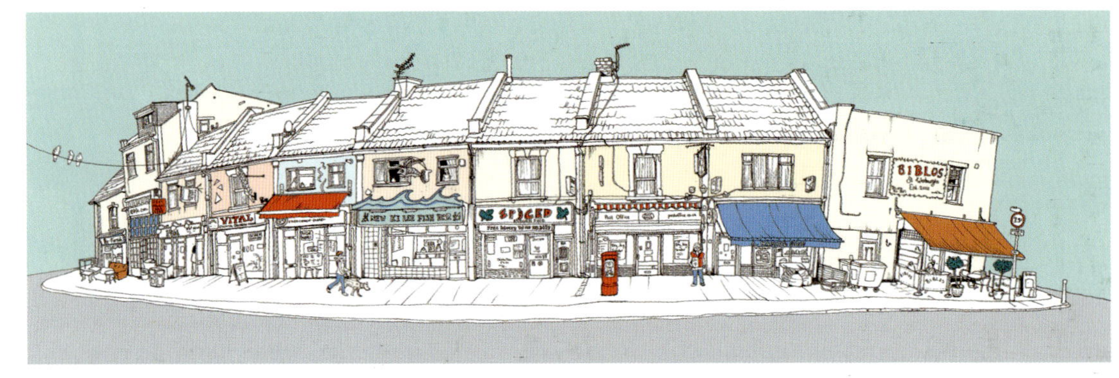

MINA ROAD, HANNAH BUNN

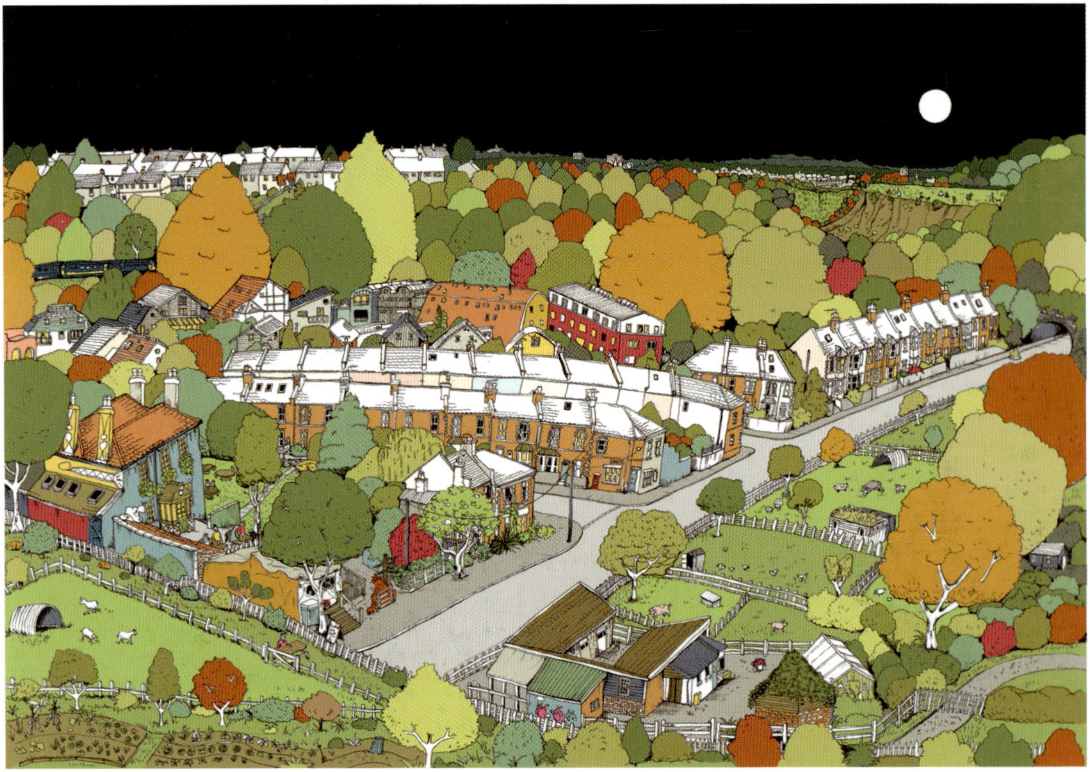

THE FARM, ST WERBURGHS, HANNAH BUNN

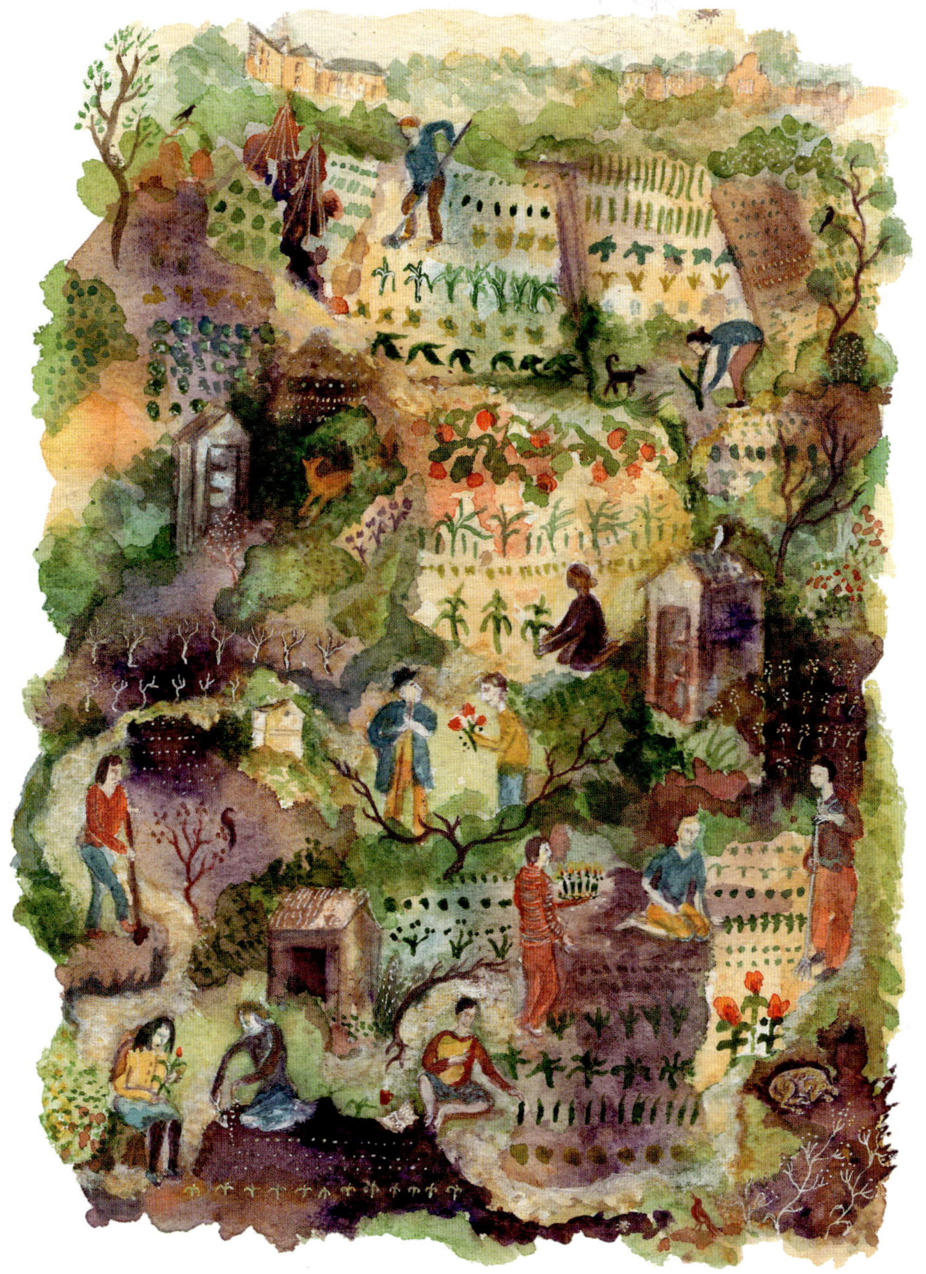

ASHLEY VALE ALLOTMENTS, EMMA BURLEIGH

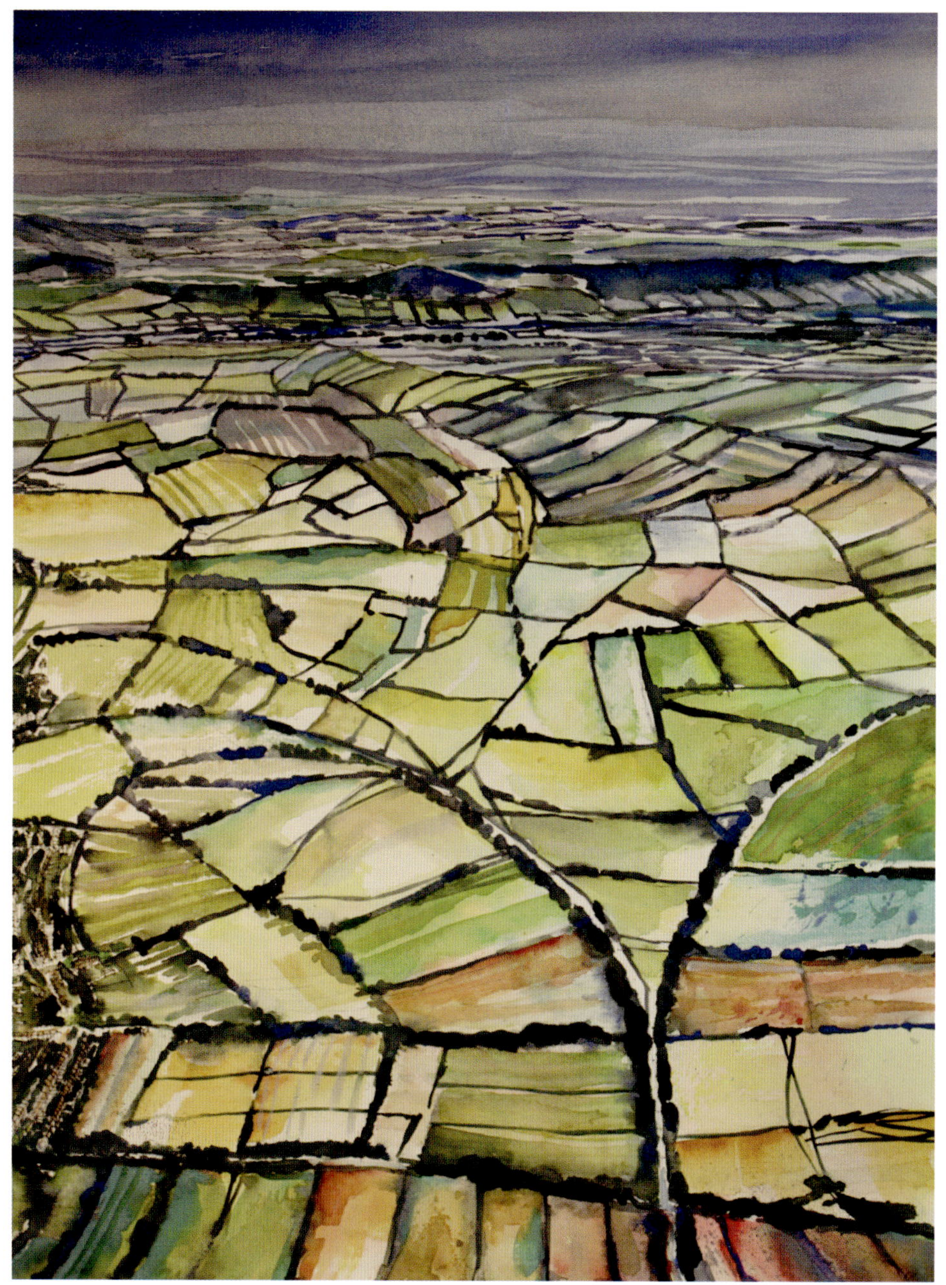

FROM BRISTOL TO BATH, SARAH BODEN

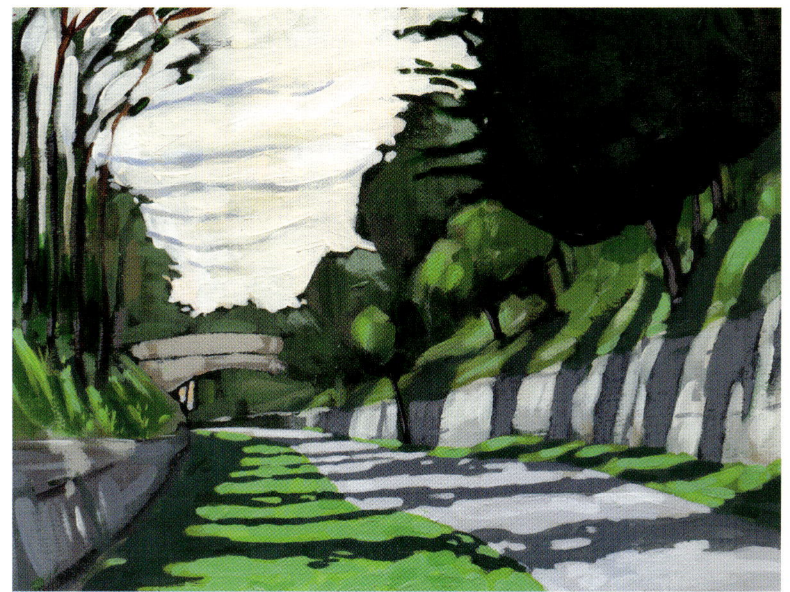

Bristol & Bath Railway Path, Nick Gerolemou

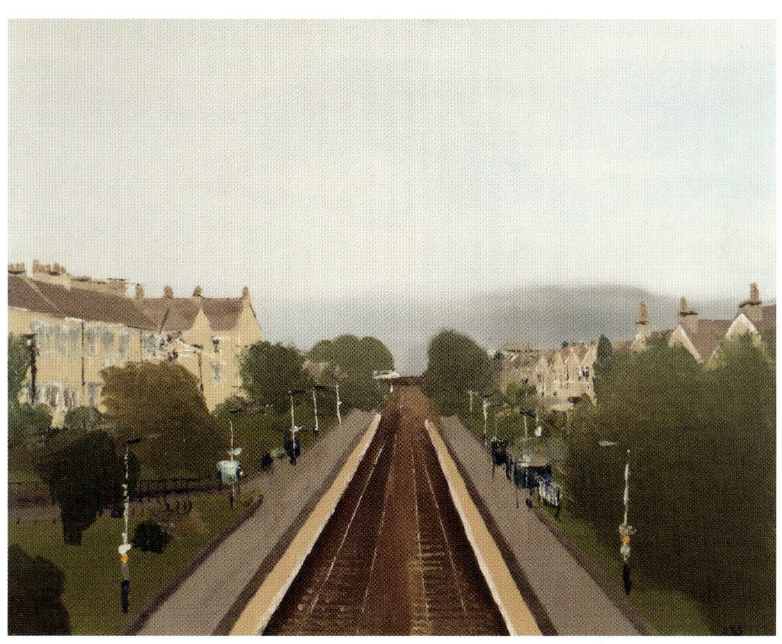

Oldfield Park Station, Kieran Luke Naish

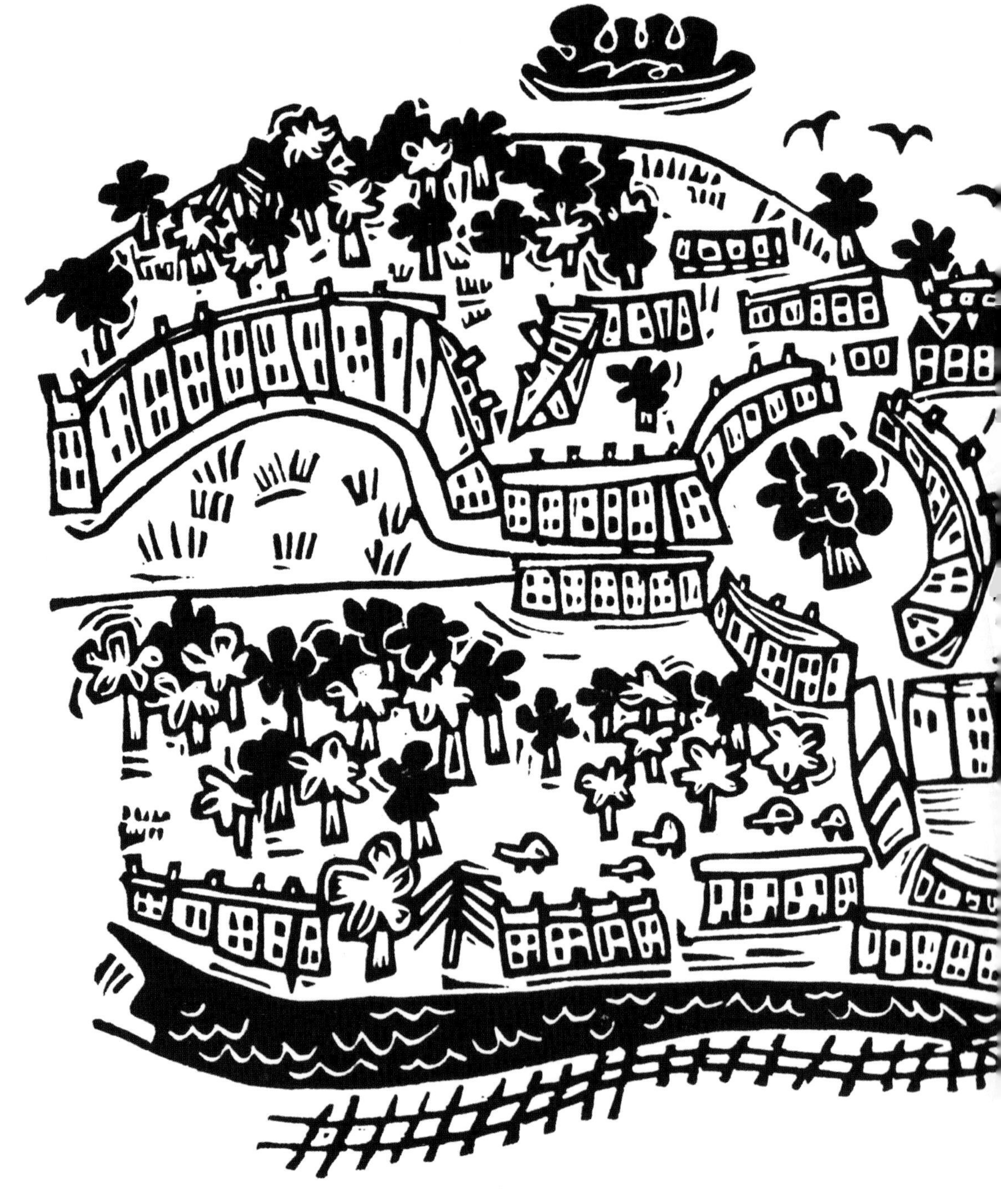

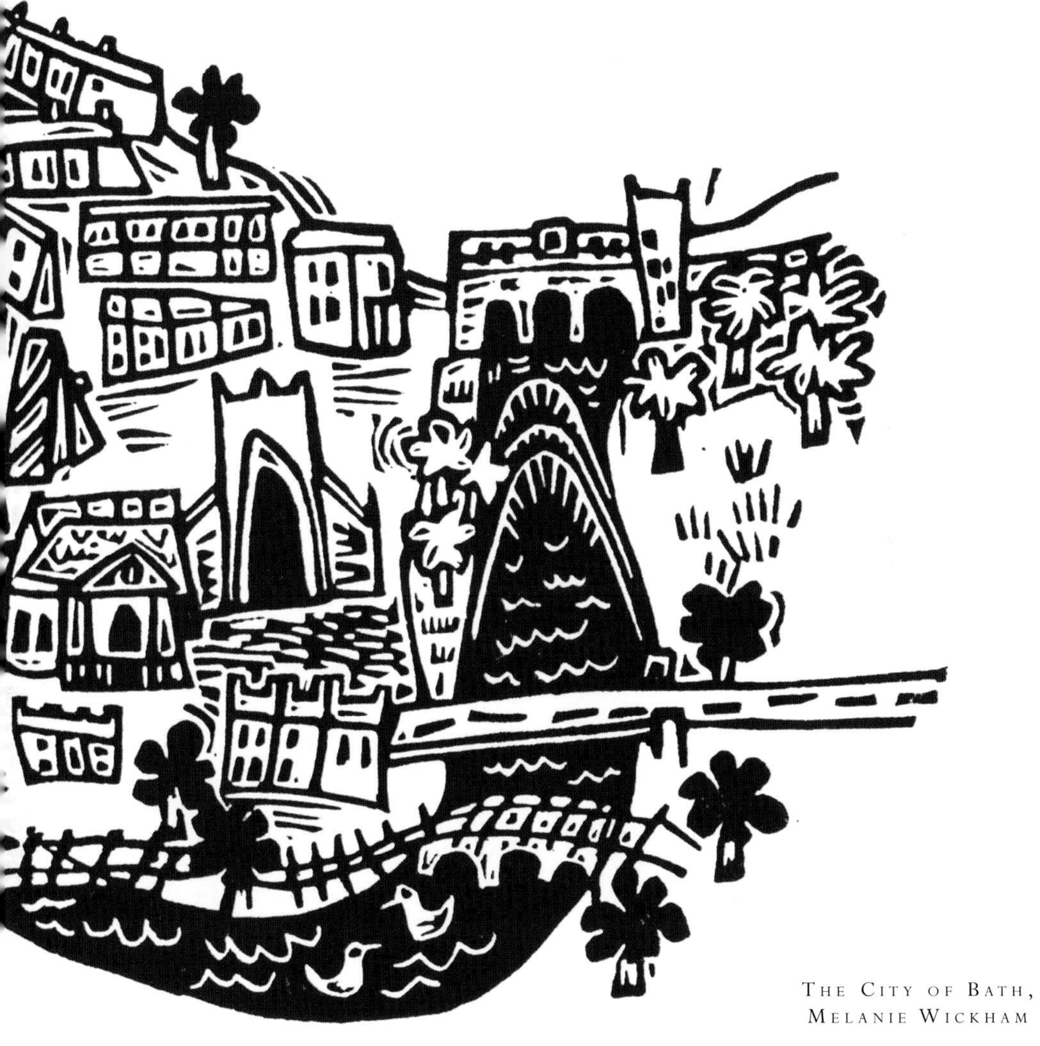

THE CITY OF BATH,
MELANIE WICKHAM

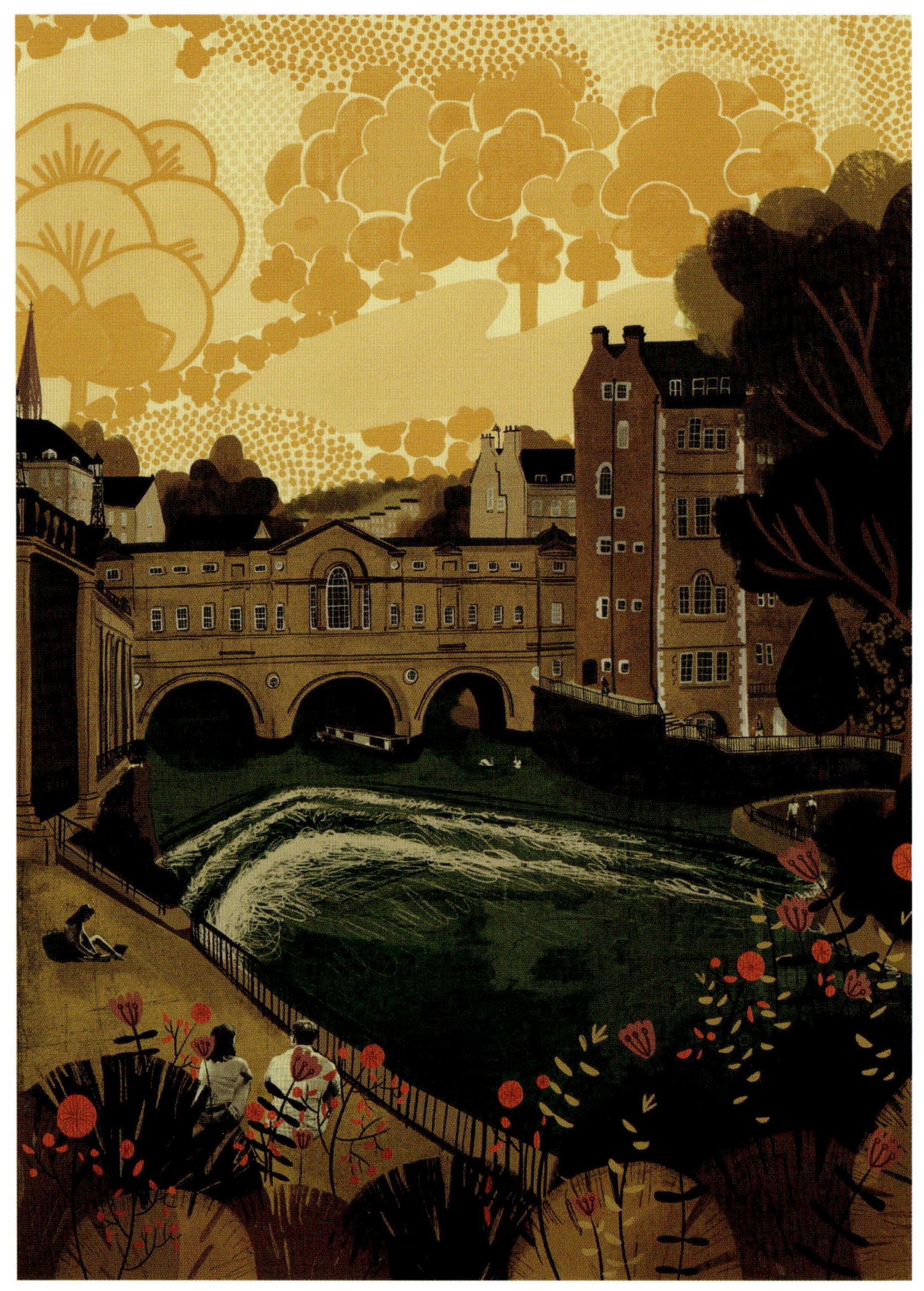

PULTENEY BRIDGE, EMY LOU HOLMES

86

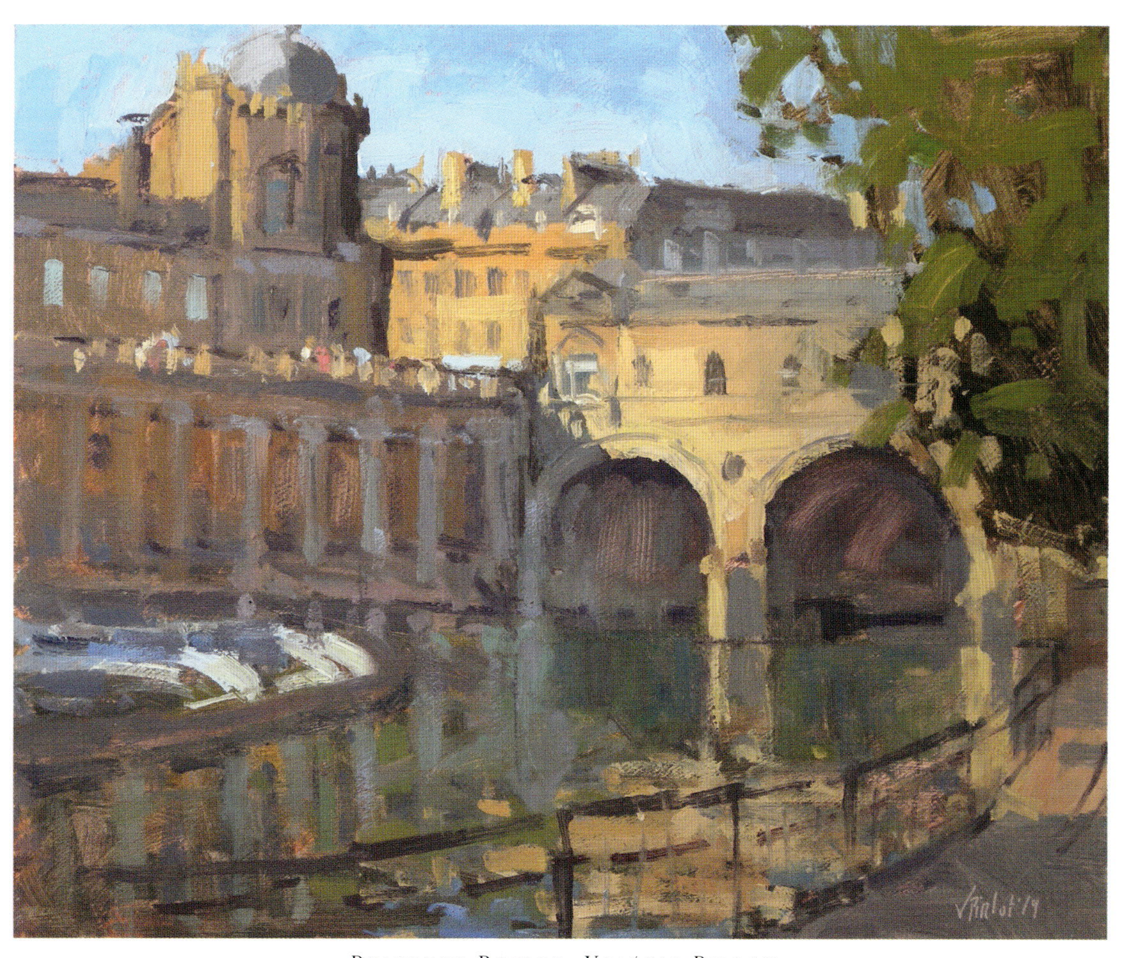

Pulteney Bridge, Valérie Pirlot

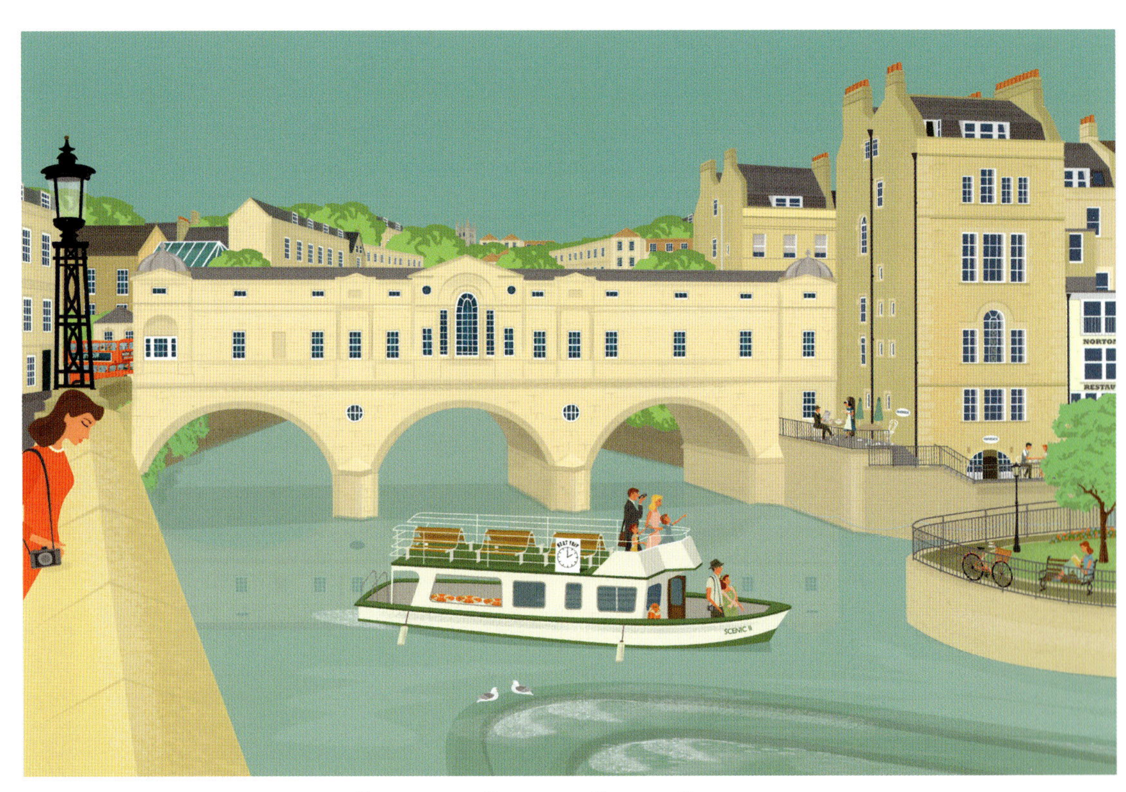

PULTENEY BRIDGE, CLARE PHILLIPS

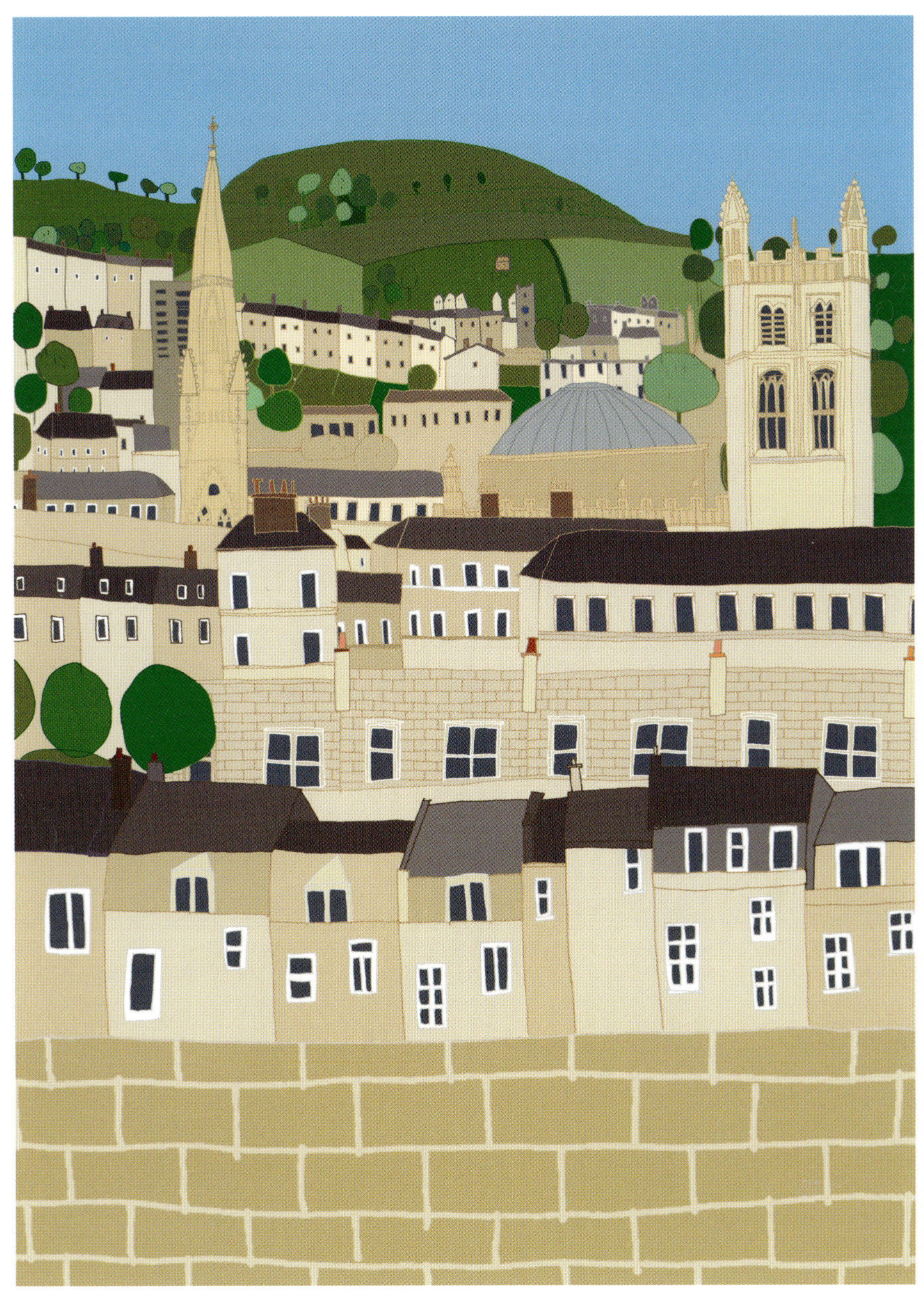

B ATH  R OOFTOPS ,  H ANNAH  B ROADWAY

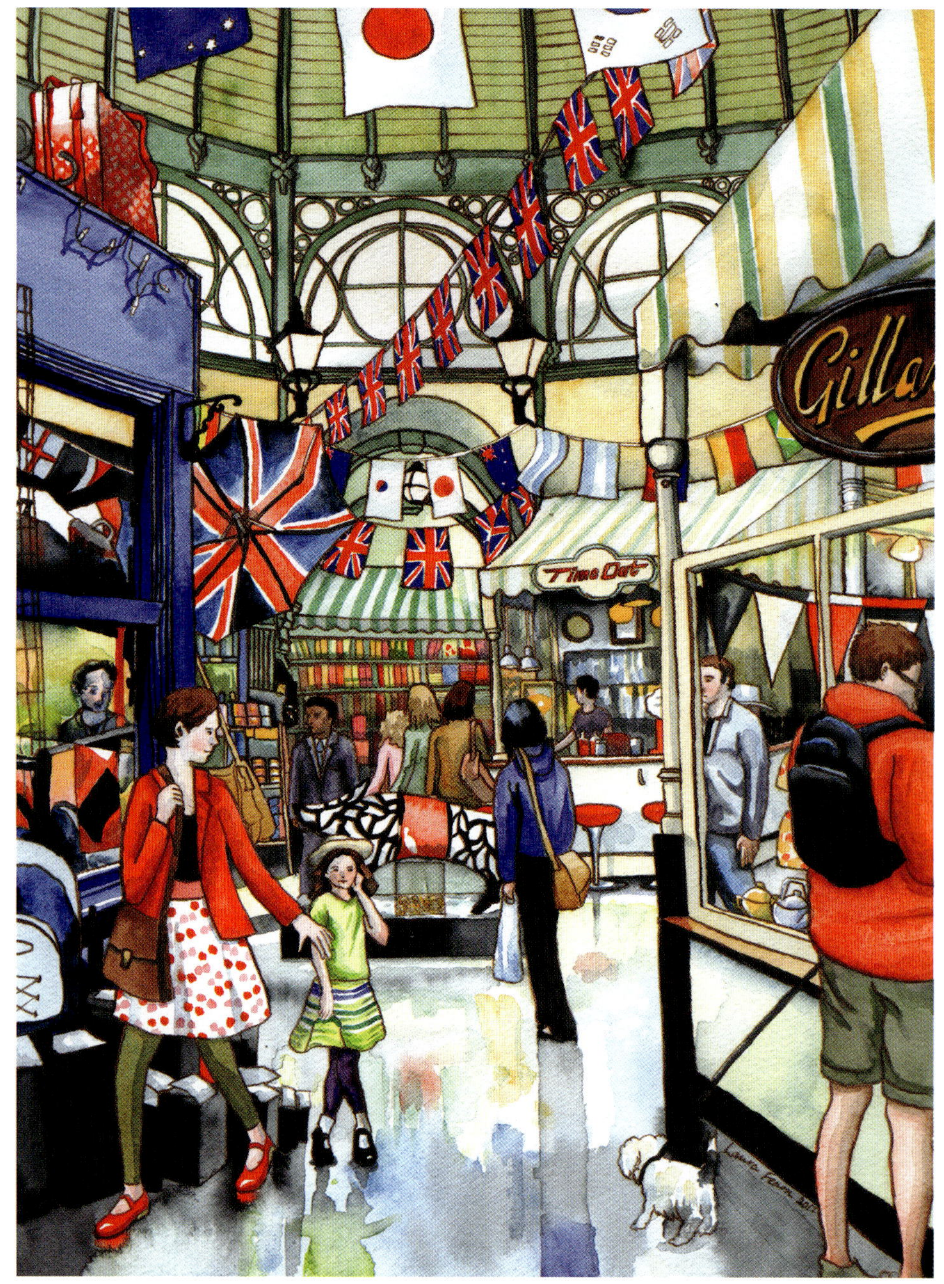

GUILDHALL MARKET, LAURA FEARN

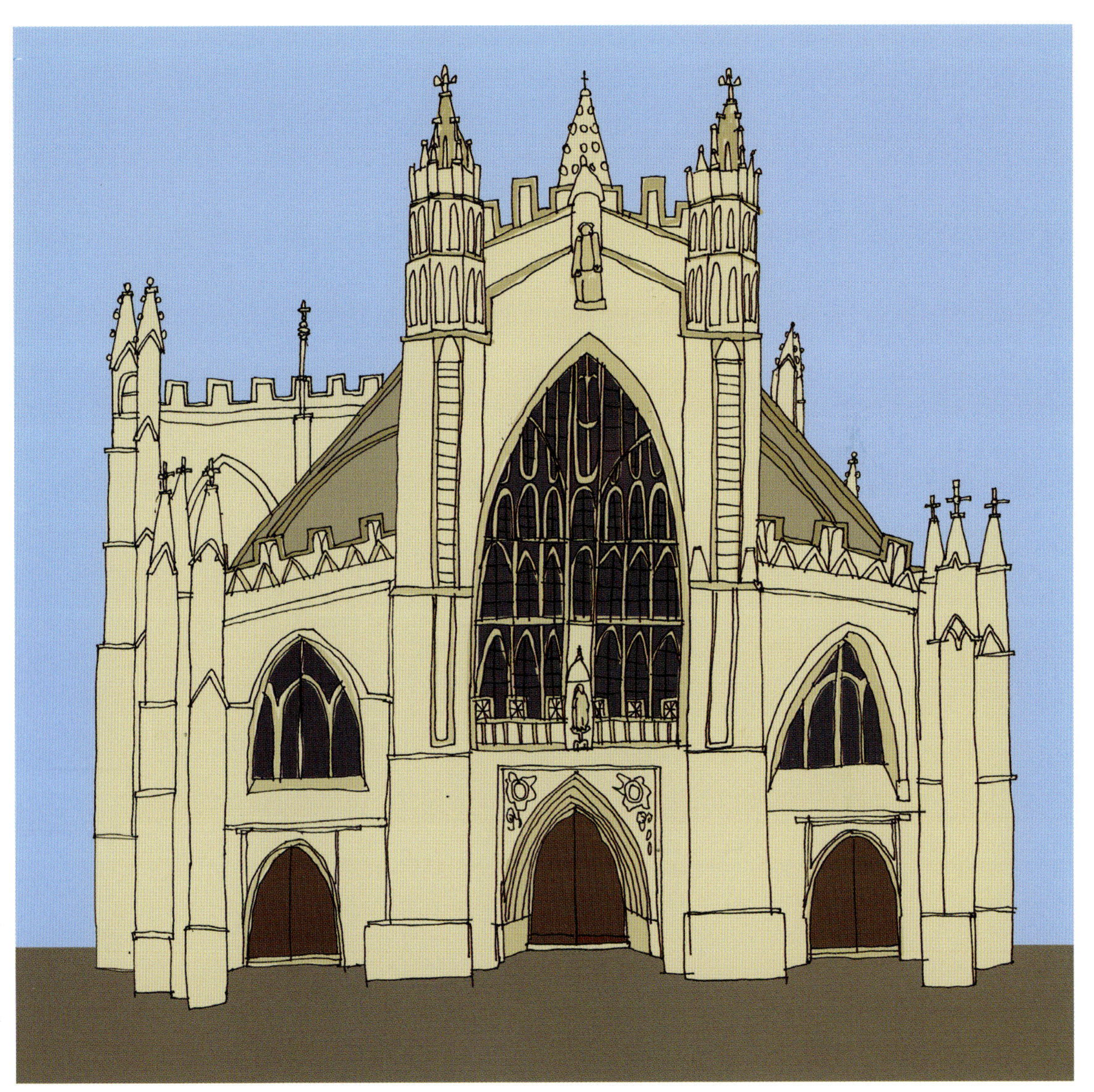

BATH ABBEY, HANNAH BROADWAY

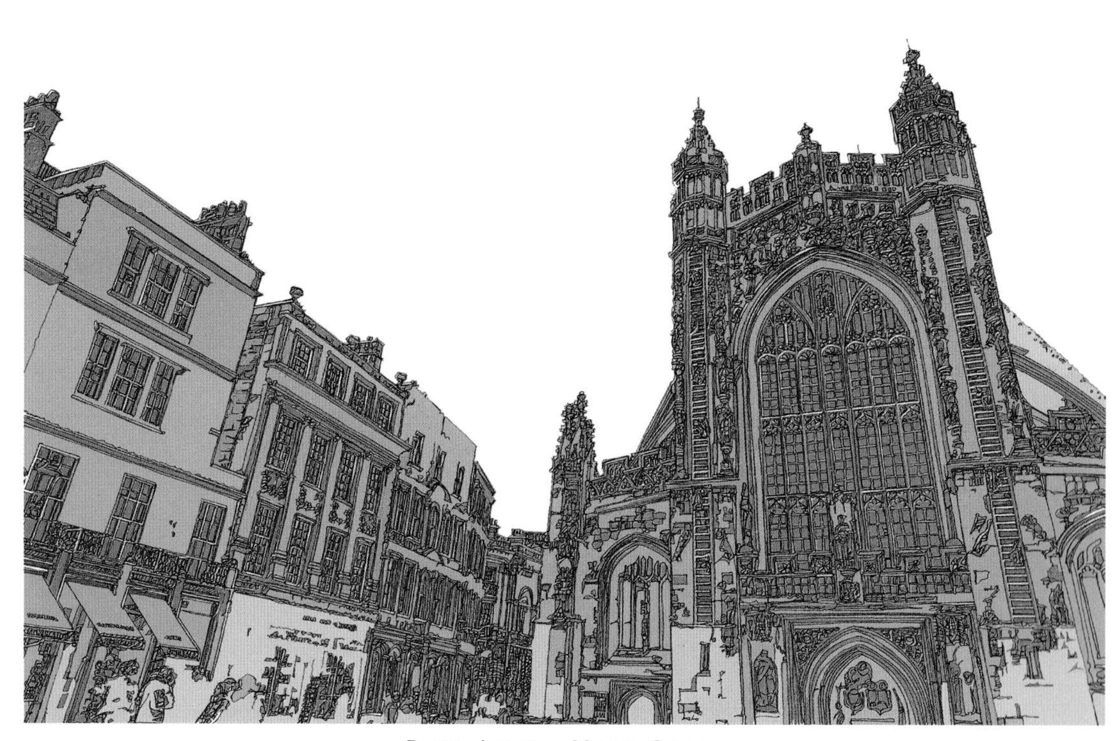

BATH ABBEY, MARY CORUM

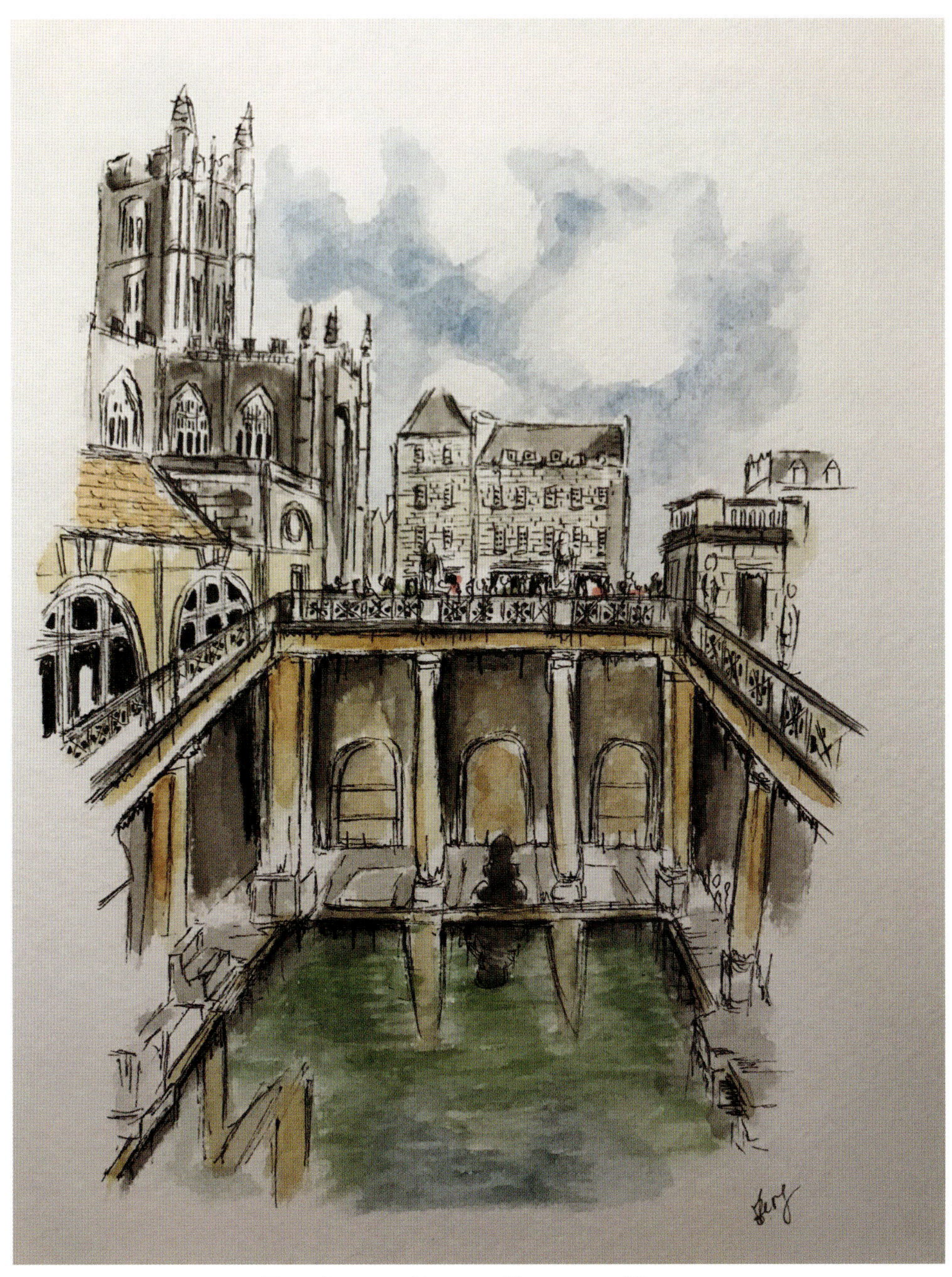


The Roman Baths, Victoria Wood

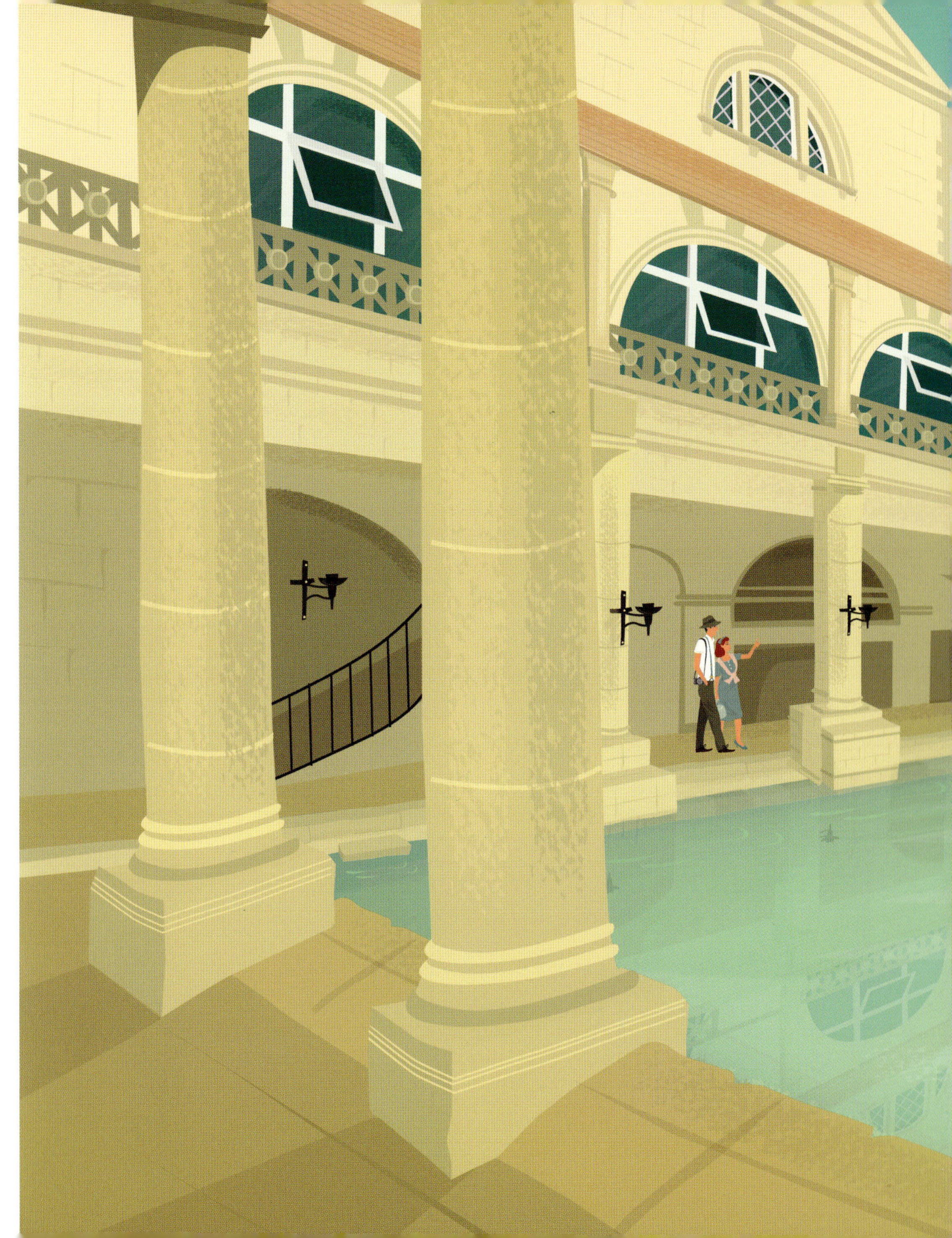

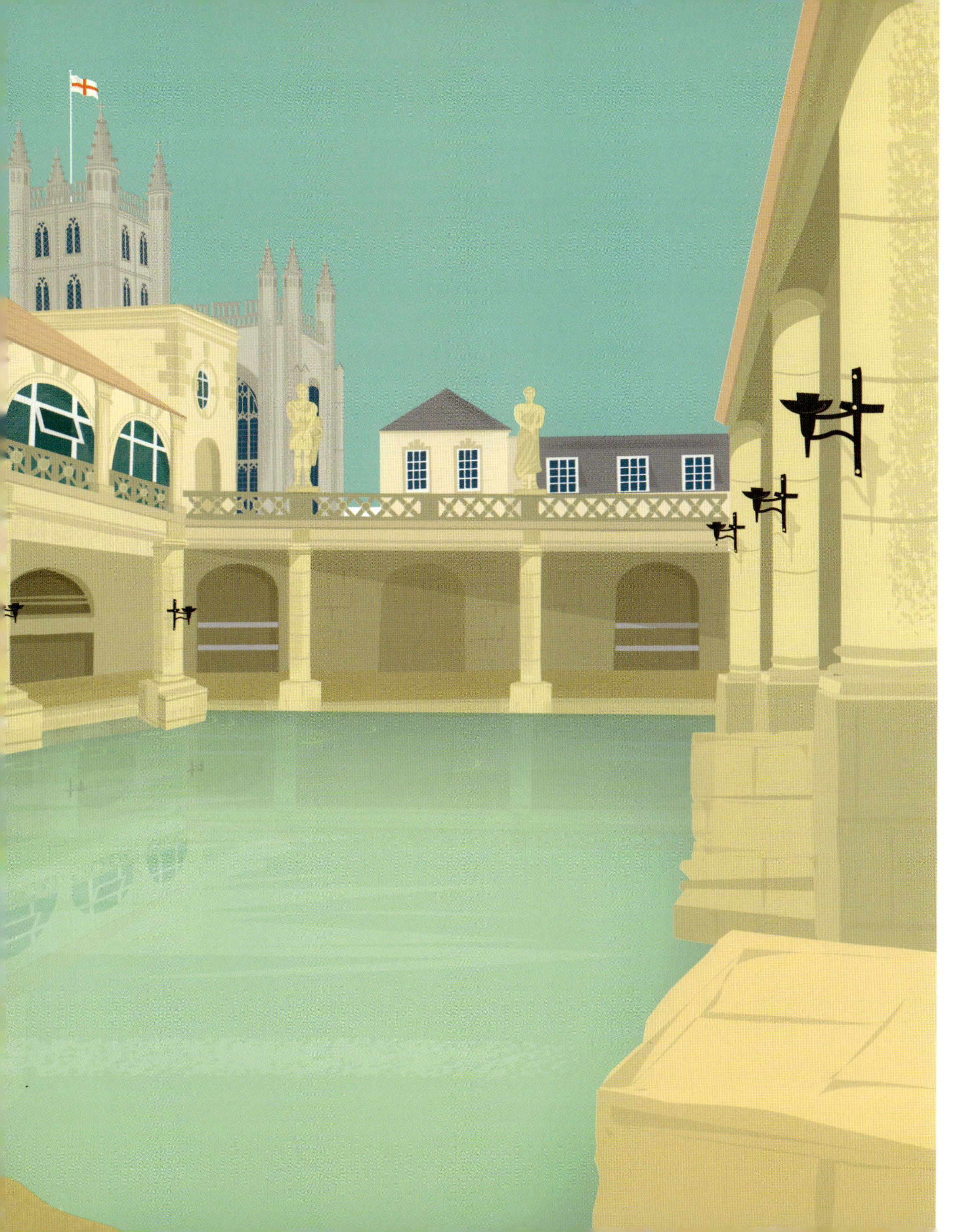

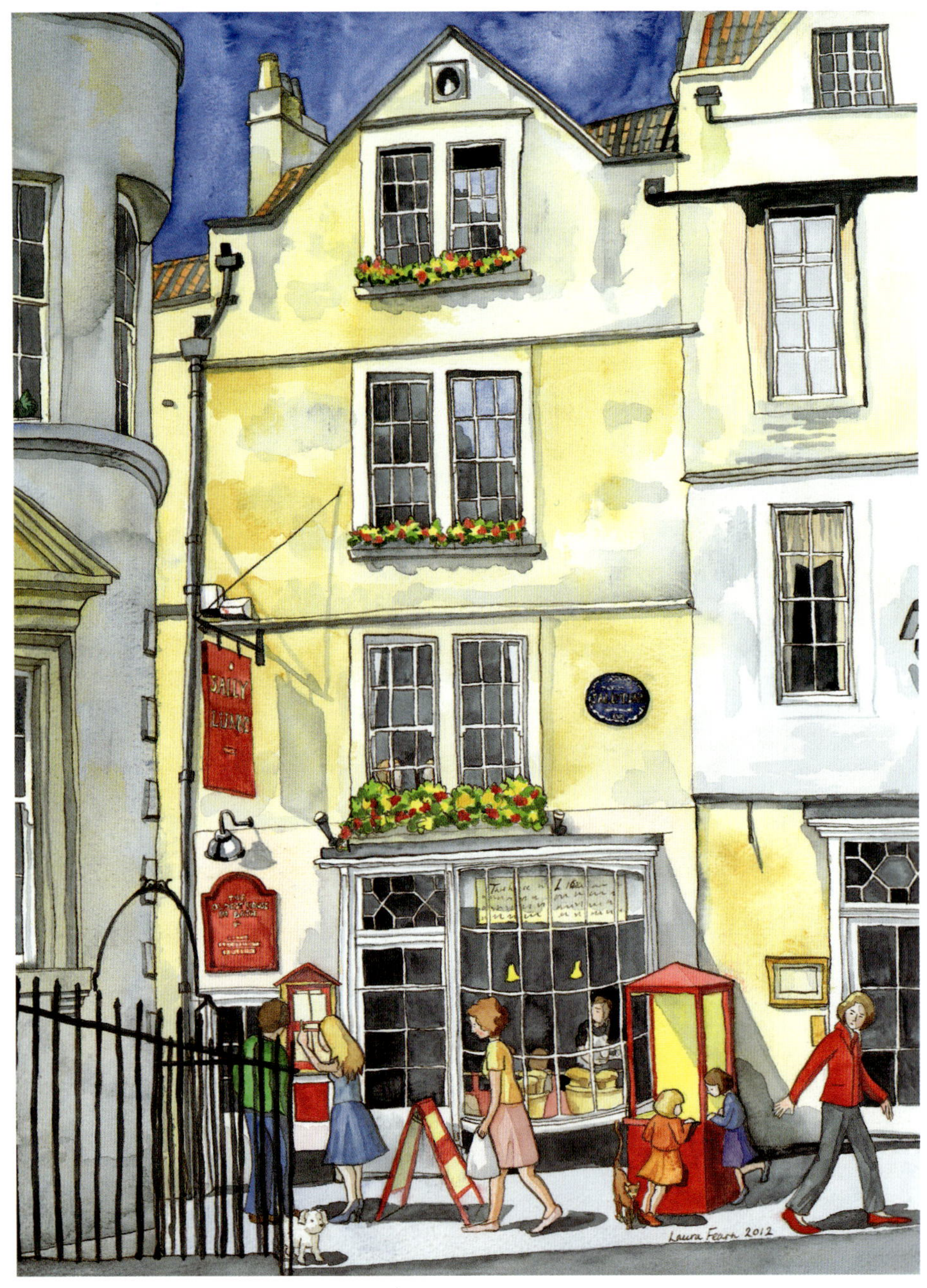



SALLY LUNN'S HOUSE, LAURA FEARN
PREVIOUS TWO PAGES, THE ROMAN BATHS, CLARE PHILLIPS

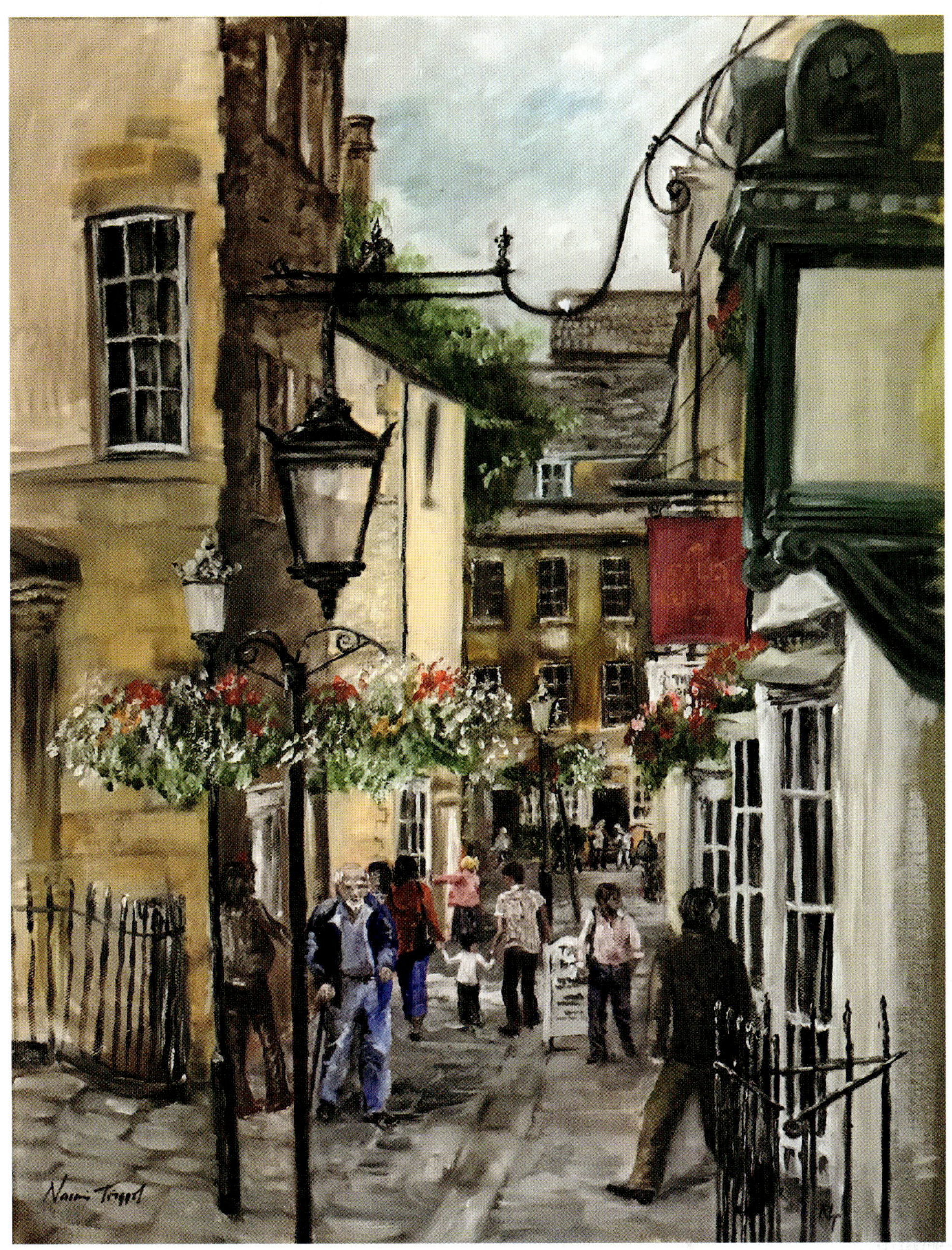

North Parade, Naomi Triggol

97

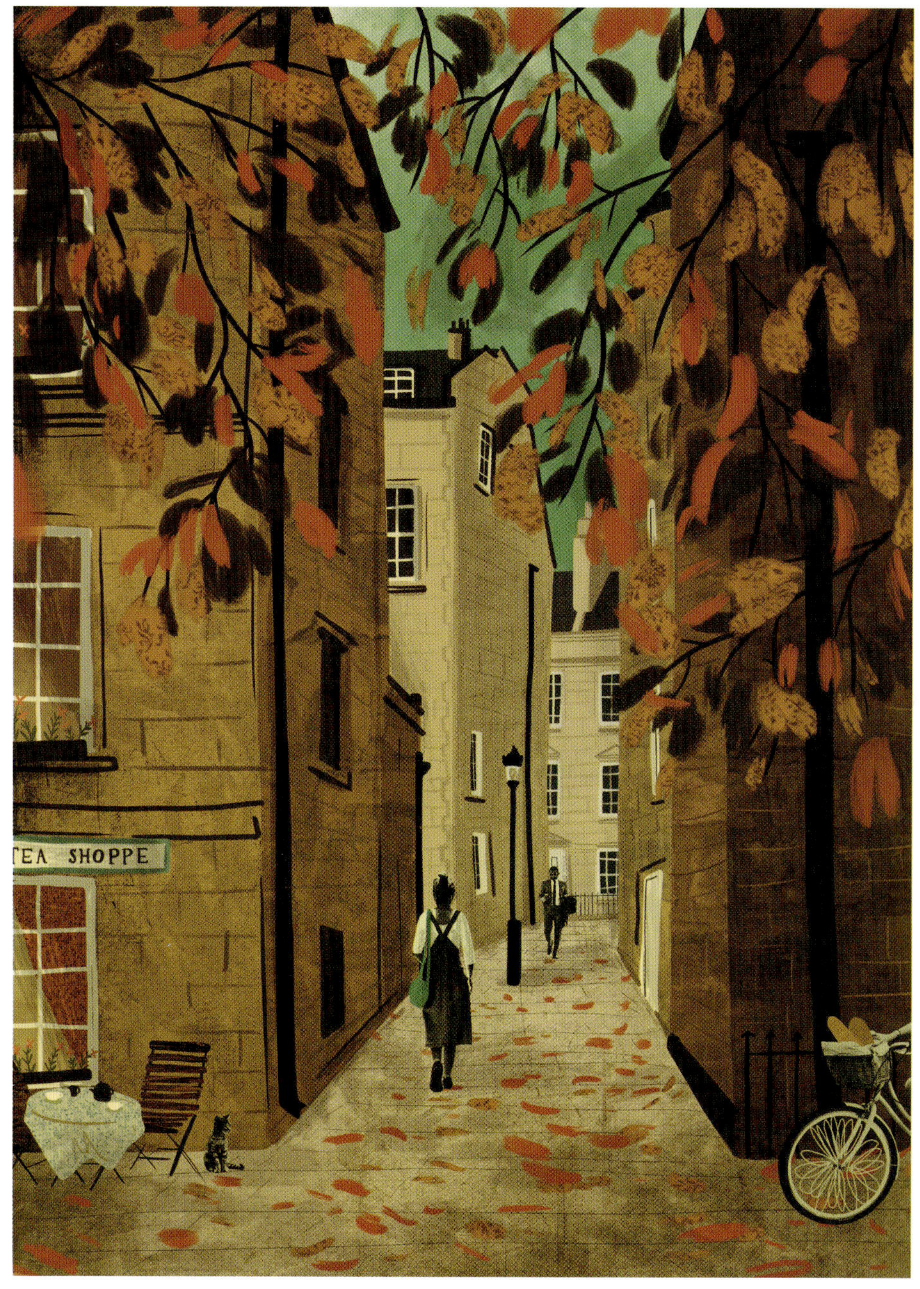

TEA SHOPPE AT ABBEY GREEN, EMY LOU HOLMES

98

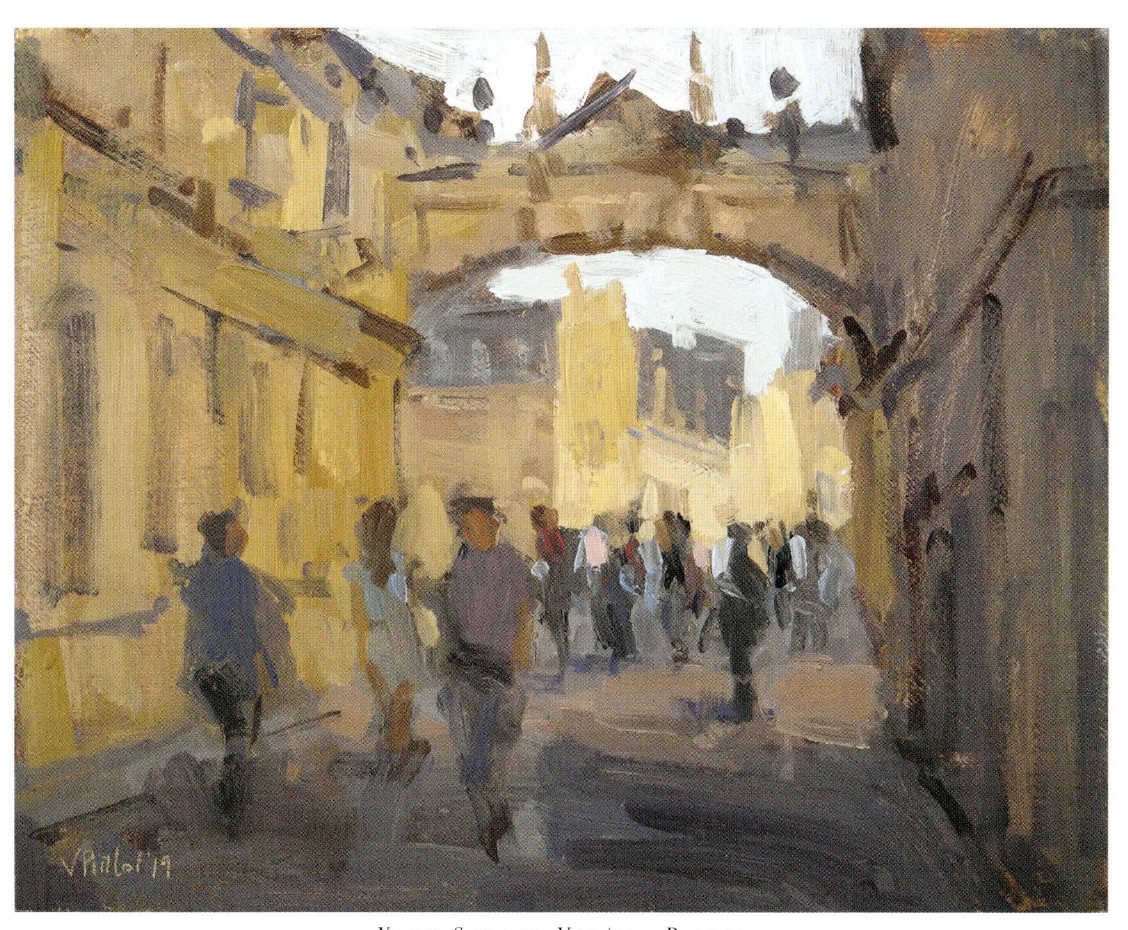



York Street, Valérie Pirlot

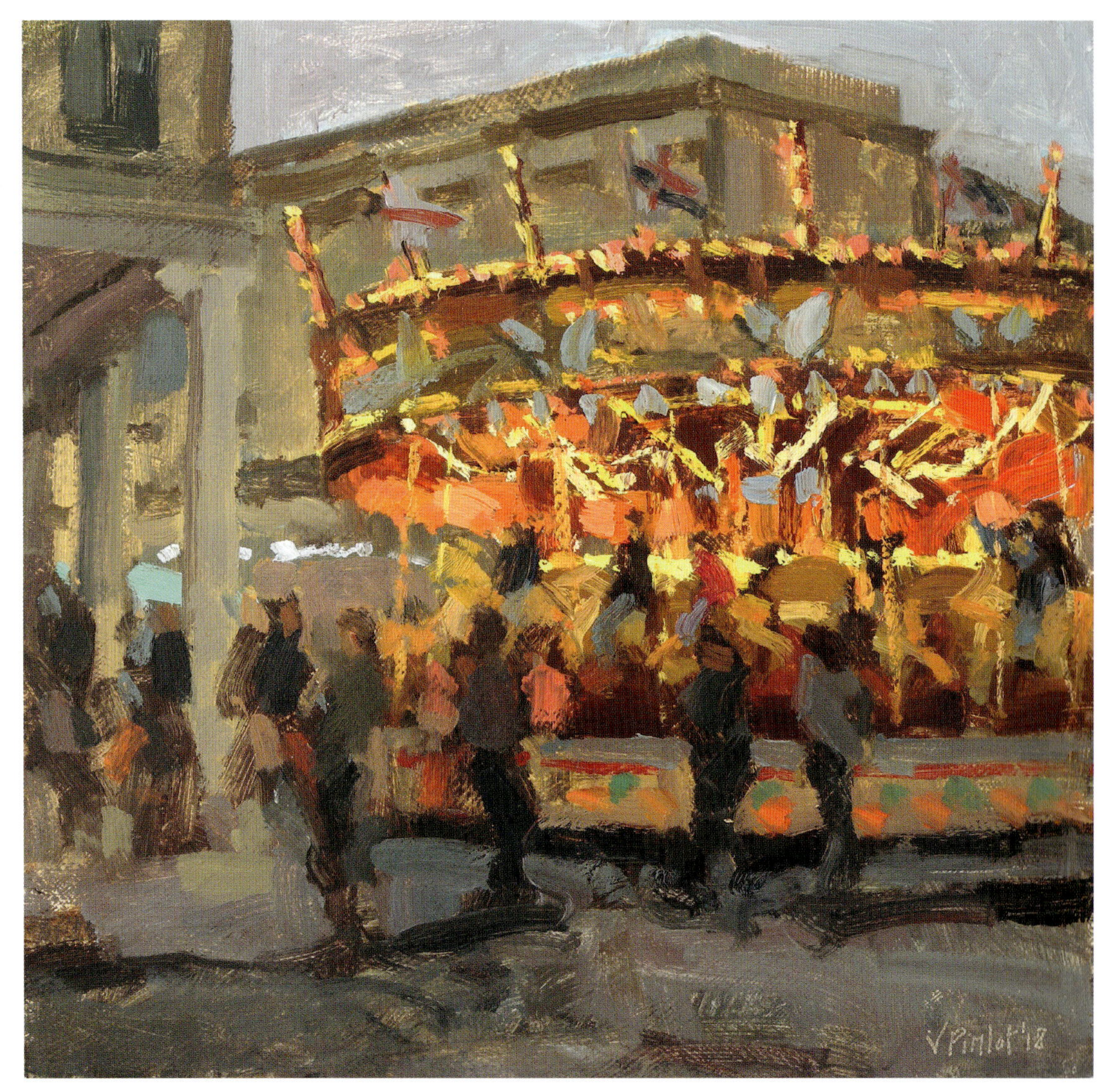

CAROUSEL, VALÉRIE PIRLOT

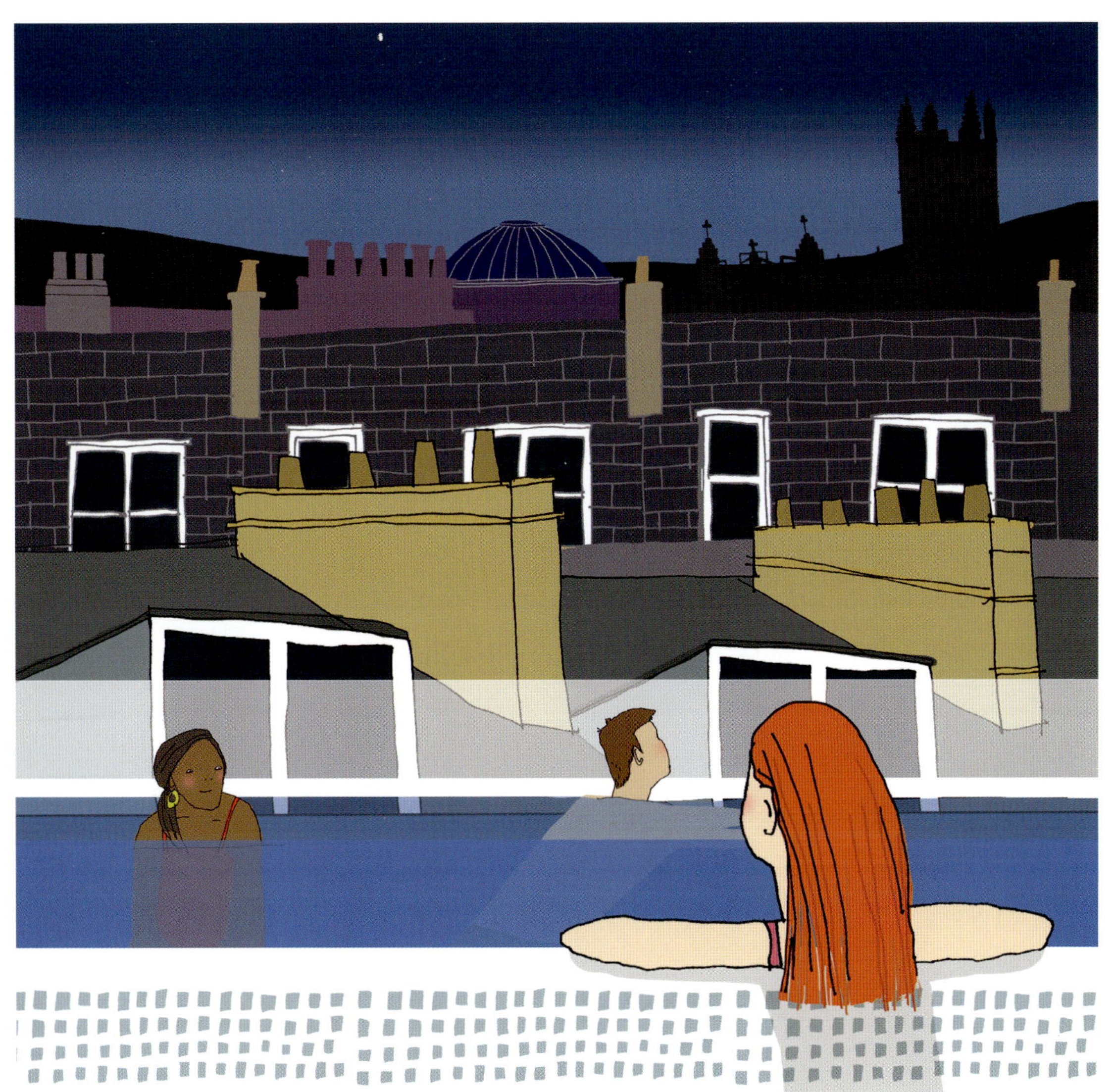

Rooftop Swimming in the Thermae Baths, Hannah Broadway

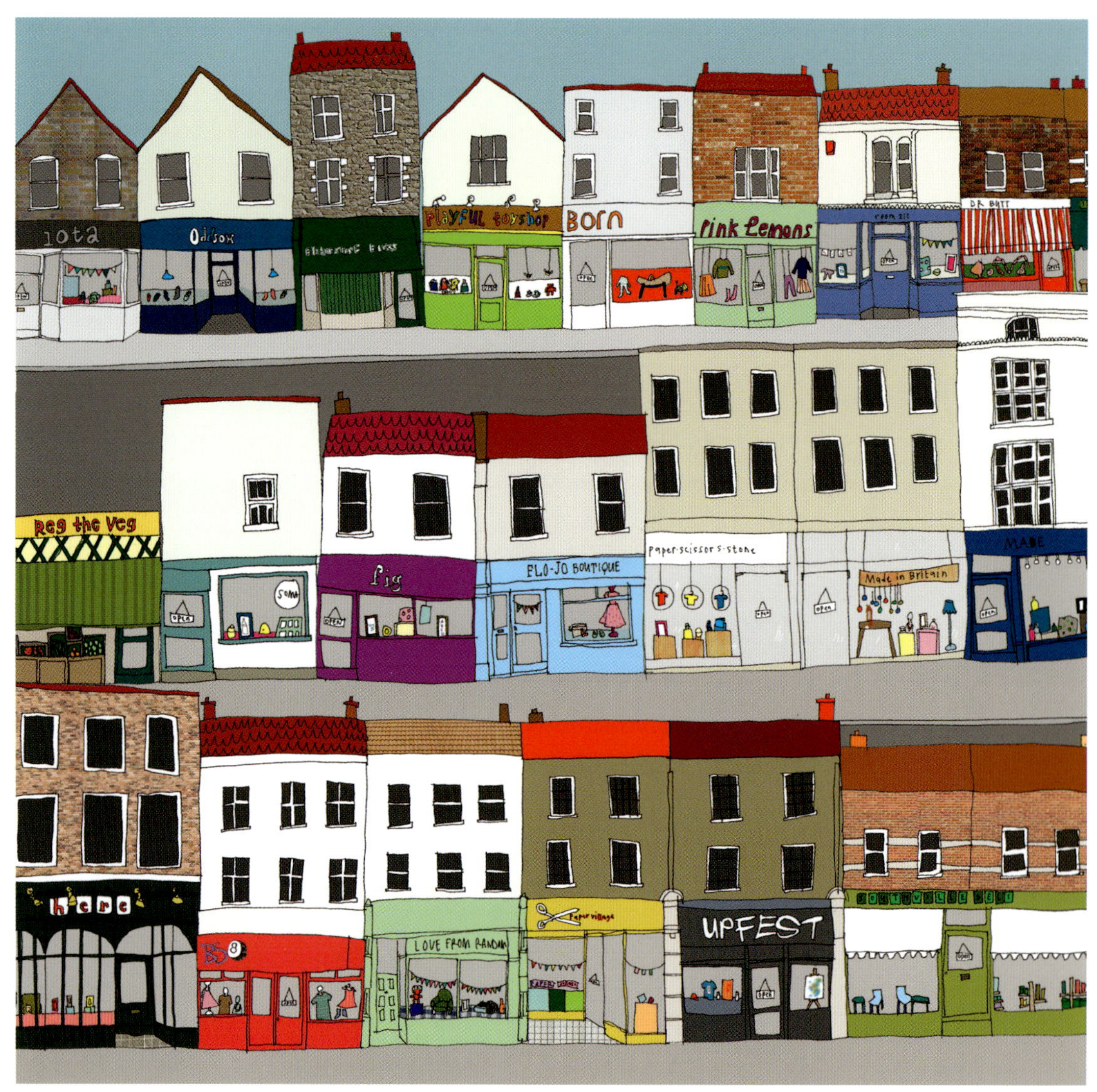



INDEPENDENT SHOPS IN BATH, HANNAH BROADWAY

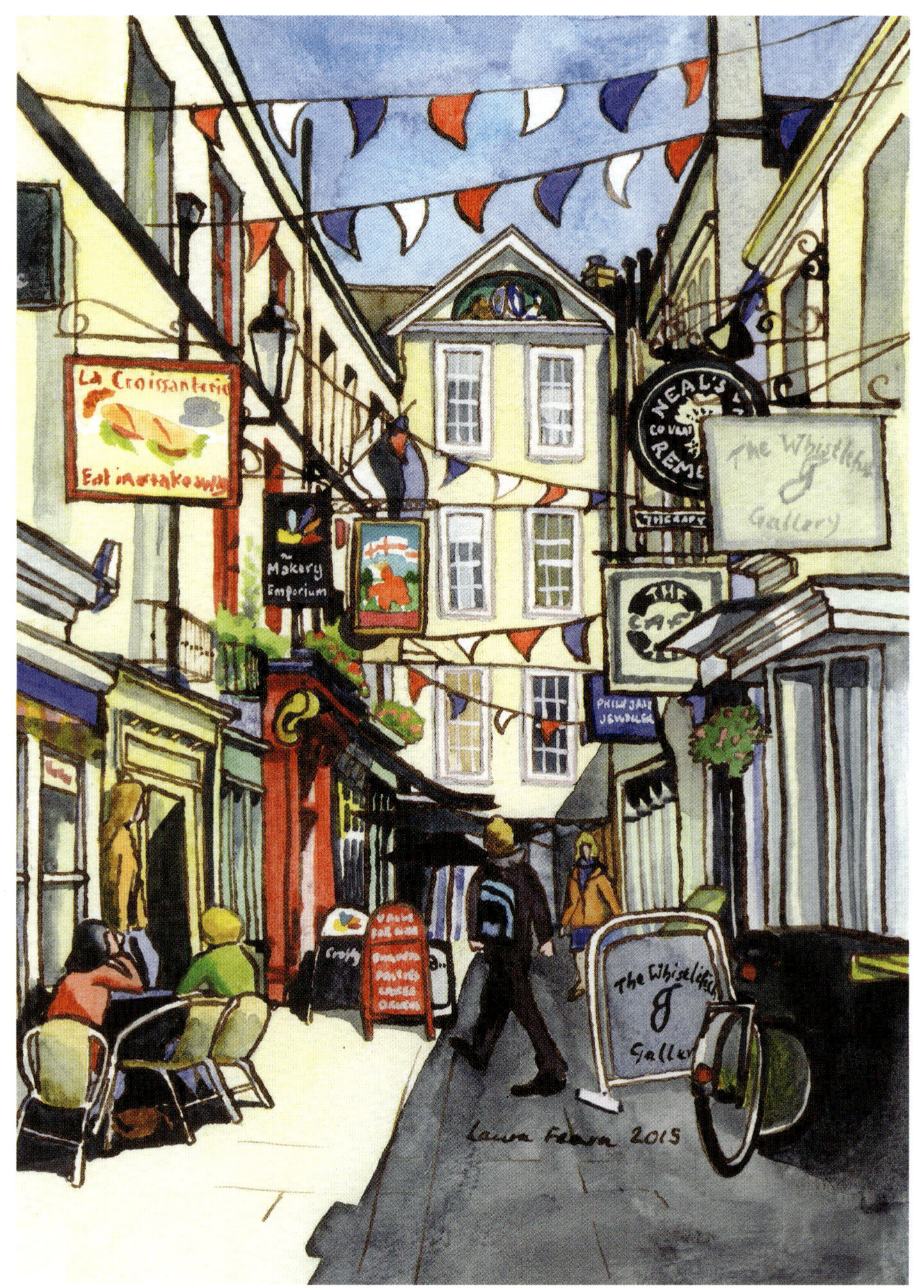


Northumberland Place, Laura Fearn

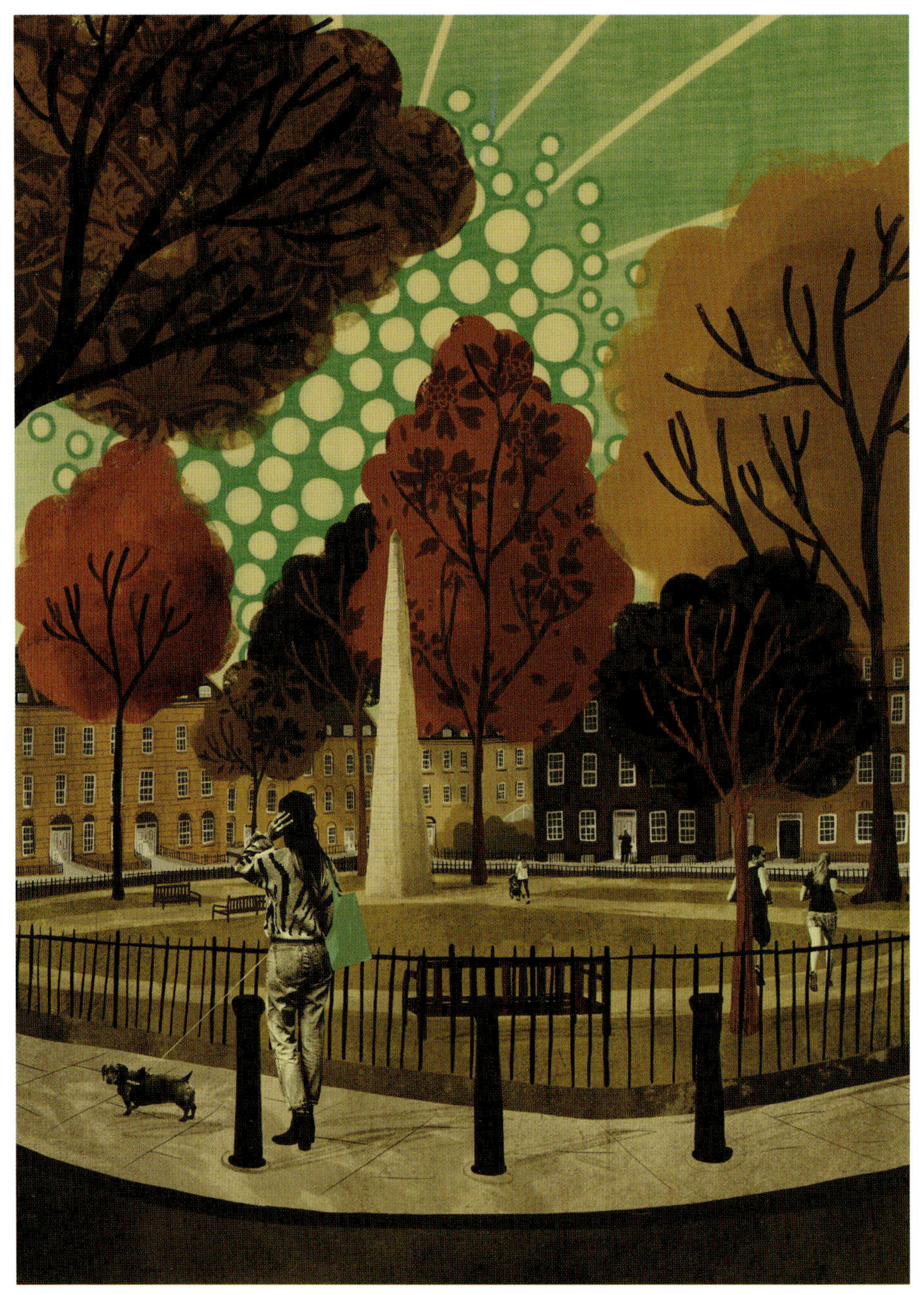

QUEEN SQUARE, EMY LOU HOLMES

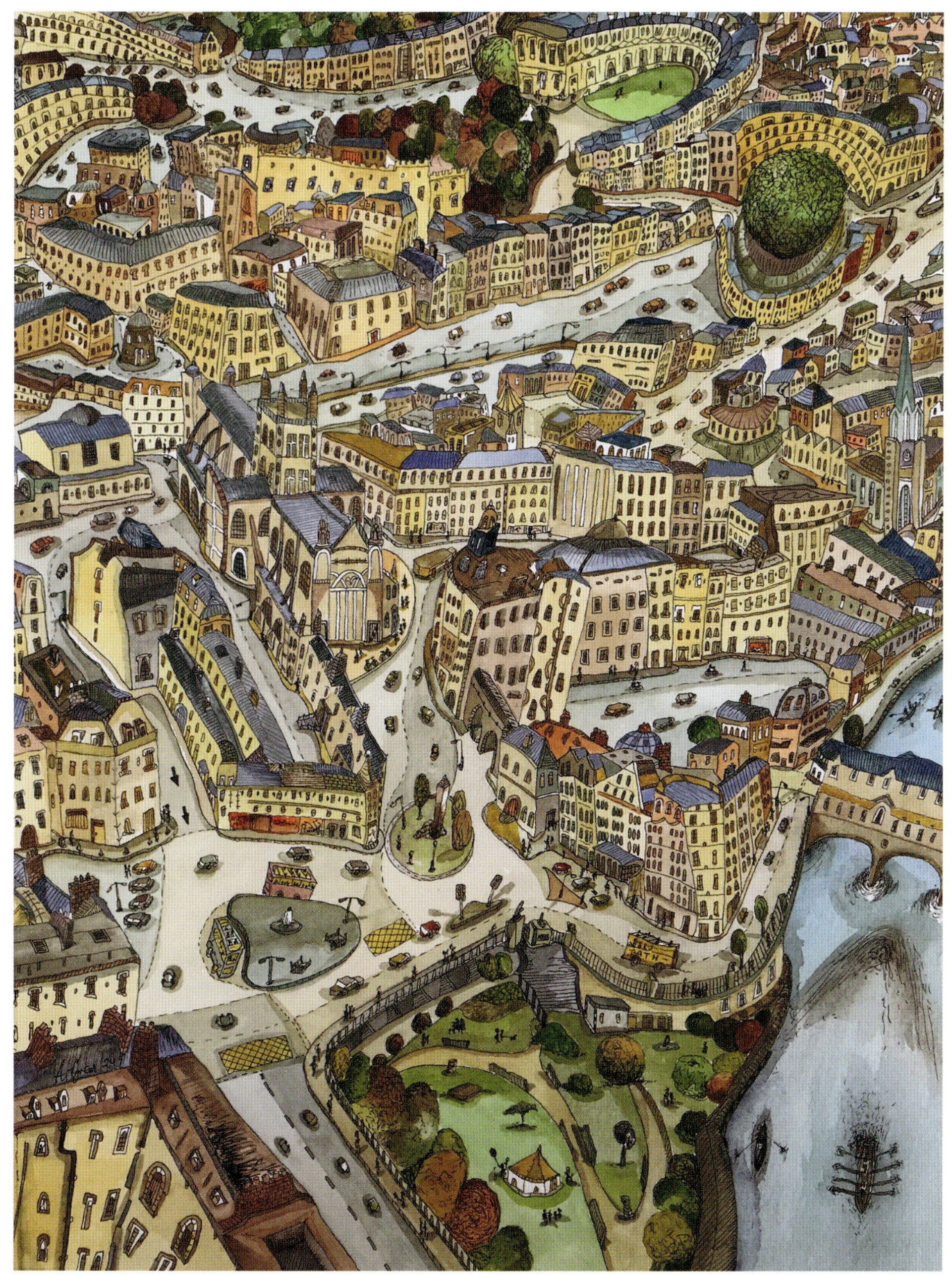

BATH FROM ABOVE, ADRIAN GREEN

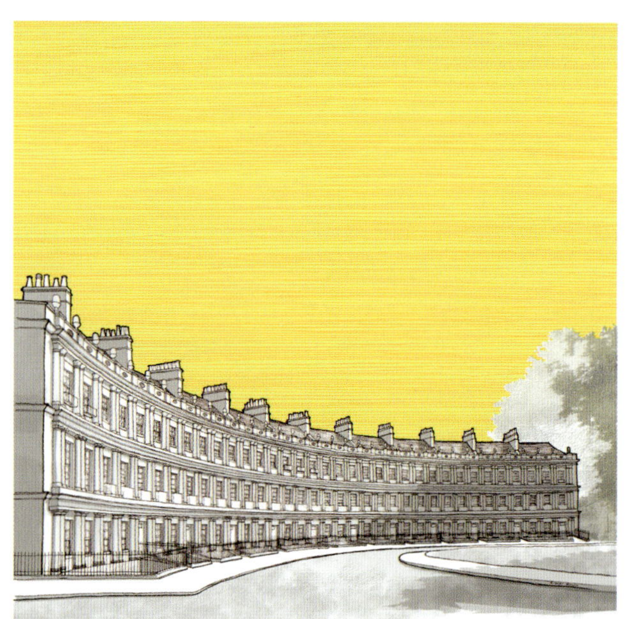

The Circus, Golden Skies, Robert Kann

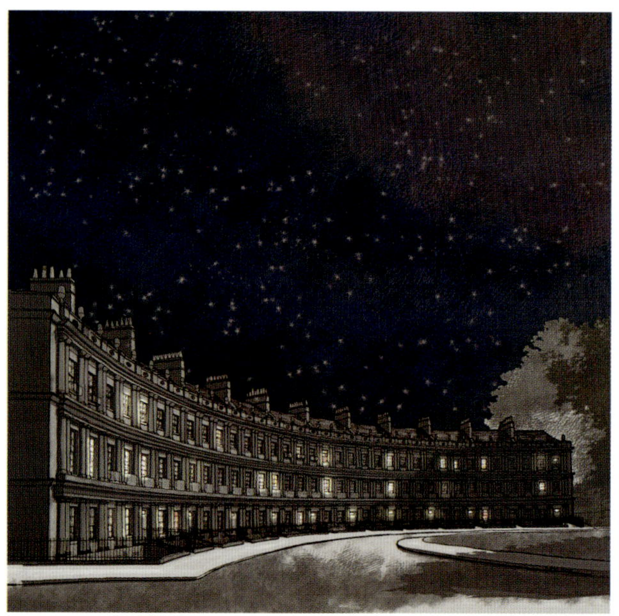

The Circus by Night, Robert Kann

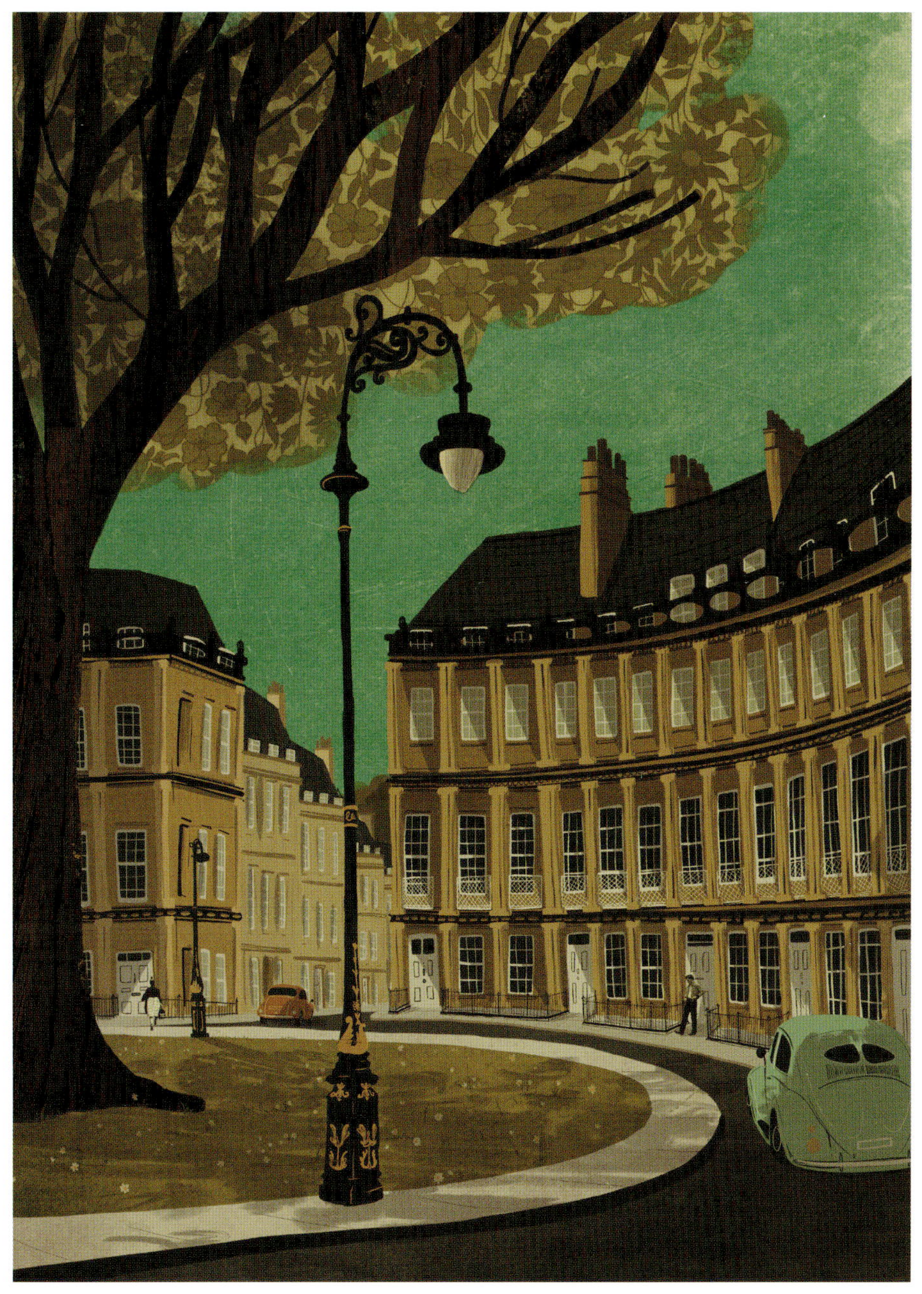



THE CIRCUS, EMY LOU HOLMES

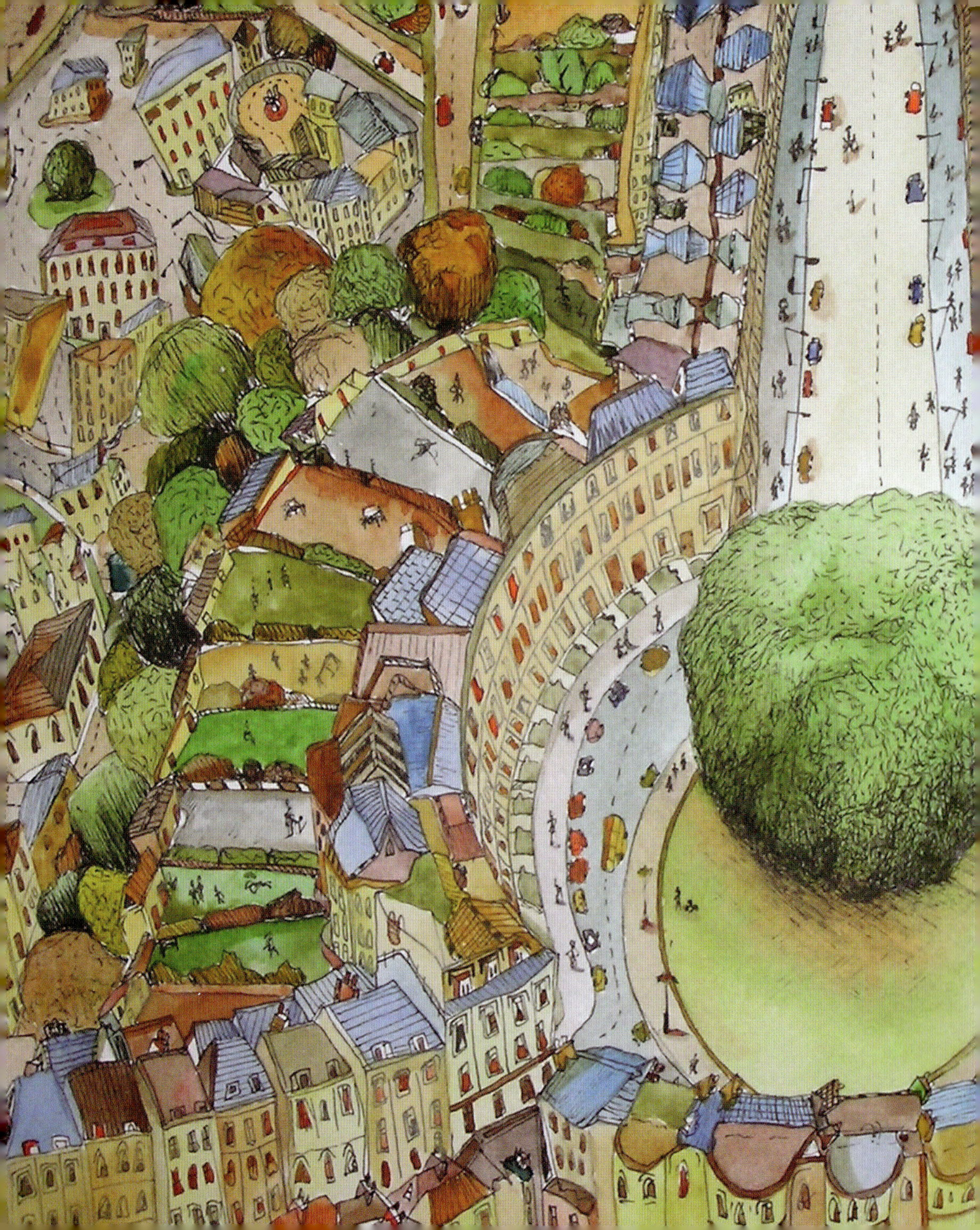

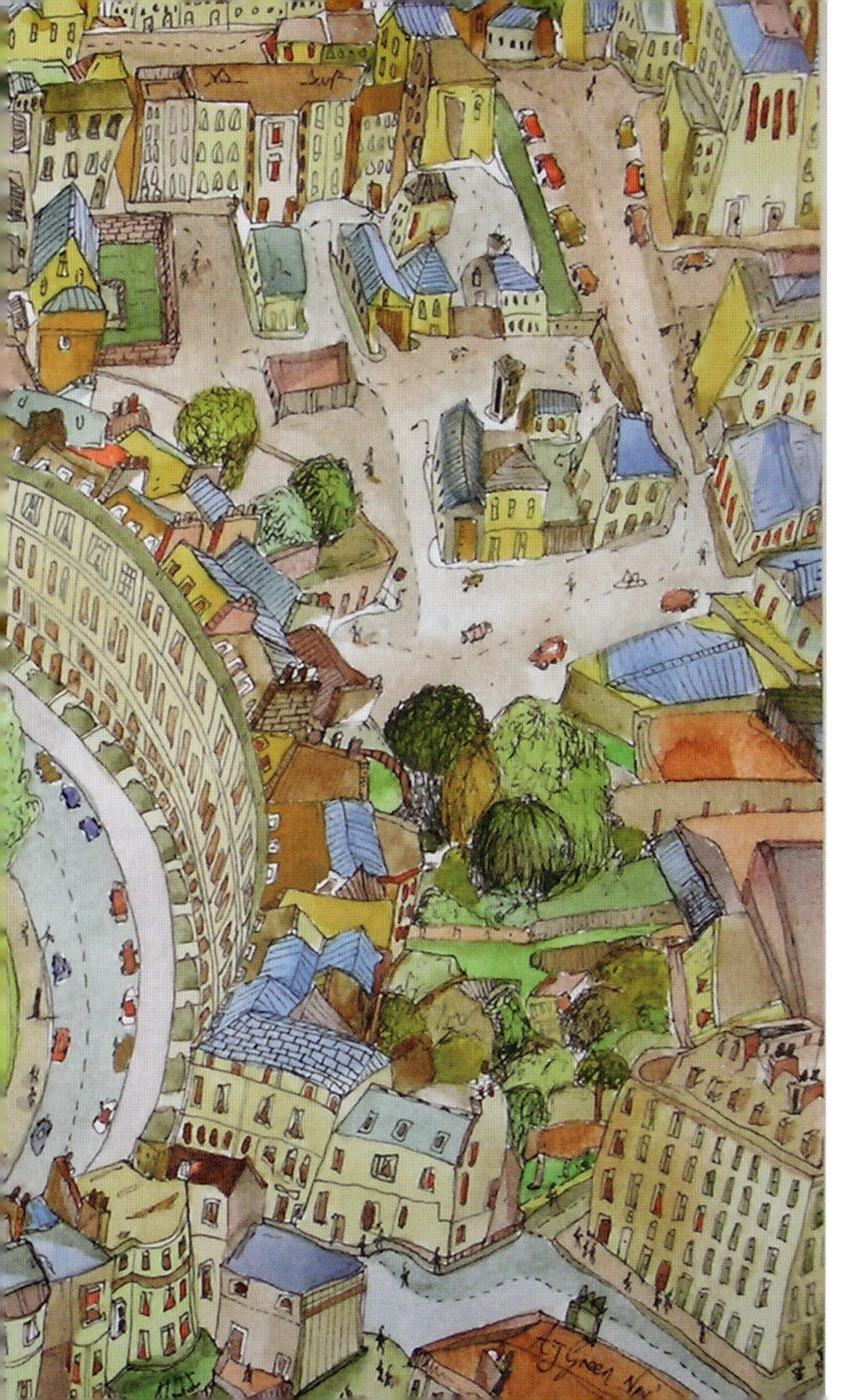

THE CIRCUS,
ADRIAN GREEN

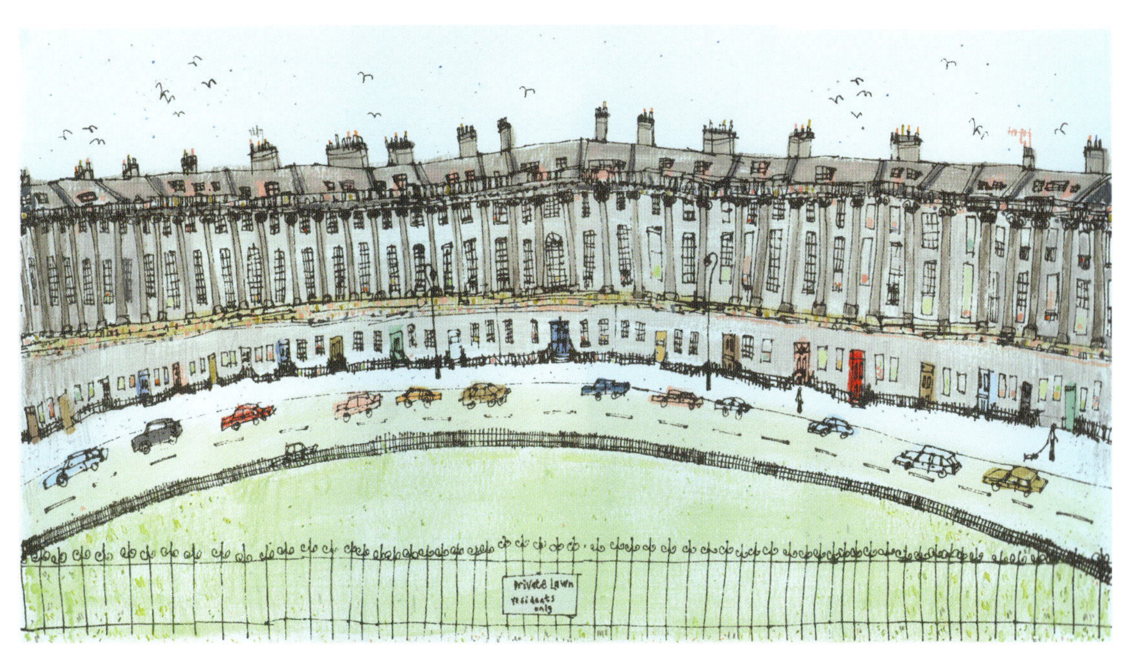



THE ROYAL CRESCENT, ·CLARE CAULFIELD

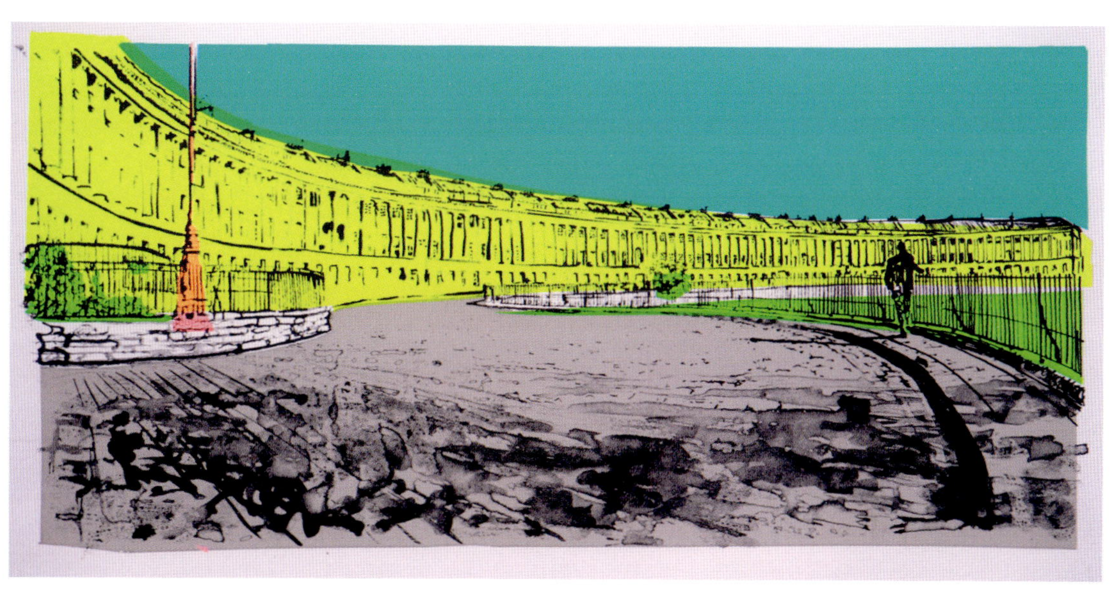

The Royal Crescent, Amy Hutchings

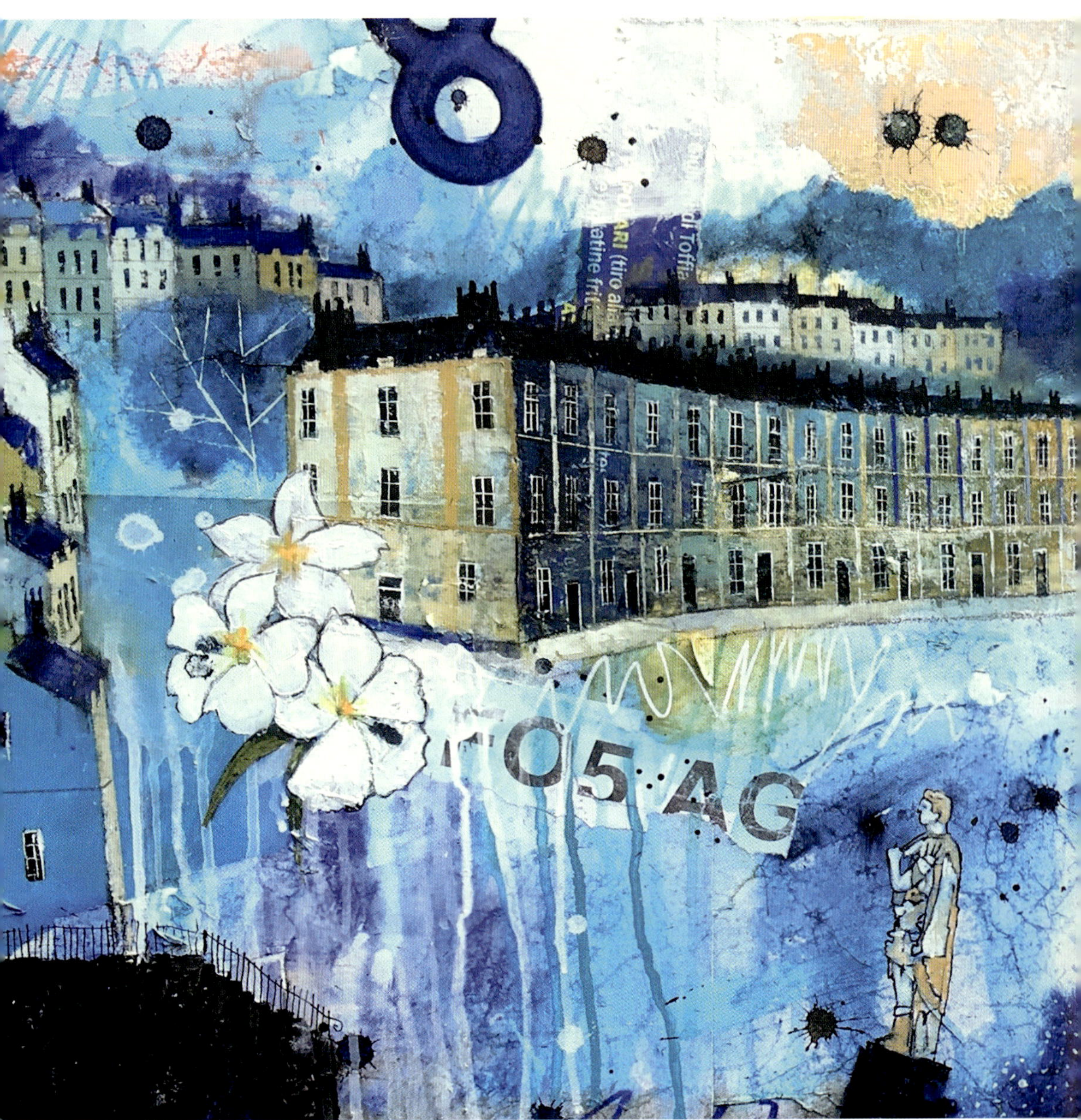

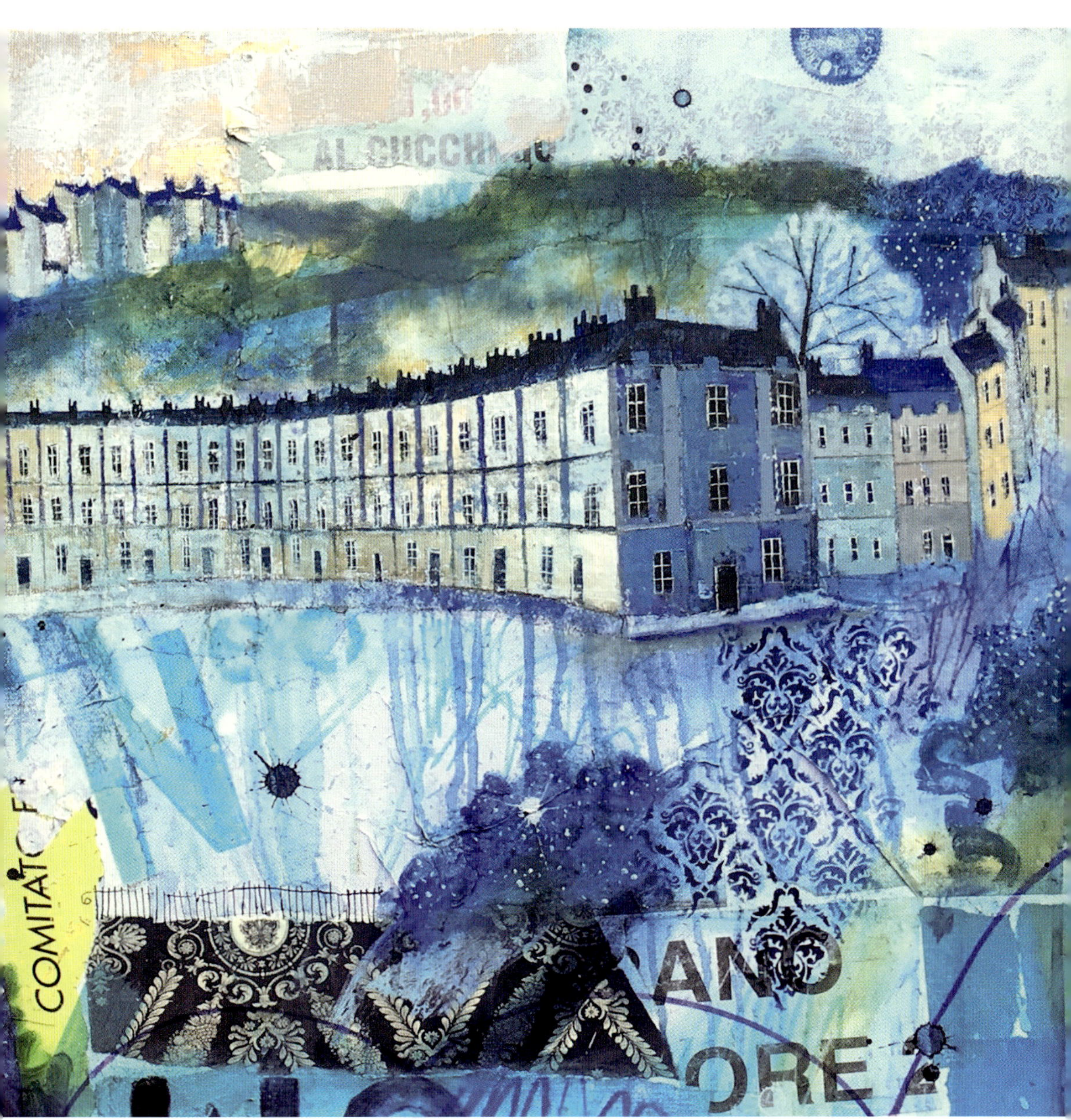



THE ROYAL CRESCENT, RICHARD BUREL

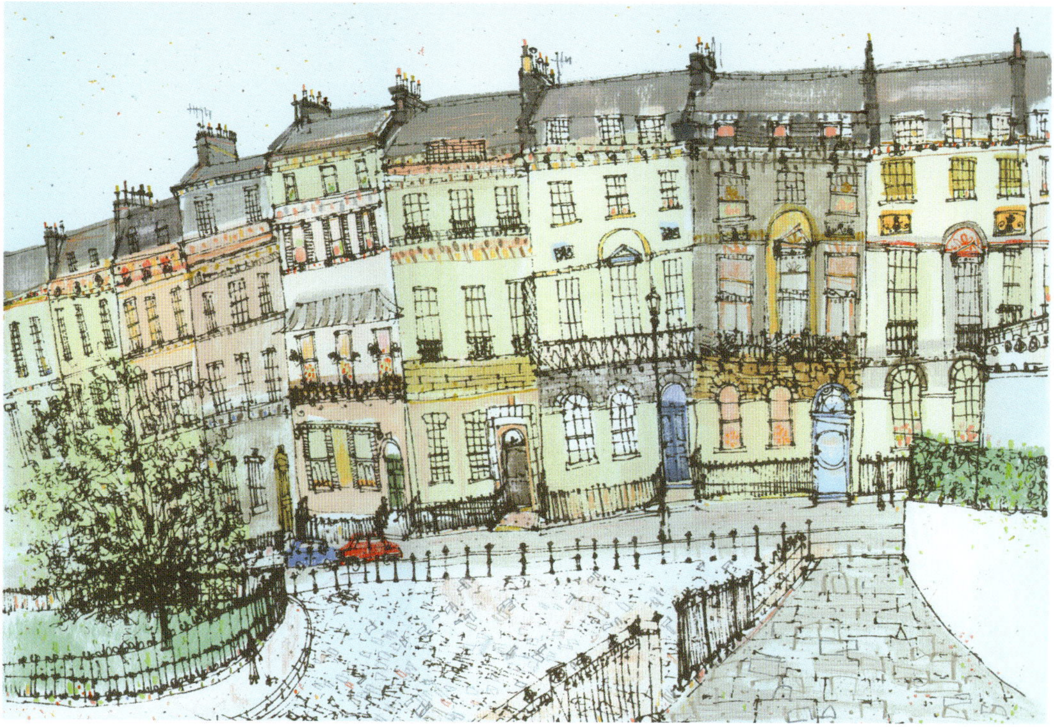

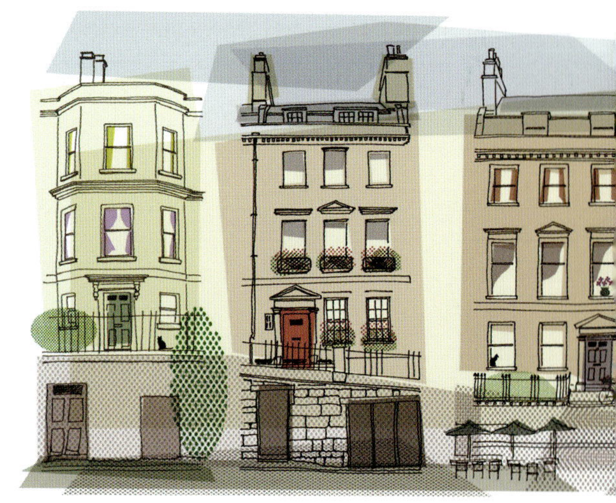

MARLBOROUGH BUILDINGS, CLARE CAULFIELD

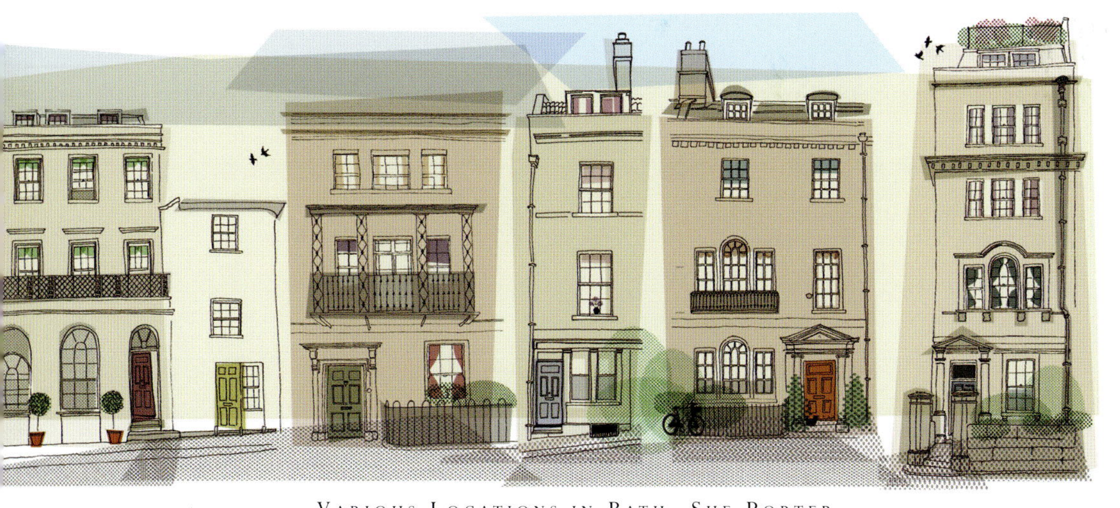

VARIOUS LOCATIONS IN BATH, SUE PORTER

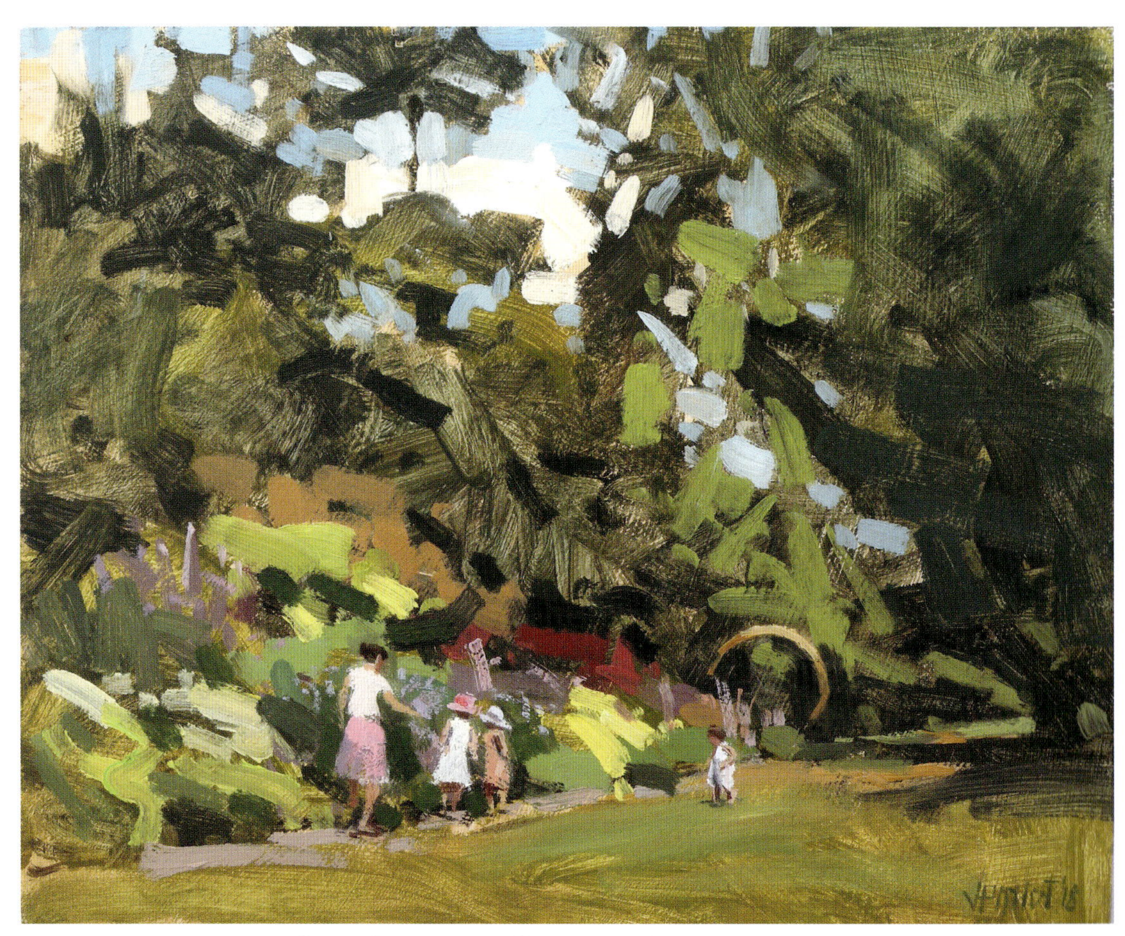

BATH BOTANICAL GARDENS, VALÉRIE PIRLOT

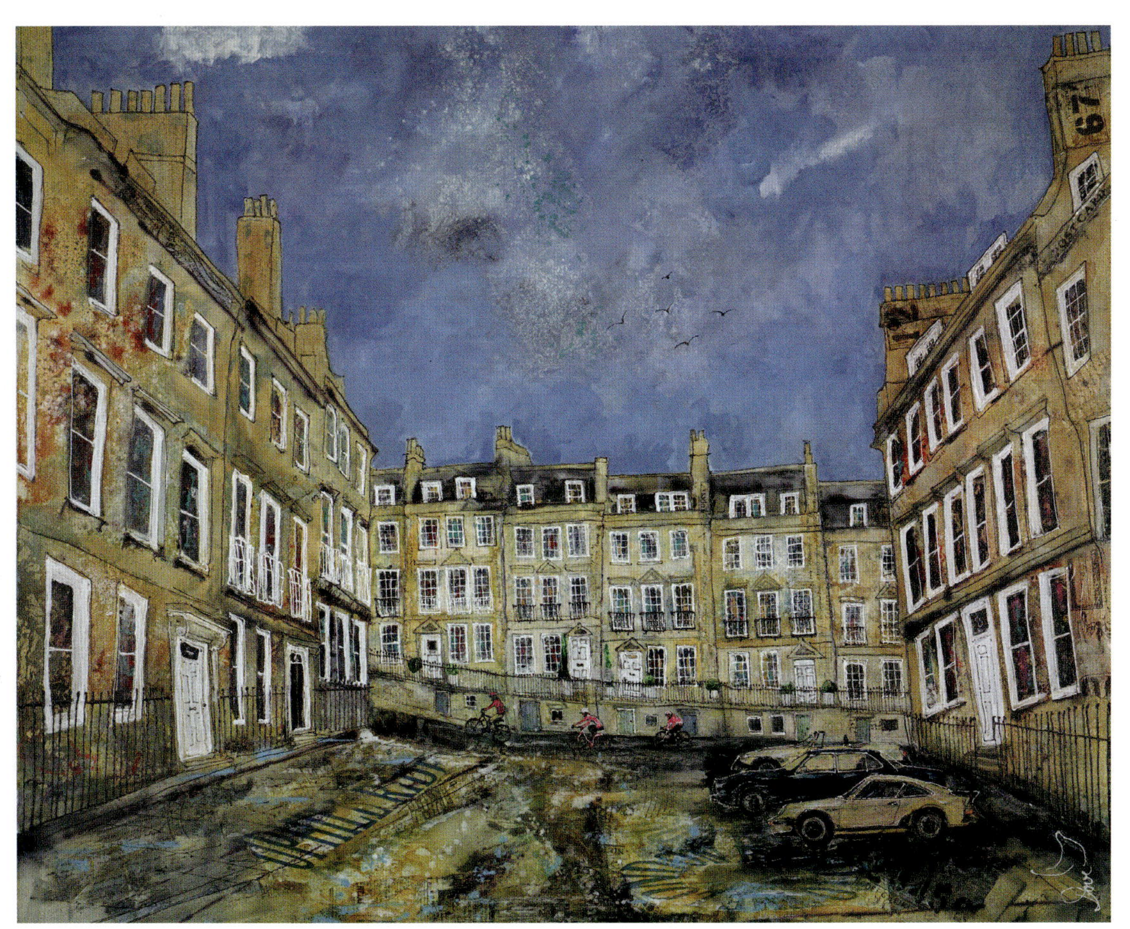


BENNETT STREET, KATHARINE DOVE

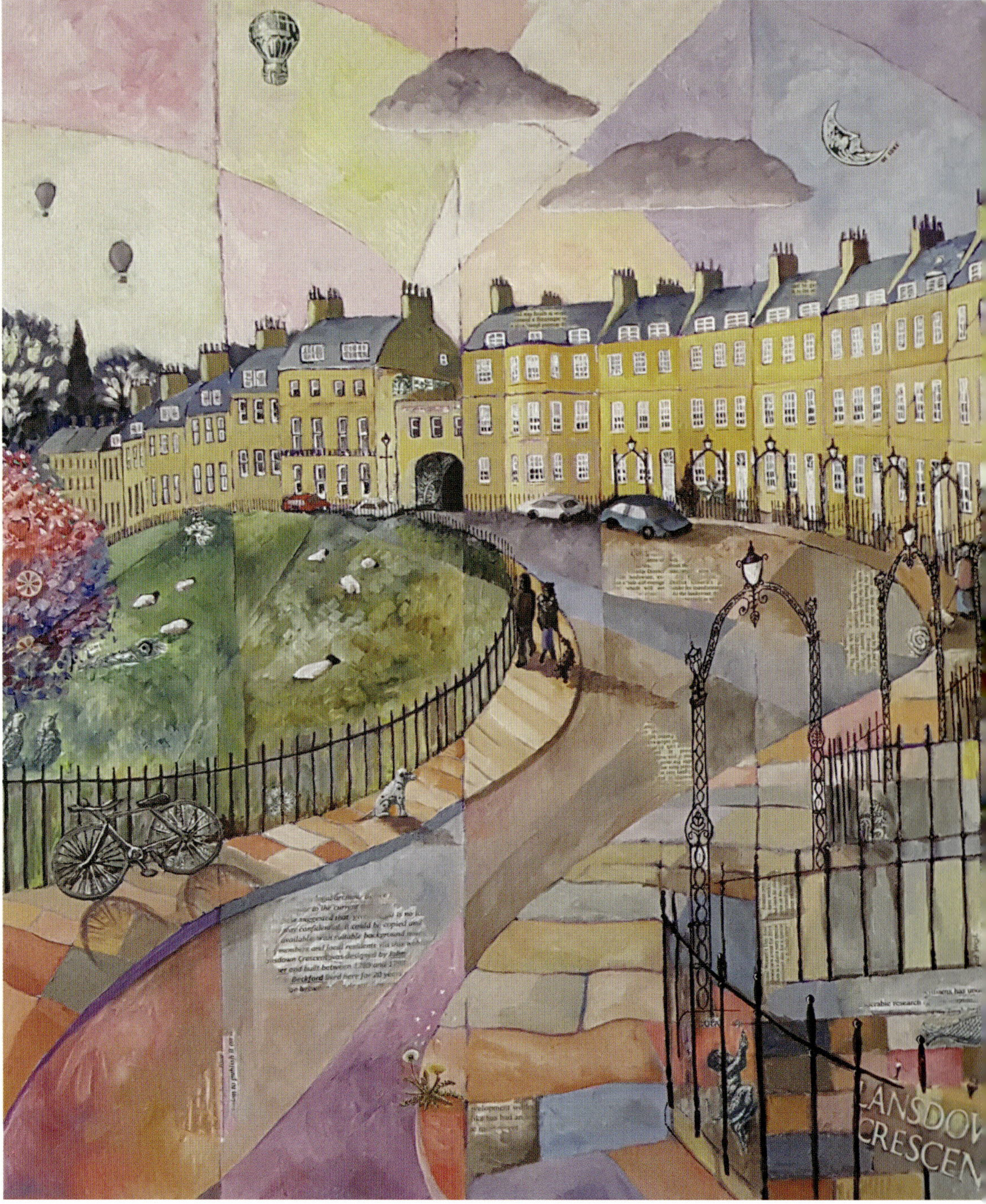

LANSDOWN
CRESCENT

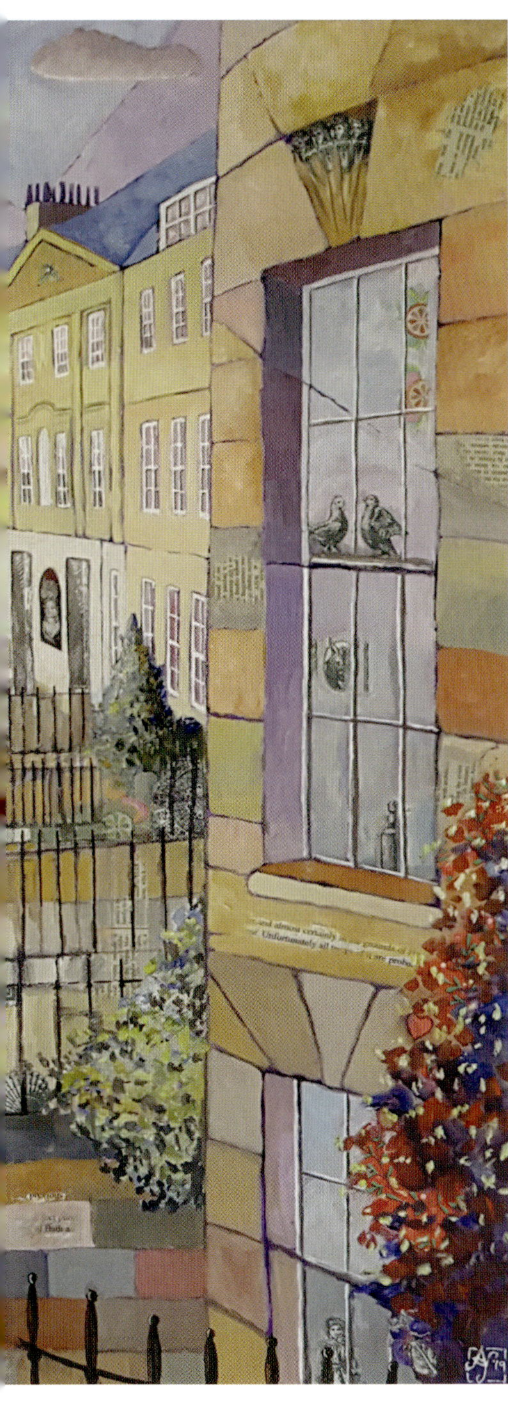

L A N D S D O W N   C R E S C E N T ,   A M Y   Y A T E S

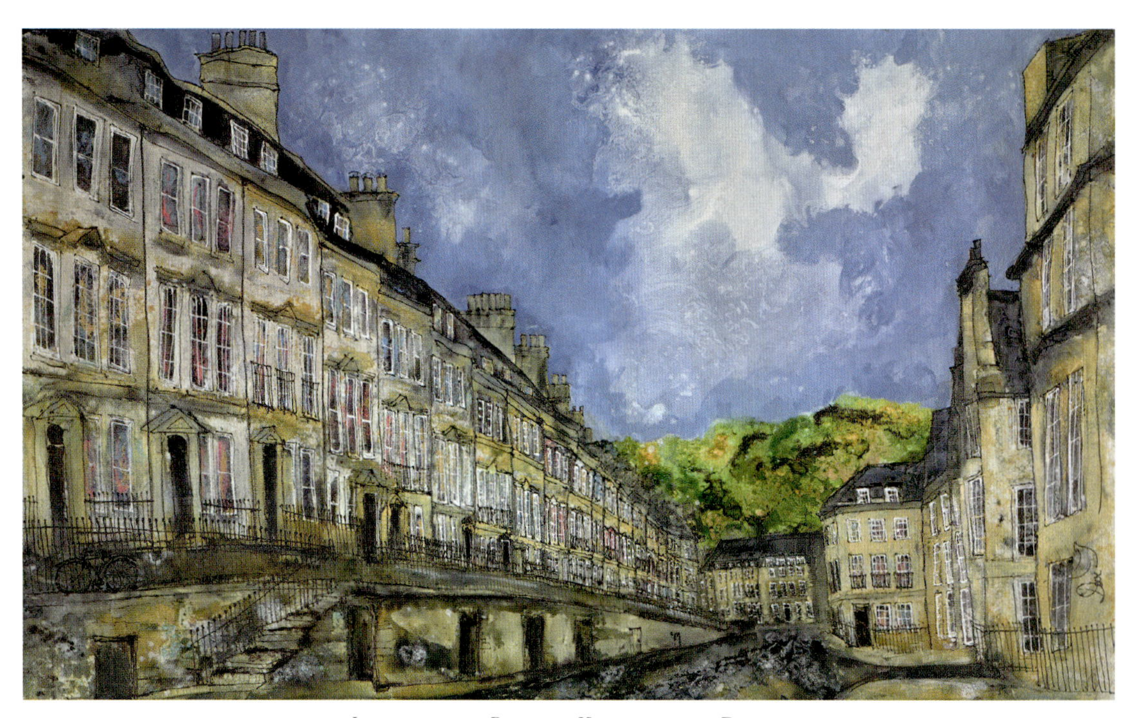

LANSDOWN ROAD, KATHARINE DOVE

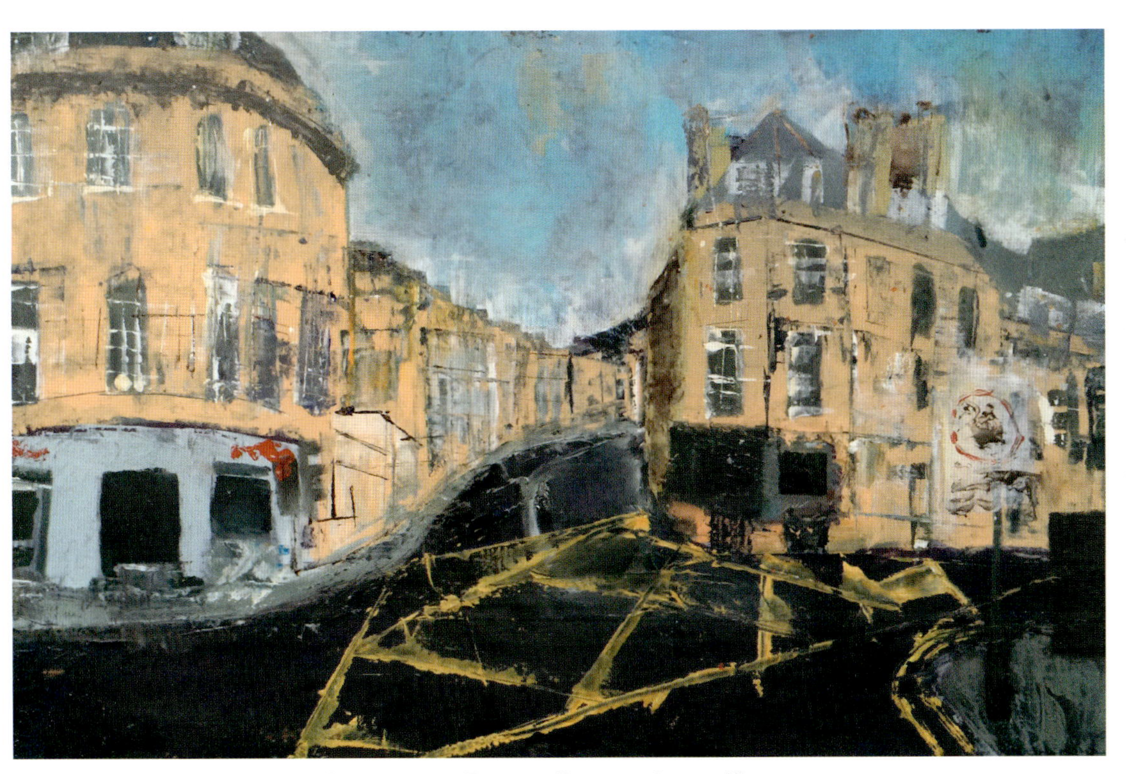

LANSDOWN ROAD, KIERAN LUKE NAISH

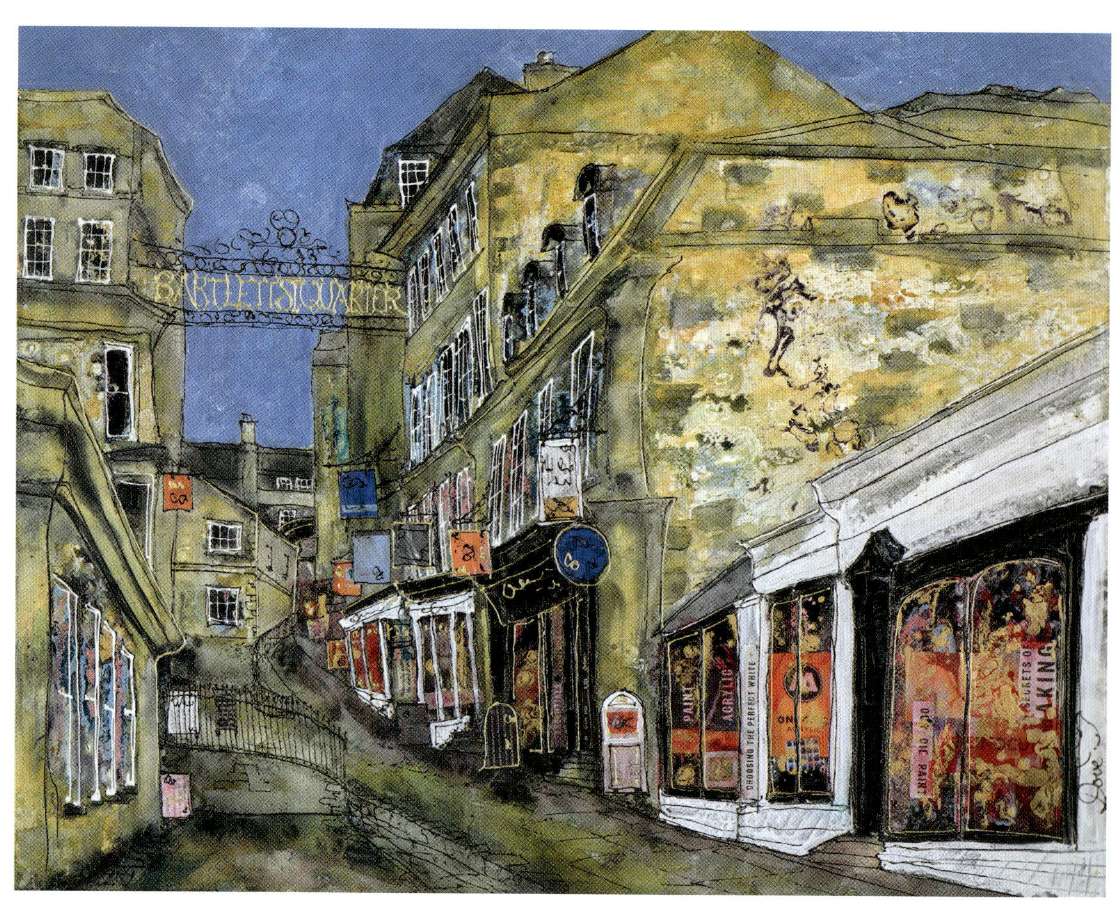

BARTLETT STREET QUARTER, KATHARINE DOVE

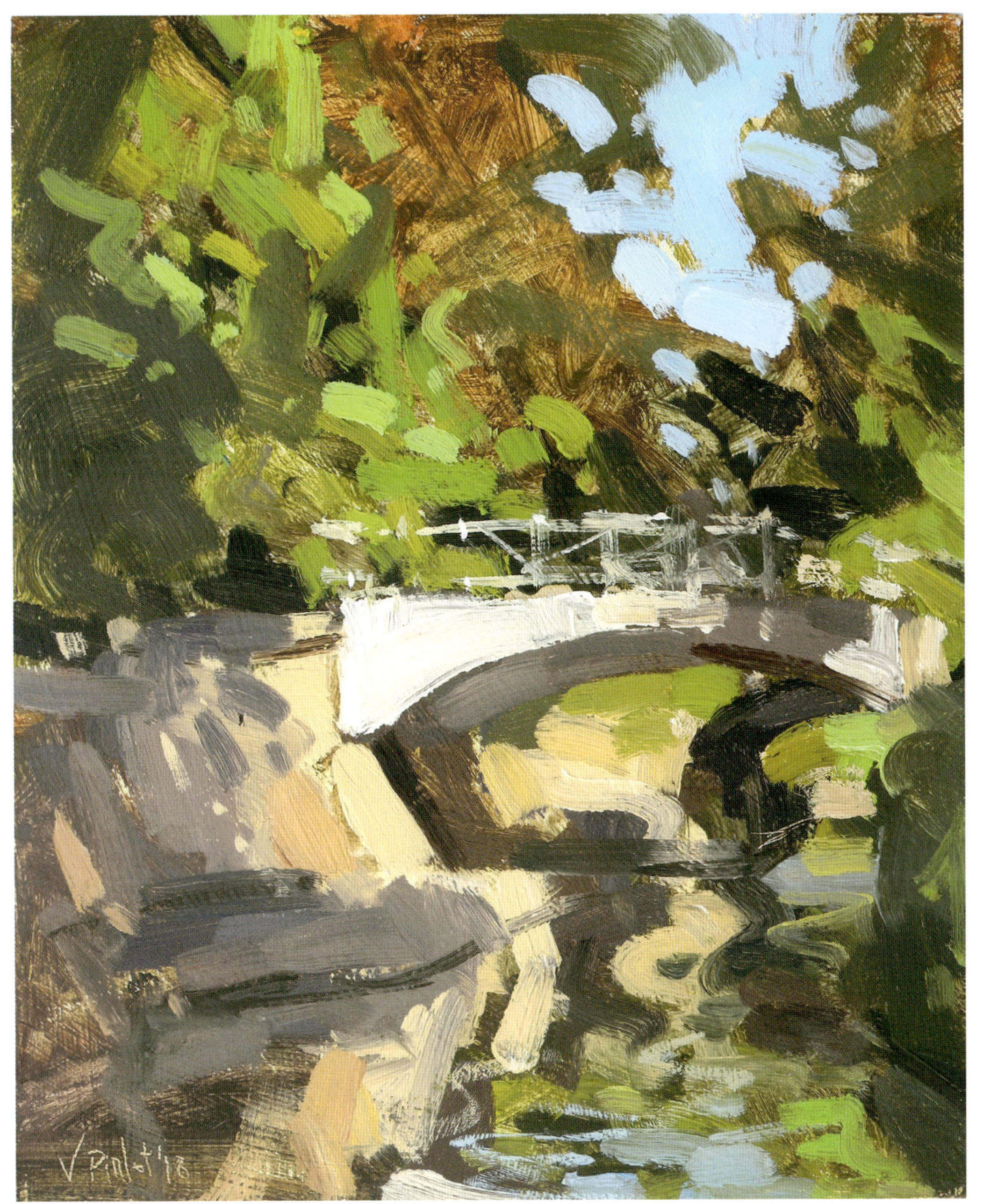



SYDNEY GARDENS, VALÉRIE PIRLOT

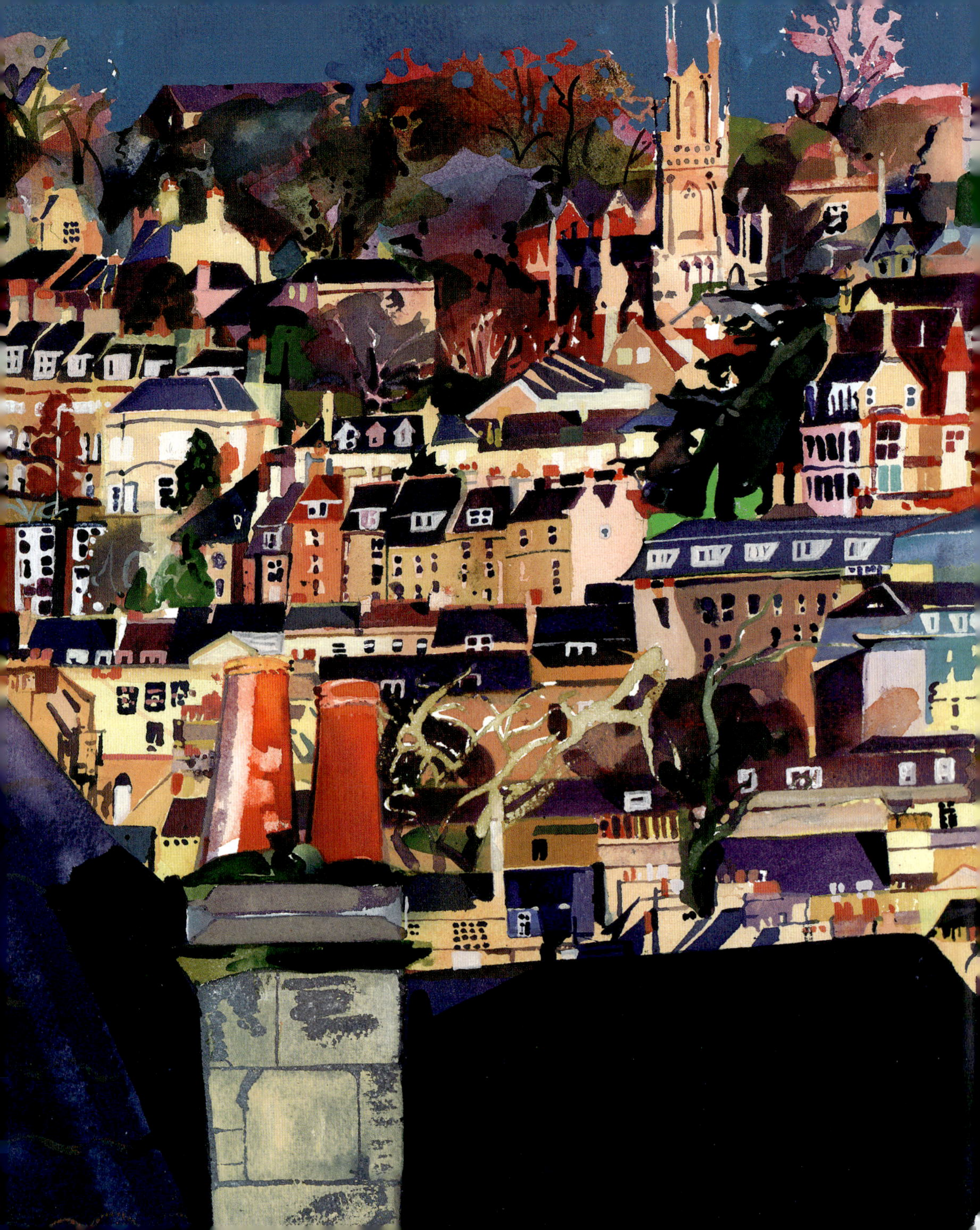

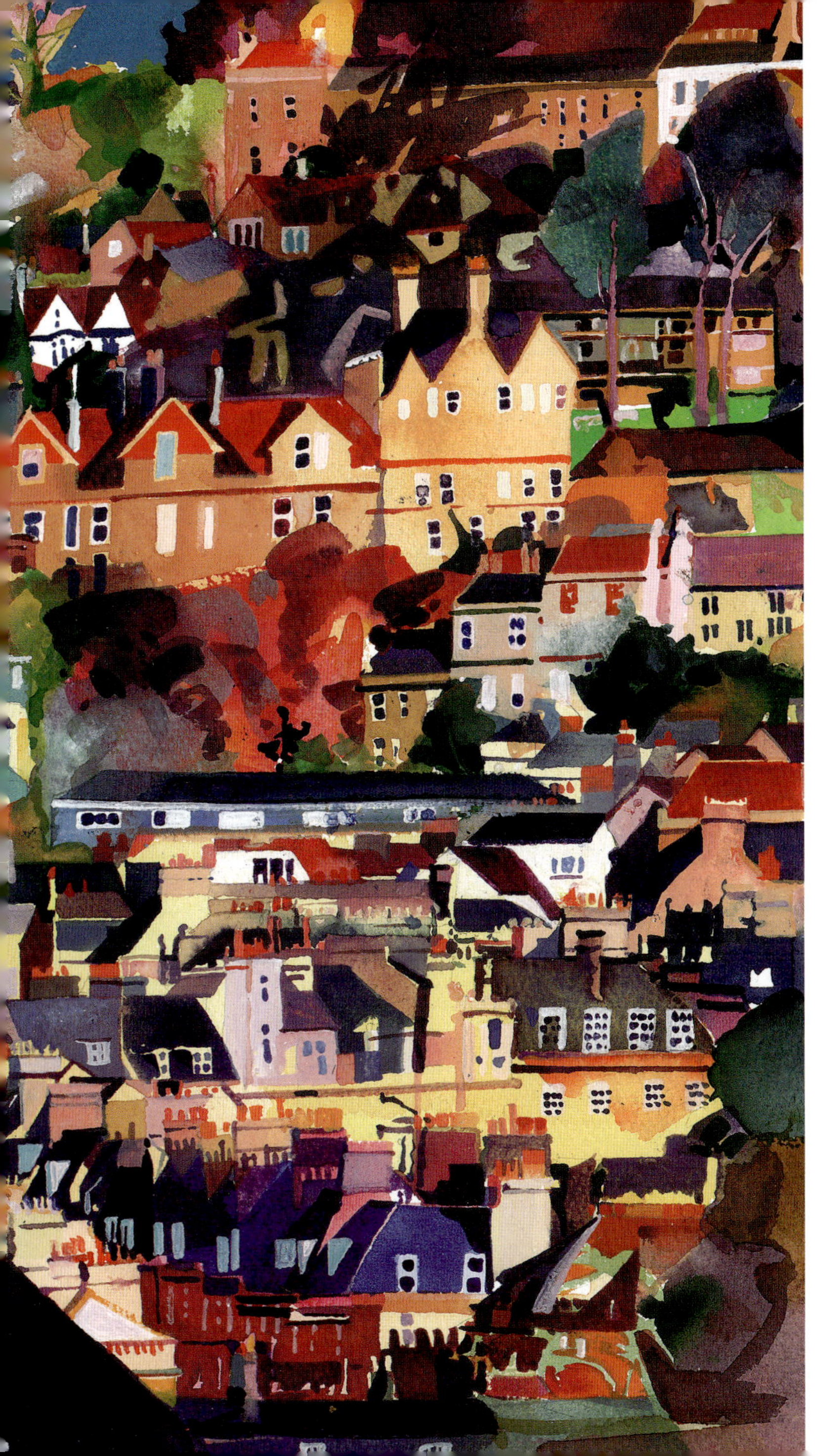


BATH ROOFTOPS,
MICHELLE SCRAGG

# ARTIST CREDITS



**Abigail McDougall (53, 57)**
Watercolour artist based in Bristol,
selling original artworks, prints and
greetings cards
www.abigailmcdougall.com

**Adrian Green (63, 105, 108)**
Original Pen and Ink watercolour
paintings capturing vibrant city life
and scenes
www.adriangreen.com

**Amy Hutchings (39, 55, 63, 111)**
Vibrant colour, line and pattern
infuse hand-drawn and hand-printed
artwork
www.amyhutchings.co.uk

**Amy Yates (49, 119)**
Colourful semi-abstract townscapes
in oil and mixed media
www.aimlessart.com

**Andrew Davies-Coward
(22, 42, 59)**
Figurative works in oils
adavieco@gmail.com

**Anna Duckworth
(27, 57, 69, 71)**
Acrylic and mixed media paintings,
prints and commissions
www.artbyanna.co.uk

**Anna Marrow (20, 26)**
Screen-prints made with a
combination of hand-drawn
and photographic imagery
www.annamarrow.squarespace.com

**Barbara Peirson (76)**
A background in theatre influences
an evocative artistic description of
everyday life
www.barbarapeirson.com

**Carrie Pooler (16)**
Semi-abstract paintings and
collages of city, landscape,
nature and still-life
www.facebook.com/p/Carrie-
Pooler-Art-100064968480687

**Clare Caulfield (110,114)**
Travel inspired mixed-media
paintings in a lively drawing style
www.clarecaulfield.co.uk

**Clare Phillips (21, 60, 88, 94)**
Digital illustrator with an MA
in printmaking, loves to create
mini worlds
www.clarephillips.com

**Diego Godoy (71)**
Colourful and detailed artwork
using a variety of media
www.diegogodoyart.co.uk

**Dona Bradley (10, 24, 37, 46)**
Architectural illustration, hand-
drawn and digital, reproduced as
prints, gifts and homewares
www.dona-b-drawings.co.uk

**Elaine Shaw (72)**
Original paintings and prints -
figurative, landscape and abstracts
in various media
www.elaineshawart.com

**Emily Ketteringham (44, 75)**
Colourful studies of the sweeping
vistas and interesting details
of Bristol
www.em-k.com

**Emy Lou Holmes
(11, 35, 61, 86, 98, 104, 107)**
Digital drawing combined with
vintage fabric/wallpaper collage and
photo montage
emylouholmes.com

**Emma Bennett (cover)**
Vibrant hand-cut collage using
recycled papers and hand-drawn
and digital illustration
www.emmabennettcollage.co.uk

**Emma Burleigh (81)**
Atmospheric watercolours and
illustrations from imagination
and observation
www.emmaburleigh.com

**Emmeline Simpson (39, 47, 60)**
Mixed-media collage illustrations
celebrating the city of Bristol
www.emmelinesimpson.co.uk

**Georgie (78)**
Colourful silkscreen prints,
paintings and murals in a
street art style
www.georgieartist.co.uk

**Hannah Broadway
(54, 89, 91, 101, 102)**
Colourful, joyful illustrations
www.hannahbroadway.com

**Hannah Bunn (23, 67, 80)**
Pen and ink cityscapes and street
scenes drawn from life, coloured
digitally
www.hannahbunn.com

**Jemal Gugunava (73)**
Oil on canvas/board/paper
www.gugunava.co.uk

**Jennifer Keeney-Blegg (19)**
Colour-inspired abstract, landscape
and still-life acrylic paintings
www.jkbleeg.com

**Jenny Seddon
(maps of Bristol and Bath)**
Illustration and screen prints
www.jennyseddon.com

**Jenny Urquhart (67, 68, 74)**
Contemporary mixed-media
landscapes of Bristol and the
South West
www.jennyurquhart.co.uk

**Juli-Anne Coward
(18, 28, 30, 31)**
Mixed-media and collage focusing
on architecture and the built
environment
juli-annecoward@sky.com

**Juliet Carmichael (52, 58)**
Landscape painting in oil and
watercolour, of some favourite
Bristol places
julietcarmichael@gmail.com

**Katharine Dove
(32, 117, 120, 122)**
Unique techniques used to
create vibrant, colourful and
textured mixed-media paintings
www.katharinedove.co.uk

**Katherine Thornton (56)**
Watercolour paintings of a range
of subjects
katherinethornton@icloud.com

**Kathy Luders (29)**
Vibrant landscape paintings,
mainly in oil, depicting nature
in all its moods
kathyluders@gmail.com

**Kieran Luke Naish (83, 121)**
Oil painting on canvas using a
palette knife
www.kieranlukenaish.co.uk

**Laura Cramer (36)**
Contemporary landscape painter
www.cramerpaintings.com

**Laura Fearn (90, 96, 103)**
Artist, designer and illustrator
based in Bath
www.laurafearn.com

**Laura Robertson (65, 70)**
Oil, acrylic and watercolour
paintings, reduction lino prints,
handmade cards, greetings cards
www.laurarobertsonartist.co.uk

**Lindsey Lavender (17)**
Exploring rhythms of light and
shade; showing the everyday in a
new light
www.lindseylavender.co.uk

**Lisa Malyon (20, 36, 45, 47)**
Contemporary architectural
drawings incorporating a
collage element
www.lisamalyondraws.co.uk

**Mary Corum (12, 92)**
Finely detailed drawings combined
with printed textile design
www.marycorum.com

**Melanie Wickham (85)**
Hand burnished lino prints of
people, animals, plants and places
www.melaniewickham.co.uk

**Michelle Scragg (125)**
Strong colour, space and shape is
her signature style
www.michellescragg.com

**Mike Rome (38, 41, 76, 77)**
Landscape, abstract, figurative,
nature and copies of
masterpieces all in oils
www.mikerome.co.uk

**Naomi Triggol (9, 97)**
Artist, educator and illustrator.
Director of Memory Maze Ltd,
illustrated histories
info@memorymaze.co.uk

**Nick Gerolemou
(29, 43, 51, 83)**
Vibrant landscape paintings
inspired by urban and disused
environments
www.nickgerolemou.co.uk

**Richard Burel (113)**
Mixed-media cityscape artist
using palette knife, oil, ink,
gold leaf, collages
www.richardburelart.com

**Robert Antell (25, 79)**
Pastel, conte and charcoal
on paper
www.robertantellartist.co.uk

**Robert Kann (106)**
Mixed-media illustrations
combining hand-drawn line
work and hand-digitised
colouring
www.pitch26.com

**Robin Richards (62)**
Beautiful, bright, original
illustrated prints and gifts
www.bemmie.co.uk

**Sarah Boden (82)**
Abstract landscapes in
watercolour, ink and
mixed-media
www.sarahbodenart.com

**Simon Tozer (34, 50)**
Printmaker specialising in
screen print
www.simontozer.co.uk

**Sonia Villiers (8, 13)**
Lively and vibrant, modern
bustling acrylic cityscape
paintings on canvas
www.soniavilliers.co.uk

**Sue Porter (48, 115)**
Ink drawings and mixed-media
creating art of architecture and
landmarks
www.vanillawhite.com

**Su Williams (70)**
Stitched textile collage and
prints in a range of media
www.suwilliams.wordpress.
com

**Tom Hughes (15, 66)**
Urban, landscape and coastal
works, painted on location in
oils
www.tomhughespainting.co.uk

**Tom Lietzau (14, 56)**
Capturing human worlds
projected onto reality using
painting and other media
www.tomlietzau.com

**Toni Burrows (79)**
Large mosaics made of broken
china, recycled materials and
found objects
www.northbristolartists.org.
uk/user/toni-burrows

**Valérie Pirlot
(87, 99, 100, 116, 123)**
Bath based oil painter and
teacher working mainly in
plein air
www.valeriepirlot.com

**Victoria Wood (93)**
Architecture and landscape
artist. Illustrations in ink and
watercolour
www.sketchpadontour.co.uk

**Zoe Billboard Gibbons
(40, 78)**
Skip-diving artist constructing
urban collages using salvaged
billboard posters and stitch
www.zoegibbons.com

Every effort has been made to correctly credit contributors. In the case of any omissions or
errors we would be pleased to make appropriate corrections in future editions.

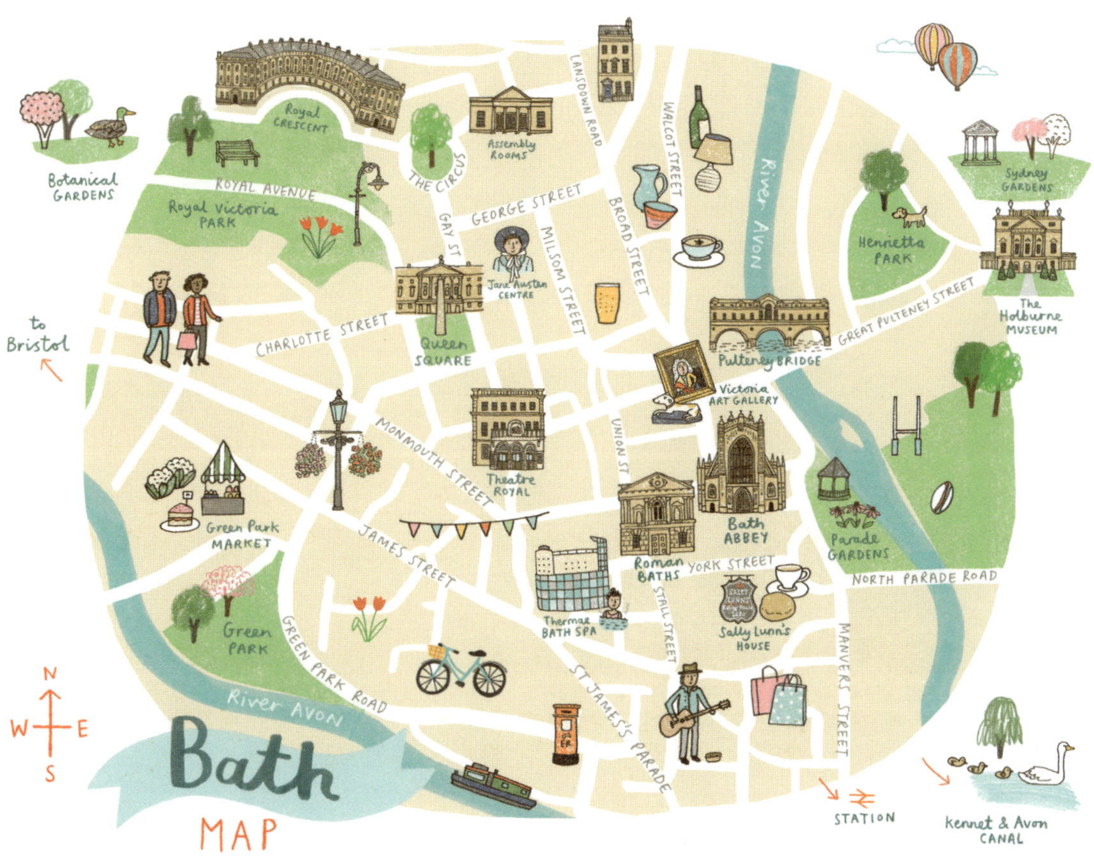

Botanical
GARDENS
Royal
CRESCENT
Assembly
ROOMS
LANSDOWN ROAD
WALCOT STREET
River Avon
Sydney
GARDENS
ROYAL AVENUE
THE CIRCUS
GEORGE STREET
BROAD STREET
Royal Victoria
PARK
GAY ST
Henrietta
PARK
The
Holburne
MUSEUM
to
Bristol
CHARLOTTE STREET
Jane Austen
CENTRE
MILSOM STREET
GREAT PULTENEY STREET
Queen
SQUARE
Pulteney BRIDGE
MONMOUTH STREET
Victoria
ART GALLERY
UNION ST
Green Park
MARKET
Theatre
ROYAL
Bath
ABBEY
Parade
GARDENS
JAMES STREET
NORTH PARADE ROAD
Green
PARK
GREEN PARK ROAD
Roman
BATHS
YORK STREET
MANVERS STREET
River AVON
Thermae
BATH SPA
SALLY
LUNN'S
Sally Lunn's
HOUSE
N
W E
S
Bath
MAP
ST JAMES'S PARADE
STALL STREET
STATION
Kennet & Avon
CANAL

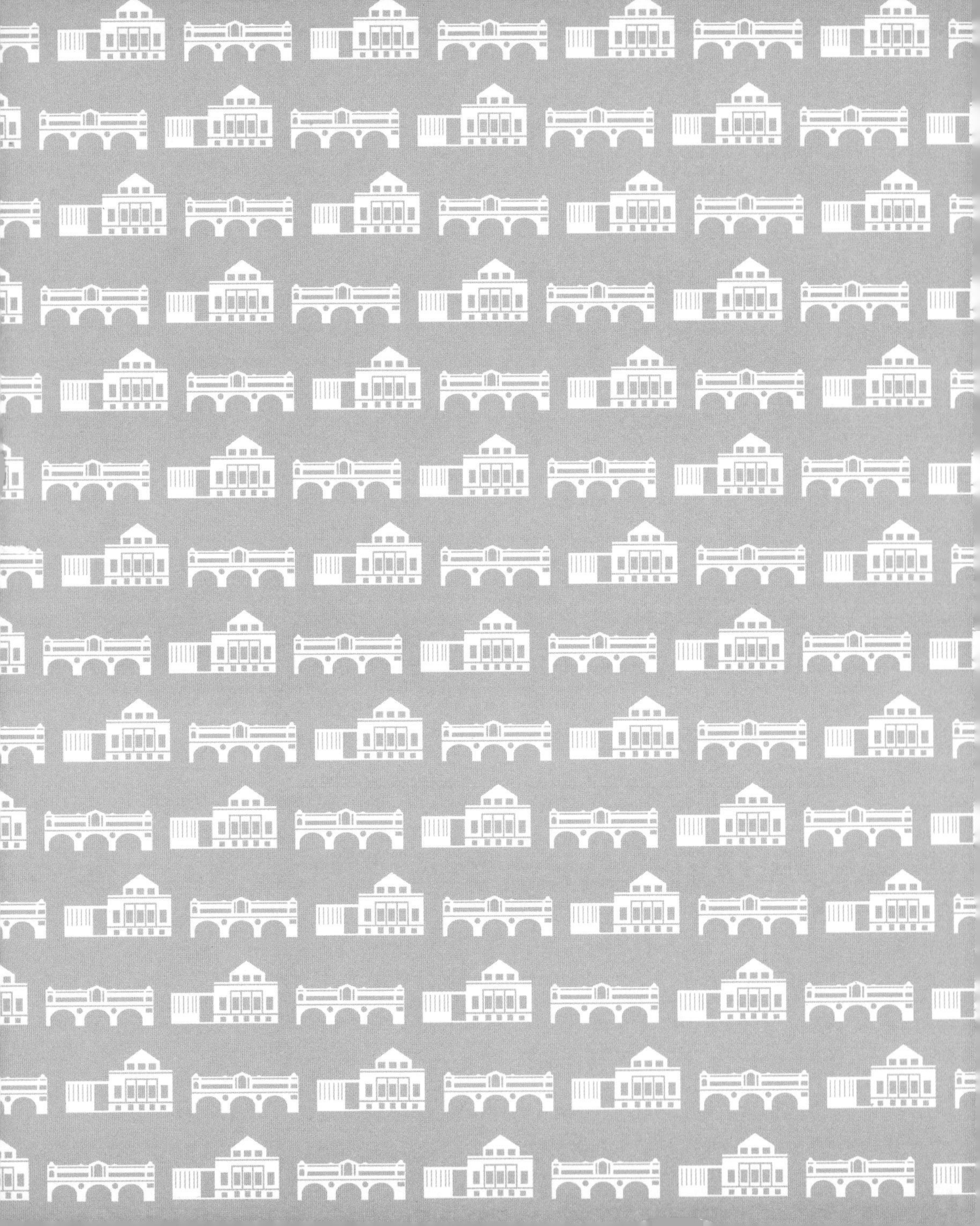